Islam and Inter-Fait

Islam and Inter-Faith Relations

The Gerald Weisfeld Lectures 2006

Edited by
Lloyd Ridgeon and
Perry Schmidt-Leukel

scm press

British Library Cataloguing in Publication data

A catalogue record for this book is available from the British Library

978 0 334 04132 0

First published in 2007 by SCM Press
13–17 Long Lane,
London EC1A 9PN

www.scm-canterburypress.co.uk

SCM Press is a division of
SCM-Canterbury Press Ltd

Typeset by Regent Typesetting, London
Printed and bound in Great Britain by
William Clowes Ltd, Beccles, Suffolk

Contents

PART III Islam and Christianity

PART IV Islam and Hinduism

PART V Islam and Buddhism

Notes on Contributors

Mahmut Aydin is Professor in the History of Religions and Interreligious Dialogue at the University of Ondokuz Mayis in Turkey. He received his PhD in 1998 from the Centre for the Study of Islam and Christian–Muslim Relations at the University of Birmingham (UK) with a thesis on *Modern Western Christian Theological Understanding of Muslims Since the Second Vatican Council* (published by the Council For Research In Values and Philosophy, Washington DC, in 2002). He is the author of several books and articles (both in English and Turkish) on religious pluralism, interreligious dialogue and modern Christian thought, for example, 'Towards a Theological Dialogue Between Christians and Muslims' (*Islamochristiana*, 26/2000); 'Is There Only One Way To God?' (*Studies In Interreligious Dialogue*, 10/2000); 'Religious Pluralism: A Challenge for Muslims – A Theological Evaluation' (*Journal of Ecumenical Studies*, 38/2–3, 2001); 'A Muslim Pluralist: Rumi' (in *The Myth of Religious Superiority*, ed. Paul F. Knitter, 2005).

Martin Bauschke is Director of the Global Ethic Foundation's office in Berlin. He received his PhD from the University of Jena with a thesis on Christian–Muslim relations (published in 2000 as *Jesus – Stein des Anstoßes. Die Christologie des Korans und die deutschsprachige Theologie*). He is researching, lecturing and providing educational training in the fields of the Global Ethic Project and the dialogue between the three Abrahamic religions. Among his publications are the books *Jesus im Koran* (2001, 2007); *Internationale Recherche zum trilateralen Dialog von Juden, Christen und Muslimen* (2001) and *Gemeinsam vor Gott. Gebete aus Judentum, Christentum und Islam* (2004, 2006).

Alexander Berzin is Director of 'Berzin Archives e.V.' and an international lecturer on Buddhist philosophy. He received his PhD in 1972 from Harvard University, Departments of Far Eastern Languages and Sanskrit and Indian Studies. He worked as a founding member of the Translation Bureau of the Library of Tibetan Works and Archives, Dharamsala, India, for 29 years and served as occasional interpreter for H.H. the Dalai Lama. Currently living in Berlin, Germany, he primarily prepares his collected works for online publication on www.berzinarchives.com. He published 17 books (mostly on Tibetan Buddhism) and his works have been translated into 18 languages. He is the author of the eBook *The Historical Interaction between the Buddhist and Islamic Cultures before the Mongol Empire.*

Asghar Ali Engineer is Chairman of the Centre for Study of Society and Secularism and Director of the Institute of Islamic Studies, both in Mumbai. He holds honorary degrees from the University of Calcutta (1993) and the Islamic University of New Delhi (2005) as well as 11 international awards and distinctions, including the 'Right Livelihood Honorary Award for Vision and Work' (Stockholm 2004). He has published more than 40 books in various languages on Islam and the contemporary world, Muslim women's rights, communal and ethical problems in India and South Asia, and is the editor of the *Indian Journal of Secularism* and the *Secular Perspective.* Among his more recent publications are: *Rational Approach to Islam* (2001), *On Developing Theology of Peace in Islam* (2003), *The Rights of Women in Islam* (2004), *Islam in Contemporary World* (2006).

Alon Goshen-Gottstein has been Director of the Elijah School for the Study of Wisdom in World Religions, and lecturer and Director of the Center for the Study of Rabbinic Thought, Beit Morasha College, both in Jerusalem, since 1997. Ordained a rabbi in 1977, he holds a BA from the Hebrew University of Jerusalem. In 1982, he did a year of research on the New Testament and ancient religions at Harvard Divinity School. He received his PhD from the Hebrew University of Jerusalem in 1986. Stanford University Press published his *The Sinner and the Amnesiac: The Rabbinic Invention of Elisha* *ben Abuya and Eleazar ben Arach* in 2000, and his *Israel in God's Presence: An Introduction to Judaism for the Christian Student* is forthcoming from Hendrickson Press.

Muhammad Kalisch is Professor for 'Religion of Islam' and Director of the Centre for Religious Studies at the University of Münster, Germany. He studied law in Hamburg and received his PhD in Darmstadt for a dissertation on 'Reason and Flexibility in the Methodology of Islamic Law'. His habilitation was in Islamic Studies with a thesis on 'Fiqh and Usul al-Fiqh in the Zaidiya – The Development of the Zaidiya as a School of Islamic Law' (2002). His special areas of research are the history and methodology of Islamic Law, the theology of the Mu'tazila and the Zaidiya, Muslim philosophy, theoretical *'irfān* (Islamic Gnosis), and perennial philosophy. He has published various scholarly articles on Islamic ethics and law, and the future of Islam in Europe.

Chakravarthi Ram-Prasad is Professor of Comparative Religion and Philosophy in the Department of Religious Studies, Lancaster University. He studied politics, sociology and history in India and did his doctorate in philosophy at Oxford. He has held research fellowships at Oxford and Cambridge, and taught at the National University of Singapore. Among his books on Indian and comparative philosophy, the latest are *Eastern Philosophy* (2005) and *Indian Philosophy and the Consequences of Knowledge* (2007). His current research includes religion and integration (commissioned by the British Home Office), theories of self and consciousness (with grants from the Arts and Humanities Research Council, and the Templeton Foundation), and comparative political theory.

Lloyd Ridgeon is Senior Lecturer in Islamic Studies in the Department of Theology and Religious Studies at the University of Glasgow. He completed his PhD at Leeds University in 1996 and his thesis was published as *'Aziz Nasafi* (1998). His subsequent books include *Persian Metaphysics and Mysticism* (2002) and *Sufi Castigator: Ahmad Kasravi and the Iranian Mystical Tradition* (2006), and he has also edited a number of works including *Islamic Interpretations of Christianity* (2001), *Major World Religions* (2003), and *Religion* *and Politics in Modern Iran* (2005). His main area of specialization is Sufism and Iranian Studies.

Perry Schmidt-Leukel is Professor of Systematic Theology and Religious Studies and Founding-Director of the Centre for Inter-Faith Studies at the University of Glasgow, and previously taught at the universities of Munich, Innsbruck and Salzburg. He studied Philosophy, Theology and Religious Studies at the University of Munich where he completed a doctorate (1990) and a habilitation (1996). He has published 20 books, among the more recent ones: *War and Peace in World Religions* (2004), *Buddhism and Christianity in Dialogue* (2005), *Buddhism, Christianity and the Question of Creation: Karmic or Divine?* (2006), *Understanding Buddhism* (2006), *God Without Limits* (forthcoming 2008).

Ataullah Siddiqui is a Senior Research Fellow at The Islamic Foundation, Visiting Fellow in the Centre for the History of Religious and Political Pluralism, University of Leicester, Director of the Markfield Institute of Higher Education, and the Vice-Chair of 'Christian-Muslims Forum' in England. He holds a PhD from the University of Birmingham and is co-editor of *Encounters: Journal of Inter-Cultural Perspectives*, a bi-annual journal published by the Islamic Foundation. His publications include: *Christian-Muslim Dialogue in the Twentieth Century* (1997), *Christians and Muslims in the Commonwealth: A Dynamic Role in the Future* (co-edited with Anthony O'Mahony 2001), *Islam and Other Faiths* (a collection of Ismail Raji Al-Faruqi's articles) (1998), '*Believing* and *Belonging* in a Pluralist Society – Exploring Resources in Islamic Traditions' in David A. Hart (ed.) *Multi-Faith Britain* (2002), 'Islam and Christian Theology' in David Ford (ed.) *The Modern Theologians* (2005).

Majid Tehranian is Director of the Toda Institute for Global Peace and Policy Research and Adjunct Professor of International Relations at Soka University of America. He has previously taught at Harvard, Oxford, Tufts, USC and Tehran universities, and is a member of the Club of Rome and the World Academy of Art and Science. A political economist by education, Tehranian received his PhD and master's degrees from Harvard University. His teaching and research have focused on international relations problems with a particular focus on communication, peace, development and democracy. His publications include over 25 books and more than 100 articles, translated into half a dozen languages. Among his publications are: *Global Civilization: A Buddhist-Islamic Dialogue,* with Daisaku Ikeda (2003 with Japanese, Italian, French, Persian and Thai editions); *Dialogue of Civilizations: A New Peace Agenda for the New Millennium*, co-edited with David W. Chappell (2002, Jap. edn 2004); *Rethinking Civilization: Resolving Conflict in the Human Family* (2007).

Jacques Waardenburg is Professor Emeritus for Science of Religions at the University of Lausanne, Switzerland, where he taught from 1987 to 1995. He received his PhD from the University of Amsterdam in 1961. After various research projects in Paris, the Middle East and Montreal, he taught Islamic History at the University of California, Los Angeles (1964–68) and Islam and Phenomenology at the University of Utrecht (1968–87). His main areas of research are the theory and methodology of religious studies, constructivist approaches to religions, Muslim views of other religions and Muslim–Christian relations. Among his numerous books and articles are *Islam et occident face à face: Regards de l'histoire des religions* (1998); *Classical Approaches to the Study of Religion: Aims, Methods, and Theories of Research* (1999); *Muslim Perceptions of Other Religions. A Historical Survey* (ed. 1999); *Muslims and Others. Relations in Context* (2003).

1. Introduction

LLOYD RIDGEON, PERRY SCHMIDT-LEUKEL

Towards a Muslim Theology of Religions

'In our day, when people are drawing more closely together . . . the church examines more carefully its relations with non-christian religions.'[1] With these words, the Roman-Catholic Church opened *Nostra Aetate*, its famous 'Declaration on the Relation of the Church to Non-Christian Religions' (1965). Since then the discussion about Christianity's relation to other faiths has developed into one of the most intensive and controversial theological discourses on a world-wide level.[2]

However, in our globalized word, where the full awareness of religious diversity is one of its most striking features, it is by no means only 'the Church' or Christianity that sees itself called to such a reflection. Something analogous to the so-called Christian 'theology of religions' is becoming more and more prominent in every major religious tradition.[3] In each religion people feel the need to clarify how they understand and assess other religions from within their own faith and whether they may have to reconsider the self-

1 A. Flannery (ed.), 1996, *Vatican Council II. The Basic Sixteen Documents*, Dublin: Dominican Publications, p. 569.

2 For an overview see J. Hick, B. Hebblethwaite (eds), 2001, *Christianity and Other Religions. Selected Readings*. Rev. edn, Oxford: Oneworld; A. Race, 2001, *Interfaith Enconter. The Twin Tracks of Theology and Dialogue*, London: SCM Press; P. Knitter, 2002, *Introducing Theology of Religions*, Maryknoll: Orbis; Veli-Matti Kärkkäinen, 2003, *An Introduction to the Theology of Religions*, Downers Grove, Il.: InterVarsity Press.

3 For an overview see Harold Coward, 2000, *Pluralism in the World Religions: A Short Introduction*, Oxford: Oneworld; J. D. Gort, H. Jansen, H. M. Vroom (eds), 2006, *Religions View Religions. Explorations in the Pursuit of Understanding*, Amsterdam – New York: Rodopi.

understanding of their own religion within the light of an increased and deepened knowledge and understanding of the others. The current volume looks at this complex issue from a primarily Islamic point of view.[4]

None of the major religions starts its reflection on a 'theology of religions' from scratch. On the one hand, their beliefs often contain certain features that, to some extent, seem to predetermine how a particular religion will, or has to, see the other faiths. On the other hand, there is the concrete encounter with the other, but an encounter that did not just start today, under the conditions of the 'global village', but occurred throughout the past in a frequently ambivalent and perhaps even more frequently rather unlucky way. Unfortunately the painful memories of mutual victimization seem to be longer lasting than the remembrance of the constructive and enriching encounters which are not absent from our common history. The past seems to weigh heavily in the bilateral relations between faiths. But it also seems as if the multilateral inter-faith encounter of the present day could put the past into fresh light reminding all sides of the more fruitful periods in history and the implicit promise thereof for a positive shape of inter-faith relations in the future. Both of these aspects, that is, the interplay between religious beliefs and the concrete inter-religious encounter on the one hand, and, on the other hand, the past and present experience of this encounter with its ambivalent potential are addressed in the present book.

Islam, with its extremely wide expansion – reached at a fairly early stage of its history and stretching from Spain to China – disposes over a broad range of experience in relation to different cultures

4 Among the influential recent attempts towards a Muslim theology of religions are for example: Fazlur Rahman, 1989, *Major themes of the Qur'an*, 2nd rev. edn, Minneapolis: Bibliotheka Islamica; Seyyed Hossein Nasr, 1989, *Knowledge and the Sacred*, Albany, NY: SUNY Press; Hasan Askari, 1991, *Spiritual Quest. An Inter-Religious Dimension*, Pudsey: Seven Mirrors; Farid Esack, 1997, *The Qur'an, Liberation and Pluralism. An Islamic Perspective of Interreligious Solidarity Against Oppression*, Oxford: Oneworld; Ismail Raji Al-Faruqi, 1998, *Islam and Other Faiths*, ed. A. Siddiqui, Leicester: The Islamic Foundation; Abdulaziz Sachedina, 2001, *The Islamic Roots of Democratic Pluralism*, Oxford: Oneworld; Asghar Ali Engineer, 2007, *Islam in Contemporary World*, Elgin, Il.: New Dawn Press.

and their religious traditions. As Harold Coward rightly states: 'Muslims probably had a far greater knowledge of all other religions than any other group during the Middle Ages and were certainly more objective than, say, medieval Christians in their representation of other faiths.'[5] Contrary to the prejudice, currently so widespread in the West, that Islam is a particularly exclusivistic religion, it did in fact not only demonstrate comparatively strong forms of inter-religious tolerance, but it also had, and made use of, the doctrinal tools to appreciate, to some degree, a religious value and authenticity in other religious traditions.[6] No part of the world was seen without divine revelation, for as the Qur'ān proclaims: 'To every people (was sent) a messenger' (10:47; similarly 16:36, 35:24). Within the mystical tradition of Islam, there were even theological theories developed according to which fairly different religions could nevertheless be understood as resting on genuine manifestations of the divine, because divine self-disclosure always reflects the nature – and thus the different cultural dispositions – of its human recipients so that 'a Christian will necessarily witness God in a Christian manner and the Buddhist realises enlightenment in a Buddhist manner.'[7] Or, as Al-Junayd had famously put it: 'The colour of the water is the same as that of its container'.[8] However, within Islam, as within every other major religion, there has always been a broad spectrum of different interpretations of the faith and, consequently, of the relation between one's own faith and the faith of one's neighbour, or, to be more precise, there was a diversity of views on whether

5 Coward, *Pluralism in the World Religions*, p. 64. The most comprehensive overview on Islam's relations to other religions in past and present is offered in: J. Waardenburg (ed.), 1999, *Muslim Perception of Other Religions: A Historical Survey*, New York – London: Oxford University Press; J. Waardenburg, 2003, *Muslims and Others. Relations in Context*, Berlin – New York: Walter de Gruyter.

6 For the distinction between 'tolerance' and 'appreciation' in inter-faith relations, cf. P. Schmidt-Leukel, 2002, 'Beyond tolerance: towards a new step in interreligious relationships', *Scottish Journal of Theology* 55, 379–91; Schmidt-Leukel, 2005, 'Tolerance and Appreciation', *Current Dialogue* 46, 17–23.

7 L. Ridgeon, 2002, *Persian Metaphysics and Mysticism. Selected Treatises of 'Azīz Nasafī*, Richmond: Curzon, p. 28.

8 R. A. Nicholson, 1963, *The Mystics of Islam*, London: Routledge, p. 88.

one's neighbour is a person of faith at all or should instead be qualified as an 'infidel'. Thus exclusivism is neither absent from Islam, nor is, or ever was it, its only choice.

Fundamental Questions and Fundamentals Questioned

God is highly exalted above everything else. From this repeated affirmation of God's transcendence in the Qur'ān two immediate conclusions are drawn. First, there can be only one God, for if there were more than one, none of them would be exalted above everything else, none of them would be truly God (23.91). Second, if God is highly exalted above everything then God must be incomparable: 'Nothing is like him' (42.11). Thus, in the Qur'ān, monotheism is a function of affirming God's transcendence, or, as Hasan Askari puts it: '"One" is not number but a form of awareness of God's Transcendence.'[9] Correspondingly, polytheism is inevitably understood as neglecting the truly transcendent nature of God. It replaces the one infinite transcendent reality by finite 'gods', which precisely for this reason can be decoded as 'idols'. Hence, polytheism and idolatry are criticized as missing the true nature of God, which is always 'greater' (so the literal meaning of *Allahu akbar*: 'God is greater'), infinitely greater than everything we can conceive of.

In relation to us the inconceivable God manifests or reveals Godself in justice and mercy. Hence the true worship of God is not only marked by avoiding idolatry or polytheism. It also needs to be reflected in just and merciful deeds (e.g. 7.29; 26.181ff; 30.36–38; 93). So even if God has sent God's messengers to every people, as the Qur'ān affirms, their message, despite possible variations in form and shape, has to be the same as far as these essentials are concerned: It needs to point to the one truly transcendent God and teach how to serve him rightly (cf. 21.25). If these essential elements are contained, it can be seen as genuine: 'The criterion . . . is . . . the message of the truth of Divine transcendence, with its moral and spiritual meaning for human life and history.'[10]

These constitutive Islamic beliefs mark the basis from which

9 Askari, 1991, *Spiritual Quest*, p. 43.

10 Mahmoud M. Ayoub, 1997, 'Islam and Pluralism', *Encounters. Journal of Inter-Cultural Perspectives* 3:2, 103–18, p. 110.

Muslims confront other religions. But there are some more fundamentals to add – which give rise to fundamental questions in the encounter with other religions.

The Qur'ān calls those who received divine revelation 'people of the book' *(ahl al-kitāb)* and mentions explicitly Jews, Christians and Sabaeans. However, is this an exhaustive list or not? As said before, the Qur'ān affirms that prophets were sent to every people in the world, but not all of these prophets are mentioned in the Qur'ān; it is even stated explicitly that not all the names of the messengers are related (40.78). Thus if there are more prophets than those who are named, there might also be more 'people of the book' than those identified in the Qur'ān. Zoroastrians, for example, were accepted as 'people of the book' by the prophet's companions despite the fact that they are not mentioned as such in the Qur'ān.[11] This was important when Islam expanded to the East (India and China), for it allowed a discussion of whether Hindus, Buddhists and others could also be understood as 'people of the book', that is as people having a divine revelation, or whether they were to be regarded just as idolaters and polytheists. Another question, of course, was how literally one has to take the category 'book'. Will all revelation have to take the form of 'a book', or should the category be understood as having a prophetic 'message'?

However, even if people were accepted by Muslim theologians as 'people of the book', or as not being without divine revelation, this did not yet automatically entail a decision about the important question of how well the divine revelation had been preserved. Islamic theology was often marked by the conviction that the divine revelation, spread by God's messengers throughout the world, had undergone various degrees of corruptions, so that the remnants of these revelations were in need of a final, definitive clarification and restoration of their original meaning – which then was, of course, identified with the Qur'ānic revelation brought by Muḥammad. If so, then the revelation at the bottom of non-Muslim religions would give those at best a preliminary validation and legitimization, that is, if these religions were ever paths of salvation – though impaired due to the corruption of the revelation – they lost their legitimacy with the advent of Muḥammad and the message brought by him,

11 Cf. Al-Faruqi, 1998, *Islam and Other Faiths*, p. 71.

as for example in the following statement on Christianity by Al-Attas: 'Those who before the advent of Islam believed in the original and true teachings of Jesus (on whom be Peace!) were true believers (*mu'min* and *muslim*). After the advent of Islam they would, if they had known the fact of Islam and if their belief (*iman*) were truly sincere, have joined the ranks of Islam.'[12] So Muslims could, at times, take a similarly supersessionist stance on pre-Muslim religions as Christians often did in relation to Judaism and the advent of Jesus Christ.

The question is therefore whether, from an Islamic point of view, the revelation of the Qur'ān should be seen as an abrogation of all previous religions so that at least from the arrival of institutionalized Islam onwards any other religion loses its legitimacy, or whether other religions could be accepted as maintaining an ongoing salvific role. Closely connected to this is the question of how to understand the Qur'ānic qualification of Muḥammad as the 'seal of the prophets' (33.40). Does this mean, as it is usually understood by the Islamic tradition, that Muḥammad is the *final* prophet – as the last and ultimate one – or is he the 'seal' in so far that he *confirms* all other valid prophecy before (2.3) and perhaps even after him? The latter part of the question becomes crucial when Islamic theology has to come to terms with newer religious developments, as for example Sikhism or Baha'i-ism.

The questions raised so far confront us with the alternative of an Islamic exclusivism, seeing all non-Islamic religions as abrogated by the advent of Islam, and an Islamic inclusivism, granting non-Islamic religions an ongoing revelatory and salvific function but nevertheless insisting on the superiority of the Qur'ānic revelation. This is not dissimilar to the self-understanding of more or less all the major world-religions who traditionally defined their position among the religions either in the exclusivistic sense of constituting the sole path of salvation or in the inclusivistic sense of admitting salvific truth to other religions in some limited sense while at the same time claiming their own superiority. However, there is currently a movement

12 Syed Muhammad Nquib Al-Attas, 1985, *Islam, Secularism and the Philosophy of the Future*, London – New York: Mansell Press, as reprinted in P. J. Griffiths (ed.), 1990, *Christianity Through Non-Christian Eyes*, Maryknoll: Orbis, p. 115.

within each of the major religions questioning both the exclusivistic and the inclusivistic option of the past in favour of a pluralistic position[13] which regards other religions as different but nevertheless as equally valid in terms of revelation and salvation/liberation.[14] As has already been indicated, contemporary Muslim theologians who tend towards a pluralistic 'theology of religions' can and do in fact draw for this on various thought models developed within Islamic mysticism.[15]

How plausible Muslim attempts to formulate an Islamic pluralistic theology of religions will be, depends, on the one hand, on what they encounter in other religions, or more precisely, on whether they succeed in pointing out that the quality of revelation preserved in other religions is not inferior to what has been preserved in Islam. On the other hand, it depends on how serious they are about the underlying conviction that the one essential and self-identical truth about divine–human relationship can and needs to be manifested in a diversity of forms. This raises inevitably serious questions about the understanding of the Qur'ān. Does belief in the Qur'ān as divinely revealed allow for the assumption of other forms of revelation that parallel and even complement the Qur'ān? Mahmut Aydin has on several occasions – and also in his contribution to this book – opted for a theological view according to which the Qur'ān should be seen as a 'universal, decisive and indispensable' but not as a 'full, definitive and unsurpassable' revelation, one of his main arguments being

13 For an exposition of this classification see: P. Schmidt-Leukel, 'Exclusivism, Inclusivism, Pluralism. The Tripolar Typology – Clarified and Reaffirmed', in: P. Knitter (ed.), 2005, *The Myth of Religious Superiority. Multifaith Explorations of Religious Pluralism*, Maryknoll: Orbis, pp. 13–27.

14 For the move to a pluralistic approach to religious diversity from within various religious traditions cf. J. Hick, H. Askari (eds), 1985, *The Experience of Religious Diversity*, Aldershot: Gower; P. Knitter (ed.), 2005, *The Myth of Religious Superiority. Multifaith Explorations of Religious Pluralism*, Maryknoll: Orbis; P. Schmidt-Leukel, 2008, *God Without Limits*, London: SCM Press, ch. 6. For a recent discussion on Islam and religious pluralism within a multi-religious setting see: R. Boase (ed.), 2005, *Islam and Global Dialogue. Religious Pluralism and the Pursuit of Peace*, Aldershot: Ashgate.

15 See for example: M. Aydin, 'A Muslim Pluralist: Jalaluddin Rūmi', in: P. Knitter (ed.), 2005, *The Myth of Religious Superiority*, pp. 220–36.

that 'no created medium can exhaust the fullness of the Infinite'[16] (cf. Qur'ān 18.109; 31.27). This emphasizes the finite or human side of the Qur'ān's nature. Muhammad Kalisch suggests that the 'holy books of mankind are the products of human spiritual experience' and that 'we can not exclude the Qur'ān from this . . .'.[17] Comparable positions have been endorsed, in more recent times, by various Muslim scholars (for example, Mohammad Arkoun, Nasr Hamid Abu Zaid). Wilfred Cantwell Smith described it as early as 1967 aptly by the words

> that the Qur'an was the word of Muhammad, historically conditioned, and that it was at the same time – being in some measure transcendentally true – the closest approximation to the eternal word of God to which Muhammad was capable of rising . . .[18]

This view makes room for the possibility of other finite representations of the Infinite which are different from the Qur'ān but nevertheless equally valid, equally authentic and equally salvific despite being different and despite being transmitted by other faiths.

Religion and Politics

Inter-faith relations do not solely depend on theological positions. Social, ethnic, cultural and political aspects are often as important as religious ones. Not all hostility between people of different religions was or is motivated by religious reasons. But the converse, that all conflicts are motivated by non-religious reasons, is also rather implausible. Religious people often like the idea that the frequent involvement of religions in violent conflicts would be entirely due to the misuse of religion, that is to its instrumentalization for other than religious motives. However, it may be asked how it is ever possible to misuse religion for instigating conflicts if religions do not harbour a very efficient potential to do so. And this, of course,

---

16 Cf. M. Aydin, 'Islam in a World of Diverse Faiths: A Muslim View', this volume, pp. 00f.

17 M. Kalisch, 'A Muslim View of Judaism', this volume, pp. 49f.

18 W. C. Smith, 1967, *Questions of Religious Truth*, London: Victor Gollancz, p. 93.

does have to do with theological positions: Do religions wish to overcome all other religions, or are they truly prepared to tolerate them, or could they even genuinely appreciate them so that they have absolutely no reason to wish for their disappearance?

For the past 200 years Muslims have been forced to take seriously questions relating to relations with non-Muslims for more than specifically religious reasons. With the advances made by non-Muslim states in socio-economic, military and political spheres, many Muslims advocated the need to 'catch-up', and one method to achieve this was by adopting the institutions that had made Western nations so powerful. In the present age, many 'Islamic' states that abide by the *shari'a* (constitutionally, at least) have adapted forms of democracy. Yet it is intriguing that even though many such states have developed in patterns that might lead one to conclude that secularization should be gaining ground, it is often the case that religion and Islam are becoming stronger.

Part of the explanation for this may have something to do with the perception that the Western states are exploiting their power to gain economic and strategic advantages at the expense of the indigenous peoples of the Middle East and beyond. In other words, the turn to Islamism and the persistence of Islam is in part a response to neocolonialism and the increasing trend towards globalization which contributes to a growing alienation from tradition. The same is often true among Muslims living in Islamic communities in the West. Why, for example, does a young girl decide to wear the hejab when her parents came to Britain from the Indian subcontinent, and who were not outwardly devotional in their religiosity? A number of reasons may explain such a hypothetical (although real) situation. These include the marginalization, discrimination and alienation that such young Muslims living across Europe feel. Political considerations then have a very large impact in the way that contemporary Muslims view other religious traditions. The situation of Muslims in the contemporary world is indeed complex, because of the immediacy of competing demands and differences.

An indication of the differences that must be addressed by Muslims and non-Muslims can be witnessed in the issues discussed at the Cairo Conference on Human Rights in Islam in 1990, in which most of the articles recognized the Universal Declaration of Human Rights (UDHR) so long as these did not contravene the *shari'a*, which in effect, gave the 45 signatories of the document carte blanche to interpret the document in any fashion that they pleased. Article 22 (points a through to c) offer an example of how differently the Cairo Declaration may be understood in relation to the UDHR:

> 22a. Everyone shall have the right to express his opinion freely in such a manner as would not be contrary to the principles of the *shari'a*.
> 22b. Everyone shall have the right to advocate what is right, and propagate what is good, and warn against what is wrong and evil according to the norms of Islamic *shari'a*.
> 22c. Information is a vital necessity to society. It may not be exploited or misused in such a way as may violate sanctities and the dignity of Prophets, undermine moral and ethical values or disintegrate, corrupt or harm society or weaken its faith.

The controversies that have continued to erupt in Europe since the Rushdie episode reveal how relevant article 22a is on both sides of the debate.

It has been quite common for Muslims to look at the West in two ways. On the one hand, it is generally perceived by Muslims that the West is corrupt and immoral (not just in the wider sphere of international politics but in a personal sense). The alternative view is that the West is Christian, and therefore it is to be accepted to a degree, but its peoples do not have the same degree of truth or the same level of spirituality as that enjoyed by Muslims. It is rare to find Muslims outside Europe who are prepared to contemplate that spirituality may be located in various religious traditions and even in agnosticism (and it is virtually unheard of for Muslims to say anything remotely positive about atheists).[19] Many states in Europe are only nominally Christian, and any meaningful dialogue in which Muslims (and for that matter Christians) are engaged should acknowledge this. The diversity of the various religious traditions and the affiliations of those who profess them must be given due weight by Muslims in their encounters with non-Muslims. Having said this, there is now

19 The only modern source that we have come across that recognizes any hope of salvation for atheists is Sachedina, 2001, *The Islamic Roots*, pp. 63–96, in particular p. 95.

a movement among intellectual Muslims (as represented in many of the subsequent articles) towards recognizing the range of spirituality within the 'Christian' West. Likewise, it is imperative that those who are engaged in dialogue with Muslims must appreciate the wide spectrum of thought within Islam, both historically and in the contemporary situation, and acknowledge that agendas are driven not just by convictions of religion but also by political considerations. It is very hard to lay to rest one's baggage, especially when one has borne the burdens of colonialism, neocolonialism, and is constantly having to engage with Western powers whose metanarratives drive the agendas at most international forums. While universal rights may be desirable, it is the manner in which these can be achieved that is important. Freedom for Iraqis, for example, is a wonderful idea, but given the historical differences between the three major groupings in Iraq (Kurds, Sunni Arabs and Shīʿites), it did not take much hindsight to realize that the vacuum left by Saddam Hussein would cause major trauma and difficulty. Dialogue needs to be conscious of culturally specific themes as well as the major theological differences and similarities between the religious traditions.

The articles in this volume acknowledge the contextual influences on religion. Some of the articles are startlingly brave and honest in this respect and push the traditional parameters to breaking point. Yet dialogue requires honesty and bravery if the aim is to take one's partner seriously. So in the interests of understanding and dialogue, in order for a statement about religion to be valid, it has to be honest and argued rationally.

'Not Without My Neighbour . . .'

This is the title of a little book written by Wesley Ariarajah, formerly Director of the World Council of Churches' dialogue programme. Drawing on a wealth of personal experience and theological insight, the book is written as an engaging *plaidoyer* for a future theology that can no longer be done in isolation but 'needs to be pursued within the practice and spirit of dialogue'.[20]

This future has already begun and the insight expressed by

20 W. Ariarajah, 1999, *Not without My Neighbour. Issues in Interfaith Relations*, Geneva: WCC Publications, p. 129.

Ariarajah is behind the structure of the current book: A Muslim theological exploration of Islam's relation to other religions cannot be done without the neighbour. There needs to be the feedback from the other side. If Muslims wish to reflect on their attitude to other religions throughout the past, and with the present and the future in view, they need the assistance of their partners from other faiths. A Muslim view of other religions can be refined, corrected, confirmed or transformed only within the concrete context of a living relationship. The Muslim understanding of other religions depends for its development of the non-Muslims' views of Islam. Genuine interest in, open listening to and creative involvement with the dialogue partner is necessary on both sides: 'O People of the Book! Come to common terms as between us and you. . . .' (3.64).

The contributions to this book are based on the actual dialogues that took place at the University of Glasgow as the Gerald Weisfeld Lectures 2006. The concept of the book reflects the structure of the lectures. That is, on each lecture day there was a presentation by a Muslim and a non-Muslim speaker followed by their mutual responses. After the lectures, the speakers rewrote their papers and, following their exchange, composed their written responses as they are now published. Some of the contributors have a long-standing involvement in inter-faith dialogue, others have been drawn into this more recently. But all of them are renowned experts in their respective field.

The challenging nature of the topic, the newness of the approach, the exploration of uncharted ground is reflected in a sort of discovery spirit sensible in a number of the contributions. Religions, of course, are not only made of theological discoverers. There are always the more conservatively minded who will call for caution and prefer to follow the approved traditional ways. But under radically changed conditions tradition needs to be transformed or otherwise it is in danger of ending up as a museum piece, nicely preserved but essentially dead. Which of the at times experimental suggestions will ultimately turn out to be of a somewhat 'prophetic' nature has to be seen – and to be discussed. The present book should be seen primarily as a contribution to this ongoing discussion.

The lectures would not have been possible without the active support of a number of people. They were jointly prepared and organized by the Centre for Inter-Faith Studies and the Centre for the Study of Islam within the University of Glasgow's Department of Theology and Religious Studies. Academics associated with both of these centres, in particular Mona Siddiqui, John Riches, Alastair Hunter, Amanullah de Sondy, Lloyd Ridgeon and Perry Schmidt-Leukel, helped in many ways to realize the project. This co-operation is also reflected in the joint editorship.

Last but not least, the lectures and the publication would not have been possible without the generous support of the Weisfeld Foundation and in particular of Gerald Weisfeld himself who accompanied the whole project with great personal interest and commitment. It is his and our wish that dialogues like these may lead the religions to more peaceful and more fruitful ways of relating to one another.

Part I

Islam in a World of Diverse Faiths

2. Islam in a World of Diverse Faiths

A Historian's View

JACQUES WAARDENBURG

A valid study of Islam in a world of diverse faiths requires not only a scholarly knowledge of different religions in their historical, cultural and social contexts. It also demands a scholarly reflection on various kinds of faiths and an awareness of various kinds of believers. Moreover, it presupposes a certain interest in them.

It is not only the faith but also the faithful that should be subject of interest at a time when religious beliefs – Islamic, Jewish, Christian – are no longer taken for granted. At present there is an urgent need for reflection on Islam, both in a world of faiths and in a world without faith, and for sympathy with Muslims as fellow human beings.

Muslims are very diverse. There are many forms and practices of the Islamic faith, just as there are many forms and practices of the Christian one. They are linked with very different histories and cultures, but also social structures and political processes that force many people into a day-to-day struggle for survival. Those who identify themselves as Muslims have their communal histories and personal stories, just as Christians and other believers have theirs.

Introductory Remarks

For empirical research, faith – whether Muslim, Christian or any other – is a tricky reality; it is not a clear concept. I use the term here to indicate a personalized religion, conviction or ideology. It implies a personal way of experiencing meaning, viewing truth and expressing identity, together with a personal way of communicating with others. Faiths in the plural suggest the presence of communities that have their own particular traditions, ways of life and resources as to true thinking and correct behaviour. People who are part of such communities may express the common faith of their community, but they will do it in their own way.

In particular, believers in religions like Christianity, Islam, Judaism or other 'prophetical' religions with messages to be listened to attach importance to being persons and having a personal faith. Those who have grown up and live in a world where people have different kinds of faith are bound to be aware of the great diversity of these faiths. They may quite naturally stress the differences but they may also recognize that 'having faith' at all is a quality in itself.

Convinced adherents of Christianity and Islam – and other religions as well – experience a certain difficulty in recognizing and doing justice to the fact that diversity among people is natural, including diversity in matters of religion. Most believers would like very much to see other people having the same identity as they do.

This desire is a tricky matter in human relations. But another matter is still trickier. In social life a religious identity is not necessarily read and interpreted as a 'faith'. Very often Islam – and also Judaism and Christianity – is read in the first place as a social or political identity, or even as an ideology or world-view. A Muslim identity – and also that of a Jew or a Christian – is then simply considered as a social fact, not as a particular – religious – faith. In the case of Muslims and Islam – and also that of Jews and Judaism – this situation has given rise to much misunderstanding of the people concerned and to an ideologization and politicization of their religions.

To conclude this introduction, let me say something about my own approach in studying faiths and religions. My starting point is that of critical enquiry, including enquiry into unscholarly assumptions in such studies. I do not assume a priori, for example, that religions exist necessarily as entities in themselves or that they are more or less closed systems that should oppose each other. Such assumptions, born in the West and often held about relations between religions, are unscholarly and simply mistaken. Religions as such are not closed but they can become closed. They are not rationalized systems but they can be made so. Religions do not exist as entities in themselves but they can be constructed as such, not only by believers and theologians but also by scholars.

In a scholarly approach, moreover, we should identify at the core of the diversity of what are called 'religions' certain basic human orientations, intentions and interests that acquire a 'religious' and possibly absolute character for the people concerned. Linked with social, cultural and other factors, this situation leads to a natural diversity of practices, readings and interpretations. Linked with economic and political factors implying tensions and rivalries, it creates complex relations between believers.

We know that the existing variety of the attitudes believers adopt to other believers is not only due to religious views, their interpretation and their practice. In many cases negative attitudes to other believers are mainly due to causes that have nothing to do with religion and empirical research should bring this to light. There are not only religious but also non-religious variables in relations between different believers.

Distinct Features of Islam when Compared with other Faiths

Let me enumerate first some basic positions in Islam that are relevant in comparison with other faiths and that consequently condition relations between Islam and other faiths. These positions can be found already in the Qur'ān and they have been further discussed in theological and juridical thinking (*kalām* and *fiqh*), with reference to scriptural texts (Qur'ān and *ḥadīths*). They are, so to speak, 'principles' of Islam by which Muḥammad's preaching distinguished itself explicitly from the religions he knew. They concern in particular:

- the belief in God, that this is the only God and that he is one in himself (rejection of polytheism and idolatry, and rejection of plurality within God),
- the belief that God is the creator, sustainer and judge of humankind and reality at large,
- the belief that he sent many messengers calling humankind to believe in God,
- the belief that he has established general laws for his creation to follow, and special rules for humankind to regulate human behaviour toward God, other human beings and nature,
- the belief that particular prophets of earlier times communicated these rules to their peoples by means of Scriptures, but that these Scriptures have not been well preserved,

- the affirmation that the Qur'ān as brought by Muḥammad is God's final and definite scriptural revelation which is to be followed by humankind,
- the affirmation that Islam is the true and definitive faith/religion (*dīn*) which should be accepted by humankind.

These are elements of the basic confession (*'aqīda*) of Islam, which Muslims should follow on both a communal and a personal level. They have been taught and further discussed in the Muslim community from the beginning, whereby different opinions have emerged. As a result, Muslim believers could later in practice adopt various attitudes to non-Muslims, in different historical situations and social contexts. Non-Muslims could be viewed as being at a lesser or greater distance from Islam.

This variety of Muslim attitudes towards others should warn us against considering Islam as a reasoned, let alone monolithic, system imposed on all Muslim adherents. It should be recalled that Islam has no central religious institution like a church and it has no organized religious authorities like a clergy; in practice it has allowed a variety of orientations towards non-Muslims. Four kinds of arguments and general orientations may be mentioned here, apart from specific rules prescribed by local authorities in particular situations:

(1) Argumentation based on scriptural texts, especially the Qur'ān. Texts from the Meccan period call to accept Islam, to leave idolatry and its pagan way of life, to recognize God's supreme authority and to obey his will, according to qur'ānic prescripts. They call (*da'wa*) people to join the religion of Islam, to accept its truth and prescripts, and to live as Muslim believers. Other religions have to be abandoned or corrected in this sense.

Texts from the Medinan period call for the establishment of an autonomous Muslim community under the banner of Islam. It should impose itself and other religious communities have to submit to it. This orientation is still the official one in Saudi Arabia, where no other faiths than Islam are allowed. Qur'ānic texts on Jews and Christians are casuistic, that is, linked to particular situations. It is difficult to derive rules from them for Muslim attitudes and behaviour to Jews and Christians in general, at all times and places.

(2) Argumentation elaborated in theological and juridical reasoning (*kalām* and *fiqh*), with reference to scriptural texts. Islamic theology refutes other faiths than Islam as well as dissident tendencies in the Muslim community as wrong doctrines when measured against the true Islamic ones. Different theological schools have given different judgements. In *sharīʿa* law, certain concrete rules for Muslim behaviour toward adherents of other religions when they live under Islamic political authority are spelled out, giving them a separate legal status. Different legal schools developed different arguments and rules in this respect.

(3) Particular orientations based on spiritual experience and insights are cultivated in Sufi communities, with particular rules of life lived under authoritative guidance. Such religious orientations can also be cultivated elsewhere, even among adherents of other faiths. This can lead to experiences of spiritual unity, such as cultivated, for instance, in the Sufi Movement founded by Inayat Khan. We find here a striking openness to other faiths in terms of common spiritual experience.

(4) Orientations based on reason and on reasoning if it does not go against the Qur'ān. Those who adopt these orientations try as much as possible to follow a rational course of behaviour, including in relation to non-Muslims. On a social level, practical co-operation can be sought without much theorizing. On a rational level, argumentations can be developed in favour of establishing particular truths, for example, in Muʿtazila thinking. On a philosophical level, revelation can be held to be in harmony with reason and Qur'ān exegesis should then conform to the rules of reason. Orientations based on reason are open to enlightenment and allow, for example, modernization of Muslim societies. Universal values such as human rights and principles of social order can be accepted as far as they are not in conflict with the Qur'ān. Such orientations can also lead to solidarity between Muslims and others to defend together basic norms and values in society and human life in general, which in turn leads to dialogue.

Islam, Middle Eastern and other Religions

Seen from a broad historical perspective, Islam corresponds with a particular *Middle Eastern* model of prophetical religions. As such it was easily recognizable as a religion when it emerged in the seventh century CE. It had a prophet, a Scripture, a notion of linear history, a law (outline of the rules of community life) and basic elements of a creed focused on obedience to one God, the creator of the world. Like other prophetical Middle Eastern religions at the time, it was considered to have been revealed through prophetical mediation. Religions like Zoroastrianism, Judaism, Christianity and Manichaeism, despite the well-known differences between them – about salvation and other crucial topics – belong to this model; Christianity would later develop itself further.

The Middle Eastern model is quite different from what may be called the model of *Indian* religions. Here the existence of various deities is recognized, reality is not necessarily seen as the result of one particular act of creation, there is a hierarchy of socio-religious castes, reincarnation after death, a prevailing monistic perspective on the world and various doctrines teaching particular ways of salvation through religious life from continuous reincarnation (*saṃsāra*). The Indian model has a great variety of religious doctrines, myths and rituals.

Buddhism developed out of this Indian model, while distancing itself from the major Hindu world-views. It focuses on the need for human beings to liberate themselves or to be liberated by a Bodhisattva from their natural attachments and the resulting doom of *saṃsāra*. Various doctrines and religious practices were developed to this effect.

The Middle Eastern model also differs from the great *East Asian* religions around China and Japan with their numerous gods and spirits, the privileged place they give to the ancestors, intimate links with nature and hierarchical views of the social order.

These models are of course very different from *religions without scripture* or written texts at all, where myths and rituals responding to the presence of spirits and the forces of nature occupy a prominent place. The 'higher' religions with a literate culture tend to despise such 'primitive' religions or even eliminate them.

The Middle Eastern model of prophetical religion tends to oppose itself to other models. Islam in particular is vehemently opposed to all forms of what it calls *idolatry*.

For our subject it is important to look at the line along which other religions are viewed in the Qur'ān and its message of the right religion to be followed by the Arabs at the time. Islam is held to be the Arab version of the basic religion (*Urreligion*) God has given to mankind. Accordingly, the Qur'ān presents a normative view of how religion should be. It contains a kind of classification of the main religions that were known in Arabia in Muḥammad's lifetime. The principal idea is that God in the course of history sent messengers calling for obedience and prophets bringing a particular law to various peoples at different times and places. Their task was to admonish their people to venerate and serve the one and only God, held to be the creator of the world and of humankind. He established general laws for his creation and particular rules which human beings should follow to be able to realise the aims for which they have been created.

The Qur'ān mentions some well-known names of the Jewish and Christian tradition, such as Adam, Abraham, Moses, David and Jesus. They are considered to have been prophets. Moses and Jesus – and also David – are said to have brought Scriptures that had been revealed (recited) to them. These Scriptures contain divine law, that is to say the rules according to which their followers, that is the Jewish and the Christian community, have to live. They are thought to have survived in a distorted way in the present-day Hebrew Bible and the present-day New Testament, specifically the four Gospels. Only the Scripture brought, that is recited by Muḥammad, considered to be the last prophet, contains the authentic divine law, without distortions. It is the Qur'ān.

Since the Jews and Christians possess at least partly revealed scriptures, the Qur'ān calls them *ahl al-kitāb*, 'people of the Book (recited Scripture)'. These two religious communities qualified for protection (*dhimma*) when living with the Muslim community established by Muḥammad and directed by Caliphs after his death. Consequently, these people were later called *dhimmīs* (protected people) and enjoyed certain rights when they lived under Muslim authority.

Since the Qur'ān also considers Zarathustra (Zoroaster) to have been a prophet, Zoroastrians too were later – after the conquest of

Iran – considered to be *dhimmīs*, though not on the same level as Jews and Christians. Other religious communities, for example in India, would later also qualify for the status of *dhimmīs*.

Lowest in the qur'ānic classification of religious communities were the polytheist tribes living in Arabia in Muḥammad's day. With their veneration of images they were regarded as idol worshippers to be brought to Islam, if necessary by force. In the qur'ānic view, polytheism is paganism, that is, a sin. The Qur'ān does not consider polytheism to be 'religion', since it has no monotheistic faith, no prophet, no revealed Scripture and no creed. Muḥammad preached monotheistic Islam precisely to put an end to the pagan polytheism that prevailed in Arabia.

Islam had some features that distinguished it from contemporary Middle Eastern religions which it judged severely. First of all, it soon developed universal claims for its message that was addressed first to the Arabs, then to non-Arabs and finally to the whole of humankind. Second, it developed into a religion that imposed social order upon Muslim societies by means of a law (*sharī'a*) considered to have been revealed and to be sacred. Islamic society had to be ordered in accordance with this law, and social and political problems had to be solved by recourse to it. The claim that public order should be ruled by the *sharī'a* took definite shape in the eighth and ninth centuries CE, when the caliphate developed into a large imperial state.

Third, there was, and still is, in Islam no overall religious organization enjoying authority in religious matters and there is no clergy. There is, however, a class of scholars (*fuqahā'*, *'ulamā'*) who are proficient in the knowledge of the *sharī'a*. They study its legal sources (Qur'ān and *Sunna* in the first place) and the methods of arguing on the basis of these sources to arrive at valid legal conclusions in Islamic jurisprudence (*fiqh*). The spiritual authority which the leaders of Sufi orders (*ṭarīqas*) enjoy applies only for members of their own orders. Fourth, last but not least, Islamic religion (*dīn*) from its beginning took into account the social interests of society and what may be called perhaps the state (*dunya*). Conversely, government policies had to respect the religious law of Islam (*sharī'a*). In this way state and religion were intertwined. In the Middle East of the early medieval period, Islam was a force for order in society.

The Muslim community consists of all those who recite the

common confession of faith (*shahāda*), whatever further differences there may be between them. This is also the sign of conversion. In the course of time numerous movements and groups developed, such as Sufi *ṭarīqas*, often with extensive networks throughout the Muslim world, each having specific orientations of spiritual and social life. They have their own leadership and lead their life more or less independently of existing political rivalries.

Throughout history, Islamic movements have been keen to realize an Islamic order in society in conformity with the *sharīʿa*, to be imposed on Muslims as well as others, if deemed necessary by force. Such movements could take tough attitudes to non-Muslims.

Followers of most other religions tend to perceive Islam as a 'political' religion. This is not quite correct, since the believers' first duty is to be obedient to God. But imposing the *sharīʿa* of course has political implications; its precise contents have always been open to debate. It is fair to say that in actual fact, all religions with a particular vision of society, favouring or resisting particular social projects, have been politicized in certain ways. Moreover, all religious communities have had to develop ways to survive, if necessary political ones.

That Islam has played a prominent role in tensions and conflicts between Muslims and others, and also among Muslims, is due to the identification of political and religious interests by Muslim communities under pressure. Islam can be instrumentalized politically without further ado in conflicts, but the same can be found in nearly all other religious communities under sociopolitical pressure, even those claiming to be spiritual ones. It is always particular groups of adherents in particular situations and contexts who politicize their religion. To see Islam as such, rather than the use made of it, as an immediate cause of political conflicts is superficial and incorrect in scholarly terms. Certain Muslim claims that base themselves on Islam as the absolute religion will create tensions with those who reject these claims. But this also holds good for other religions with absolute claims. Especially if such claims have political implications, they constitute a most sensitive issue in interfaith relationships. The clue to deal with it is, I think, to look at the ways in which the faithful hobnob (go about) with their own religions.

Changing Contexts

Islamic norms for judging other faiths and Islamic criteria for proper Muslim behaviour toward other believers were established and further developed between the seventh and the thirteenth centuries CE, that is to say in a medieval context. This means that the social and intellectual framework within which Muslim views and judgements pertaining to non-Muslims were developed was conditioned by traditions mostly from early medieval times.

These traditions started to be questioned when the modernization of Muslim societies, which developed roughly speaking in the nineteenth century, created new conditions. The many contextual changes that have occurred since that time in Muslim countries that had non-Muslim communities have had considerable consequences for inter-faith relations. This has also been the result of increasing communication with non-Muslims in the context of the new nation-states, through travel and through the impact of European culture. Moreover, a better knowledge of other religions found its way into the Muslim world in the second half of the twentieth century. All of this has worked together to bring about new interfaith relations.

From the 1960s to the 1990s, in particular, inter-faith dialogue between Christians and Muslims was high on the agenda of a number of both Christian and Muslim organizations. Political and other developments in the Middle East and elsewhere, however, have led to a revitalizing of puritan forms of Islam and an increasing distance between the West and the Muslim world in general. The situation has become even more serious since Islam has been instrumentalized in Muslim countries seeking to defend themselves against Western economic and political interests that impose themselves in the Middle East and support Israel. The attacks of 11 September 2001 brought about more or less open 'war' between Islamist terrorist groups, notably al-Qaida, and some Western countries like the USA conducting global anti-terrorist operations.

The rising tensions have had negative consequences for Muslim–Christian inter-faith relations, which had improved considerably since the 1960s. They have led on the Muslim side to new ways of ideologizing and politicizing Islam, new forms of Muslim apologetics against other religions, a new prominence of Islam in Muslim political discourse and an instrumentalization of Islam for all sorts of purposes. Distrust of Western initiatives in the region has increased, as have explicit acts of defence against any form of Western (neo-) imperialism and increased denunciation of Israeli policies, for example, directed against the Palestinian population, and resistance to American models and interests imposing themselves in the region. Since the late 1980s, authoritarianism in Middle Eastern countries has been on the rise, with a sad human rights situation and ever lessening freedom of the people. Violence and war, the result of foreign intervention, have largely devastated the Palestinian territories, cities in Iraq and parts of Afghanistan and South Lebanon. To the extent that solutions cannot be found, hatred is directed against America and Israel. Armed conflicts among the victims – between factions in Iraq and Lebanon, and now among the Palestinians – result largely from the desperate situation of the population, without any perspective of relief. I shall not discuss here the responsibilities for this – criminal – state of affairs.

Such developments give force to further attempts at communication, dialogue and common action. The problem of this paper – Muslim views of other faiths – acquires a new relevance if we do not speak of Islam in general but of those persons of Muslim background who are able and prepared to work together with people of another faith. Whatever the news that the media report as facts about sensational but revolting events in other countries and among other peoples, it increasingly evokes common concerns among people of different faiths who want to unite in creative thought and constructive action in the face of these events. Whatever destructive political forces and negative ideologies impose themselves, a deeper feeling for interaction, communication and the need for action is shared by people of different faiths who are worried about endless tensions and conflicts that bring meaningful human life to a bitter end.

Whatever interests lie behind destruction and terrorization, people with Muslim and other backgrounds and faiths need to meet each other and come to dialogue on what should be done. There are cultural links, human bonds and creative affinities between them.

If at certain times Muslim people have been sensitive to existing boundaries between the world of Islam and the rest of the world, and if they have often closed themselves off from others, it may very well be that nowadays or in the near future non-Muslim people will close themselves off from Muslim regions and Muslims. Largely because of fear of each other, both groups will have difficulties in seeing each other – and themselves – as they are.

Whoever may be the terrorists and anti-terrorists, the fact of terrorization exists. Muslims as well as non-Muslims risk being paralysed: being 'terrorized' by violence from those who are called terrorists and from those proclaiming themselves anti-terrorists but using terrorists' methods.

I would like to make a serious appeal to people of Muslim and other faiths to open up to each other on the human level, using social and cultural expressions, precisely when the fixed interests of political and religious parties and authorities lead to the proclaiming and sustaining of conflict. It is an appeal to all persons to descend to a deeper level of human community and personal faith, where people of Muslim and other backgrounds can view each other with respect, and where this mutual respect can further develop.

Cultural and Religious Encounters

Interaction

Just as commercial exchanges between Europe and the Muslim world had awakened interest in Muslim cultures since the seventeenth century if not earlier, the missionary activities in the nineteenth century and beyond awakened interest in life in Muslim societies. Their work comprised schooling and further education, health services and social work in the broadest sense. In the independent states, many of these originally missionary activities were simply transformed into public services.

After independence, various Catholic, Protestant and neutral study centres were founded in Muslim countries. Libraries with reading rooms were established. The other way around, Islamic institutes and centres were established by Muslim organizations in Europe and North America. They often started as a local resource for Muslim immigrants but could then also reach out to the local non-Muslim population.

In the 1960s initiatives were taken for further co-operation and dialogue between Muslims and Christians. High-level international dialogue meetings with experts on both sides were organized, sponsored by religious institutions, cultural bodies and official delegations. These activities of co-operation and dialogue between Muslims and Christians could also be linked to initiatives taken to inform the Western public about Islam and to stimulate the integration of Muslim immigrants in Western societies.

Common movements and meetings were typical of the momentum to further dialogue between the West and the Muslim world, Christians and Muslims, especially from the 1960s onwards. Many other initiatives were taken for cultural contact and interaction, including exchange visits of students, scholars and authors; translations of important texts; exhibits of art and historical objects. A complete 'World of Islam Festival' was held in Britain in the 1970s and an 'Islam Expo' took place in London in July 2006 and 2007. Annual inter-faith meetings take place in Doha, Qatar. Paris witnessed the establishment of the Institut du Monde Arabe, many of whose events are connected with Islam. In the West numerous books appear on Islam and Muslim countries, and Muslim speakers are increasingly invited to speak to Western audiences.

Study of each other's culture and religion

Muslim students in Europe and North America evidently became familiar with the language, history and culture of the particular country where they studied. Unless they were at private institutions, they would not learn much about Christianity. Yet they could become interested in the historical and comparative study of religions as carried out at Western universities.

Apart from some exceptional scholars in the medieval period, like al-Mas'ūdī (before 893–956), al-Bīrūnī (973–after 1050) and al-Shahrastānī (1086–1153), Muslim interest in obtaining fair knowledge about religions other than Islam remained limited for a long time. Such knowledge was generally considered to create confusion among faithful Muslims. Muslim views of other religions were largely subject to the norms and values of Islam and the Islamic tradition. After World War Two, however, especially in Turkey, Egypt and Iran, but also in Pakistan and Indonesia, Muslim scholars became interested in studying other religions.

During the last half-century Muslim scholars have familiarized themselves with more scholarly approaches in the study of Islam as well as other religions. In the University of Cairo, for example, debates have taken place about studying the Qur'ān as a literary text. Scholars can discuss problems of linguistics and hermeneutics of religious texts. The history of Islam can be studied now in the same way as the history of any religion. A start has been made with the study of the social history of Muslim countries, including its religious aspects, and with social scientific research into present-day Muslim societies and their religious communities. New approaches in the study of Islam have developed, including those paying attention to phenomenological methods. Books on other religions attract increasing interest and are widely sold.

From 27 September until 3 October 2004 an important international conference on the study of religions took place in Yogyakarta and Semarang, in Indonesia. Its theme was 'Religious Harmony: Problems, Practice and Education', and the participation was predominantly Muslim, especially from Indonesia. Whereas in the Western cultural tradition, research and scholarship – including that on cultures and religions – have acquired a somewhat autonomous status but also excessive specialization, Muslim scholars in this field tend to place the study of religions in broader frameworks. Some demand coherence between a scholar's views of his or her own Islam, of other religions, and of religion in general. Others postulate the need for a normative theological or philosophical framework for the study of religions. Others again insist on certain commitments – for example to harmony and peace, freedom of expression, justice, a minimum standard of living – for a truly humanistic study of religions.

Over against irrationalism, Muslim philosophers have always put their trust in reason as a quality common to human beings and linked to a spiritual dimension in human life. To the extent that studying religions has also become a search for reasonable insight through scholarly knowledge, it can lead to ongoing exchanges between Muslim and other researchers, between scholars of Islam and scholars of other faiths.

Insight

The invitation for this lecture series asked contributors to address the important question of 'what Islam can give to and might receive from the other great faiths'. This question, of course, goes beyond the general need for honesty, knowledge, co-operation and solidarity. Islam can contribute to moral standing, true knowledge and solidarity among scholars and students.

On the level of faith, it seems to me that Islam can stimulate fruitful exchanges in particular about the notion of God and the search for social justice. The presence of Islam as a religion incites reflection on these matters.

And what might Islam receive from the other great faiths? As I see it, nearly all faiths have wrestled with the problem of evil, its nature and origin, and its links with the use of force. Islam can be enriched by discussions on human responsibilities with regard to such matters.

Let me end with a call for insight. Once upon a time certain thinkers held that religions as such lead their adherents to the holy, the absolute, God. The study of religions, in a way, should lead into this direction. There was also a time when thinkers denounced religion as such as an illusion and a cause of alienation, a trap to be avoided or fought against. The study of religions, in a way, should be used as a remedy against it. At present, most scholars take a more modest position. We study religions and religious data professionally because they should be known. And we do it according to particular disciplines, in fields of specialization.

Some scholars, however, happen to have further intentions in studying religions and faiths. They see them, for example, as traditions that have conveyed 'meanings of life' to particular communities in particular contexts. Scholarly speaking, religions are human phenomena that are worth studying. We can enquire about meanings, derived from religious traditions, that people have given life. Such meanings are indeed worth knowing.

Select Bibliography

Goddard, Hugh, 1996, *Muslim Perceptions of Christianity*, London: Grey Seal Books.

——, 1998, 'Christianity from the Muslim perspective. Varieties and changes', in *Islam and Christianity. Mutual Perceptions since the Mid-20th Century*, ed. Jacques Waardenburg, Leuven: Peeters, pp. 213–55.

Moussalli, Ahmad S., 1998, 'Islamic fundamentalist perceptions of other monotheistic religions', in *Islam and Christianity. Mutual Perceptions since the mid-20th Century*, ed. Jacques Waardenburg, Leuven: Peeters, pp. 121–57.

Omar, Irfan A. (ed.), 2006, *Islam and Other Religions. Pathways to Dialogue. Essays in honour of Mahmoud Mustafa Ayoub*, London and New York: Routledge.

Pye, Michael; Franke, Edith; Wasim, Alef Theria; Mas'ud, Abdurrahman (eds.), 2006, *Religious Harmony. Problems, Practice, and Education.* Proceedings of the Regional Conference of the International Association for the History of Religions, Yogyakarta and Semarang, Indonesia, 27 September – 3 October 2004. (Religion and Reason, vol. 45), Berlin and New York: Walter de Gruyter.

Ridgeon, Lloyd (ed.), 2001, *Islamic Interpretations of Christianity*, Richmond, Surrey: Curzon Press.

Shboul, Ahmad, 1979, *Al-Mas'ūdī and his World. A Muslim Humanist and his Interest in Non-Muslims*, London: Ithaca Press.

Steenbrink, Karel A., 1990, 'The Study of Comparative Religion by Indonesian Muslims. A Survey', *Numen*, 37, pp. 141–67.

Stümpel, Isabel, 1999, 'Christianity as described by Persian Muslims', in *Muslim Perceptions of Other Religions. A Historical Survey*, ed. Jacques Waardenburg, New York and Oxford: Oxford University Press, pp. 227–39.

Waardenburg, Jacques (ed.), 1998, *Islam and Christianity. Mutual Perceptions since the mid-20th Century*, Leuven: Peeters.

——, 1998, 'Observations on the scholarly study of religion as pursued in some Muslim countries', *Numen*, 45, pp. 235–57.

—— (ed.), 1999, *Muslim Perceptions of Other Religions. A Historical Survey*. New York and Oxford: Oxford University Press (see also by the same author the chapters on 'Muslim Studies of Other Religions', pp. 1–101, and the 'Selected Bibliography', pp. 309–40).

——, 2003, *Muslims and Others. Relations in Context* (Religion and Reason, vol. 41), Berlin and New York: Walter de Gruyter.

——, 2006, 'Classical attitudes in Islam towards other religions', in *Religions View Religions. Explorations in Pursuit of Understanding*, ed. Jerald D. Gort, Henry Jansen and Hendrik M. Vroom (Currents of Encounter, vol. 25), Amsterdam and New York: Rodopi, pp. 127–48.

——, 2007, *Muslims as Actors. Islamic Meanings and Muslim Interpretations in the Perspective of the Study of Religions* (Religion and Reason, vol. 46), Berlin and New York: Walter de Gruyter.

Wide, Clare, and McAuliffe, Jane Damman, 2004, 'Religious Pluralism and the Qur'ān', in *Encyclopaedia of the Qur'ān*, Jane Dammen McAuliffe, General Editor, Volume Four, Leiden-Boston: Brill, pp. 398–419.

Wismer, Don, 1977, *The Islamic Jesus. An Annotated Bibliography of Sources in English and French*. New York: Garland.

3. Islam in a World of Diverse Faiths

A Muslim View

MAHMUT AYDIN

As is well known our contemporary intercommunicating and interdependent universe has started to make Muslims aware, more clearly but also more painfully than ever before, of the multiplicity of diverse faiths and of the many different ultimate answers given by these faiths. Because of this fact we, as Muslims, are facing some theological questions and challenges we never had to confront before. These questions and challenges force Muslims to develop an Islamic theology not in isolation but in relation with other religions and theological visions. For that reason we believe that an Islamic understanding that considers and expresses itself within the context of world religions can make sense in our world of diverse faiths. It seems rather difficult for Muslims to assume an Islamized world in the sense of the institutionalized religion of the Prophet Muḥammad. Instead of this imaginary vision we need to take into account realistically the present situation of our pluralistic world and should reconsider our traditional attitudes towards the others.

In this paper I will try to formulate a new Muslim theology of religions that would provide a foundation for a better relation with people of other faiths by asking the following questions about the traditional Muslim belief that only those who follow the teaching of the Prophet Muḥammad can be saved or can go to Paradise. If God's grace and mercy is limited only to the followers of the institutionalized religion of the Prophet Muḥammad, does this mean that all those who are outside of this particular religion will be exposed to eternal punishment? Have all those who consider themselves as 'the people of the right way' attained this way as a result of exploring the other ways and concluding that these are false or invalid? Is one's religious identity as a Muslim the result of one's free will or of the cultural identity given to him/her by birth? If being born as a Muslim is not the result of one's free will but the result of his/her cultural identity, can this be regarded as a privilege for salvation? If it is a privilege for salvation, why has God given it only to a small minority by depriving the majority? While trying to answer these and other similar questions we will focus our attention on the qur'ānic teaching. The main reason of this is that, as Fazlur Rahman strongly underlines, 'a more positive and a more open Muslim attitude towards the others can only be achieved by hearkening of Muslims more to the Qur'ān than to the historic formulations of Islam'.[1] Because of this fact at the very outset of my paper I would like to make a clear distinction between the original teaching of Islam and its interpretations given by its commentators and the behaviour of its followers in different historical and political situations.

Exclusivist and Inclusivist Muslim Attitudes towards the Others

The term 'exclusivism' maintains that only one religion holds the absolute truth that leads to salvation, while others are considered to be in error in varying degrees and unfit as vehicles of salvation. The exclusivist line finds its roots among Muslims from the belief that Islam is the final and full religion for humanity as put forward in the Qur'ān as the way of life. Although Muslims believe in the continuity of revelation and of prophecy throughout history, this does not mean Muslims accept other religions as they are. In fact, in explaining why a new religion in the form of Islam was needed, Muslims usually appeal to the verses critical of the 'other' such as Jews and Christians. While Jews were accused of 'altering the scripture',[2] Christians were accused of overstepping 'the bounds of truth' in their religious beliefs by attributing divinity to Jesus, Son of Mary.[3] Thus Muslims traditionally believe that as far as they were aware,

1 Fazlur Rahman, 1989, 'The People of the Book and the Diversity of "Religions"', in Paul J. Griffiths (ed.), *Christianity through Non-Christian Eyes,* Maryknoll: Orbis Books, p. 110.

2 Qur'ān 4.46f.; 2.75; 5.13, 41.

3 Qur'ān 4.171; 5.72, 73.

other religions were corrupt and there was a genuine need for a new universal religion. This is Islam, revealed in the Qur'ān and proclaimed by the Prophet Muḥammad. As we will see below, according to qur'ānic teaching, although the Prophet was no different from other prophets in explaining the religion of Abraham,[4] exclusivist Muslims strongly argue that those who want to attain salvation must follow him as the last and final prophet. Since his teaching as the perfected version of the true religion of Abraham effectively abrogated and invalidated all religions before it, the natural conclusion of an exclusivist Muslim view is that today only Islam, the institutionalized teaching of the Prophet Muḥammad, mediates the salvific knowledge of God which brings people to eternal salvation. According to this argument, religions apart from Islam are in error and could not bring their followers to God. So, it is not possible to go to paradise unless one follows the teaching of the Prophet Muḥammad strictly in one's own daily life.

Inclusivism holds that there is one surest way to salvation, which is Islam in Muslims' case, and others may also be led to salvation but their ways are not as good as Islam. In other words, God's salvific knowledge is mediated not only by Islam, but by other religions/ways as well. But among these ways only the way of the Prophet Muḥammad mediates this salvific knowledge in a uniquely superior way because Allah perfected and elected it for the Prophet Muḥammad and his followers. When we look at the history of Islam we can say that the inclusivistic approach could be regarded as a common Muslim approach towards other religions. Sociologically, Muslims have set good examples of integration with other religions throughout history;[5] a good illustration of this was the Andalusian Moorish Empire in Spain where Muslims, Christians and Jews produced a highly sophisticated, civilized and advanced society. Another example was the Ottoman *millet* system in which people from different faiths and cultures lived together in peace and harmony.

Theologically speaking inclusivism, too, was not considered an option for non-Muslims. This is because, according to inclusivist Muslims, although there is a hope for everybody concerning salva-

4 Qur'ān 2.285.

5 H. A. R. Gibb, 1957, *Mohammedanism: An Historical Survey*, London: OUP, pp. 3–5.

tion, both the opportunities and the end result are likely to be better for the followers of institutionalized Islam.[6]

When we look at the history of Muslims we see that apart from those who were pursuing experience-centred religiosity, that is, Sufis such as Rūmī[7] and Ibn 'Arabī, all Muslim thinkers (especially those who were pursuing truth-centred religiosity, namely, jurists and theologians) argued that institutionalized Islam which was proclaimed by the Prophet Muḥammad is the most perfect revelation. While the former were giving priority to orthopraxy rather than orthodoxy the later regarded religion only as fixed rules and tried to defend Islam against other religions dogmatically. According to these thinkers, although other religious traditions may contain some truth, they are meaningless without Islam.[8] Today, while few creative thinkers try to reconsider this traditional Muslim belief in order to reconcile it with the necessities of religious pluralism and a dialogical world view in which people of different faiths live together by keeping their own differences, the great majority still considers institutionalized Islam as the final dispensation or sacred law revealed by God to the Prophet Muḥammad and maintains that this final dispensation is meant for all humanity, and for all time until the Day of Judgement.

As we have seen above, exclusivist and inclusivist Muslims put the teaching of the Prophet Muḥammad at the centre and evaluate other teachings according to their distance from this centre just as traditional Christians put Christianity, Jesus Christ or the Church at the centre and evaluate the others according to their relation and closeness to this centre. However this traditional Muslim world-view contradicts not only the necessities of religious pluralism and inter-religious dialogue but also the main teaching of the Qur'ān concerning the others, which we will elaborate below. For example, in chapter 2, verses 111 and 113, while the Qur'ān condemns those

6 Rifat Atay, 1999, *Religious Pluralism and Islam: A Critical Examination of John Hick's Pluralistic Hypothesis* (unpublished PhD thesis, St Andrews University, August 1999), p. 36.

7 See, Mahmut Aydin, 2005, 'A Muslim Pluralist: Jalaluddin Rūmī', in Paul F. Knitter (ed.), *The Myth of Religious Superiority: Multifaith Explorations of Religious Pluralism*, Maryknoll: Orbis Books, pp. 220–36.

8 Al-Maturidi, *Kitāb-al Tawīḥīd*, İstanbul, 1979; see also, Hanefi Özcan, 1999, *Maturîtî'de Dini Çoğulculuk*, İstanbul: MUIFV.

Christians and Jews who made exclusive claims about the uniqueness and superiority of their own faiths and states that salvation cannot be achieved by mere claims but by true belief and right actions, it also urges Muslims not to make this kind of exclusive claim about their own faith or salvation. In another verse, the Qur'ān clearly underlines that 'it may not accord with your wishful thinking – nor with the wishful thinking of the followers of earlier revelation – that he who does evil shall be requited for it, and find none to protect him from God, and none to bring him succour'.[9] With this clear statement the Qur'ān underlines that religious patriotism that limits being a chosen nation and a community or being acceptable to God only to its followers has no value with God.

Diversity of People and Varieties of Prophets

Islam emphasizes not only the unity of God as its basic teaching but also the unity of mankind, since the Qur'ān underlines that 'humankind is a single nation'.[10] However this is a unity within diversity and this diversity was the result neither of the gradual change of mankind from an ideal to a utopia nor of the lack of divine guidance. This is because the Qur'ān points out that the diversity of mankind was a normal human situation that came about as a result of the varieties of cultures, languages and environments of people.

> All mankind were once one single community; (then they began to differ) whereupon God raised up the prophets as heralds of glad tidings and as warners and through them bestowed revelation/book from on high, setting forth the truth, so that it might decide between people with regard to all on which they had come to hold divergent views. Yet none other than the self same people who had been granted this (revelation) began, out of mutual jealousy, to disagree about its meaning after all evidence for the truth had come unto them . . .[11]

As is seen from this highly significant verse, the Qur'ān does not use the term 'books' in the sense of plurality of God's revelation or

---

9 Qur'ān 4.123
10 Qur'ān, 2.213.
11 Qur'ān, 2.213.

holy book but uses it as a singular in the sense of heavenly sample and fundamental source of all the divine revelations. According to this fact all the revelations starting with the first prophet Adam to the last prophet Muḥammad have been the worldly examples of this fundamental source.[12] The Qur'ān states that all the revelations emanate from a single source, namely 'the Mother of the Book'[13] and 'the Hidden Book'.[14]

This verse also points out that humanity's religious journey is from unity to diversity and this diversity of the nations and differences among the people was not the result of their disobedience to God's orders but was the result of jealousy and enmity of people to each other. Because of this fact the Qur'ān does not condemn the diversities and varieties of people and nations, but it does condemn enmity, jealousy, conflict and arrogance among the people. So, according to qur'ānic teaching if the diversity of people does not lead to conflict and war it is a good thing, since God appointed different laws and ways of life to every nation to compete with one another in doing good works.[15] So the Qur'ān accepts and appreciates the diversity and the variety of religions and cultures within the context of the unity of believing in one God and submission to His will. The qur'ānic view of diversity is neither total relativism nor chaos but it is a *diversity within unity*. This unity has continued its existence starting with the first prophet Adam and finishing with the final prophet Muḥammad.[16] The Qur'ān underlines that God has sent a prophet to every community with this message: 'worship God and shun the powers of evil'.[17] The Prophet Muḥammad pointed out that 'prophets are brothers in terms of their father (*awlād al-allāt*); their mothers are different, but their religion is one.'[18] So according to the Qur'ān different prophets have come to different nations but their fundamental messages are identical and universal, since their

12 Fazlur Rahman, 1989, 'The People of the Book and the Diversity of "Religious"', pp. 103–4.

13 Qur'ān, 43.4; 13.39.

14 Qur'ān, 56.78.

15 Qur'ān, 5.48.

16 Mahmoud M. Ayoub, 2000, 'Islam and the Challenge of Religious Pluralism', *Global Dialogue*, 2/1, pp. 56–7.

17 Qur'ān, 10.48; 4.41; 16.36.

18 Al-Bukhārī, *Anbīyā*, 48; Al-Muslīm, *Fażā'īl*, 145.

messages stemmed from a single source, namely the 'Mother of the Book'. That is why the Qur'ān invites the Prophet Muḥammad and his followers to believe in the prophethood of previous prophets such as Noah, Abraham, Moses and Jesus, since God's religion and the prophethood are indivisible. For that reason it does not matter which faith we belong to, it is incumbent on all of us to believe in all the messengers without making any distinction among them.[19] As Fazlur Rahman rightly points out just as 'the Prophet Muhammad and his followers believe in all the prophets and their teachings, all people must also and equally believe in him',[20] since disbelief in Muḥammad would be equivalent to disbelief in all the prophets.

The Function of the Prophet Muḥammad

Both exclusivist and inclusivist Muslims forget the fact that the mission of the Prophet Muḥammad was neither to establish a new religion nor to make Jews and Christians his followers but to follow and complete the religion of Abraham and confirm all the previous prophets.

> Say: 'I am not the first of God's apostles'[21] . . . who could be of better faith than he who surrenders his whole being unto God and is a doer of good withal, and follows the creed of Abraham who turned away from all that is false – seeing that God exalted Abraham with His Love.[22]

In another verse the Qur'ān explains the main features of Abraham's creed and invites the Prophet Muḥammad to obey and follow it.

> Verily, Abraham was a man who combined within himself all virtues, devoutly obeying God's will turning away from all that is false, and not being of those who ascribe divinity to aught beside God, (for he was always) grateful for the blessing granted by Him

19 F. Rahman, 1986, 'A Muslim Response: Christian Particularity and the Faith of Islam', in D. G. Dawe & J. B. Carman (eds), *Christian Faith in a Religiously Plural World*, Maryknoll: Orbis Books, p. 71.

20 F. Rahman, 1989, 'The People of the Book and the Diversity of "Religions"', p. 104.

21 Qur'ān, 46.9.

22 Qur'ān, 4.125.

> who had elected him and guided him onto a straight way. And so We vouchsafed him good in this world; and verily in the life to come he shall find himself among the righteous. And lastly we have inspired you (o Muhammad with this message) Follow the creed of Abraham who turned away from all that is false, and was not of those who ascribe divinity to aught beside God . . .[23]

As is seen from these verses God invites the Prophet Muḥammad and his followers to accept the creed of Abraham as the model for the right and true faith just as previously He invited Jews and Christians to do the same. Furthermore the Qur'ān underlines that Abraham is not a model just for the followers of one faith but those who have true faith in one God by refusing the monopolizing claims of Jews and Christians about him.[24]

Thus while rejecting the monopolizing claims of Jews and Christians concerning Abraham, the Qur'ān also warns Muslims not to make similar exclusive claims by arguing that Abraham was a Muslim like themselves. As we have said above, the Qur'ān does not limit Abraham to one faith by inviting all people to obey and follow the creed of Abraham which is true submission to the will of the Lord of the Universe and worship of Him alone by rejecting all kinds of polytheism. Muhammad Arkoun makes the following comment about the qur'ānic presentation of Abraham as the first *muslim*:

> When the Qur'ān says that Abraham was neither Jew nor a Christian but a *muslim*, it clearly does not refer to Islam as defined by theologians and jurists in their interpretations of the Qur'ān and the teaching of the Prophet Muhammad. In that context, *muslim* rather indicates an ideal religious attitude symbolised by Abraham's conduct in conformity with the Pact or Covenant described in the Bible and the Qur'ān. It is for this reason that Abraham is called the Father of Believers.[25]

If the Prophet Muḥammad was not a founder of a new religion but a follower and fulfiller of the creed of Abraham just like the previ-

---

23 Qur'ān, 16.120–124.

24 Qur'ān, 3.65–67.

25 Muhammad Arkoun, 1994, *Rethinking Islam: Common Questions, Uncommon Answers*, London: Westview Press, p. 15.

ous prophets, and if the Qur'ān rejects all kinds of exclusive and superiority claims which depend on mere absolutist claims instead of submission to the will of God and doing righteous works, it seems that the following question should be answered by us as Muslims: Can we, as Muslims, still continue to argue that the institutionalized religion of the Prophet Muḥammad is the only teaching that is supposed to be for all mankind just as the exclusivist and inclusivist Muslims have argued in our religiously pluralistic world? If we continue to do this, are we then not making the same exclusivist claims against which the Qur'ān so strongly warns Jews and Christians?

Islam or 'islām'?

Those Muslims who declare that the institutionalized religion of the Prophet Muḥammad is the only true way acceptable to God and who argue that only those who accept the Qur'ān as the unique word of God and the Prophet Muḥammad as the final prophet and follow his teaching can go to Paradise, always quote the following Qur'ānic verses to support their arguments.

> The Religion before God is Islam (submission to His Will).[26]

> If anyone desires a religion other than Islam (submission to God), it never will be accepted of him.[27]

> This day have I perfected your religion for you, completed my favour upon you, and have chosen for you Islam as your religion.[28]

Because of this fact, first of all we will deeply examine these verses in order to make clear what 'islām' means in these verses in order to put forward whether the Prophet Muḥammad's aim was to establish a new religion or fulfil Islam, '*dīn al-fiṭrah*' (or, as Ismail R. al-Faruqi calls it, '*religio naturalis*' or '*Ur-Religion*'[29]) which all the prophets

---

26 Qur'ān 3.19.
27 Qur'ān 3.85.
28 Qur'ān 5.3.
29 I. R. al-Faruqi, 1978, 'Islam and Other Faiths', in A. Gaufar (ed.), *The Challenge of Islam*, London: Islamic Council of Europe, pp. 93–6.

proclaimed. Furthermore, we believe that developing a more tolerant and open Muslim attitude towards the others depends on whether Muslims differentiate between the wider, literal, meaning of *islām*, namely submission to the will of God, and the colloquial use of it in a limited sense as the name of the institutionalized religion of the Prophet Muḥammad. As Muhmoud Ayoub rightly states, if *islām* in these verses is taken to refer to Islam the religion, the verses relating the message of the Prophet to the earlier prophets from Adam onwards and of their '*islām*' are 'meaningless.' Furthermore, if we also take the meaning of the term *islām* in the above verses at face value, namely that 'no other manifest or institutionalised religion will be acceptable to God except Islam as we have it today and have had it for the last 1500 years,' the qur'ānic verses which declare the principle of plurality and the unity of faith are meaningless words.[30]

In order to understand fully what the term *islām* means in these verses, we need to explain what the Qur'ān means by the term *dīn*. When we look at the Qur'ān, we see that the term *dīn* is used in the following ways: management, obeying, judgement, adoration, Unity (oneness of God), submission, law (*sharī'a*), boundary, custom and punishment. Besides these meanings, the term *dīn* is also used as the meaning of 'true religion',[31] 'right religion',[32] 'sincere religion',[33] 'being sincere in religion/professing submission to Allah'.[34] It is also used in the Qur'ān to express not only Muslim belief but also the beliefs of others as well. For example, in chapter 109, verse 6, which was revealed in the Meccan period the ethical values and the practical lives of infidels (*mushrikūn*) was defined as 'dīn'. In the Medinan period, too, non-qur'ānic ways of life were presented as separate ways of life besides the qur'ānic one.[35]

In the light of these different usages of the term *dīn*, we can say that it covers the belief and faith dimension of religion. According to this view, the religion that Allah wanted to establish was the religion that was shaped within the context of faith, worship and ethics, and was addressed to all times. From God to man, it articulates God's

30 Ayoub, 2000, 'Islam and the Challenge of Religious Pluralism', p. 61.
31 Qur'ān 48.28; 61.9.
32 Qur'ān 9.36; 30.30, 43; 98.5.
33 Qur'ān 39.3.
34 See, Qur'ān 7.29; 10.22; 29.65; 31.32; 40.14, 65; 98.5.
35 Qur'ān 48.28.

sovereignty and order; from man to God, it states man's submission to God's will and obedience to His orders. At the horizontal level, man's obedience to God's orders reflects the ethical relationships between human beings and goes beyond time and space. For that reason, established structures such as revelation, sacred book, prophethood, sacred places, religious community and law (*sharī'a*) are not religion per se but its concrete forms. Unlike the universality and unhistoricity of religion, these established structures are bound to time and place.[36]

Now, we move to explain the meaning of the term *islām* in order to understand what the above verses really mean. But before doing this, we would first like to point out three different levels and understandings of *islām*, as indicated by Ayoub. The first and the widest sense 'signifies the attitude of the entire creation before God' and 'applies to the heavens and the earth and all that is in them'[37] including human beings. The second level is the more common meaning, namely 'any human being or human community which professes faith in the One God and seeks to obey God in all they do and say.'[38] Finally at the most specific level, it is 'the Islam of a given community following a particular divine law revealed to a particular prophet, the Prophet Muhammad (peace be upon him).'[39]

The term *islām* is employed in the Qur'ān in order to express the submission and self-surrendering of one's own will to God's will, God's authority and God's orders. Thus, *islām* as verb indicates an attitude and behaviour that goes from human being to God. Within this context, the word *islām* used in the above-mentioned verses can be understood as a faith sent by God first of all through the prophet Abraham to all humankind and then approved by later prophets such as Moses, Jesus and Muḥammad. So, we may conclude that the term *islām* embraces all of those who submit themselves to the will of God. So, as a religious system, Islam is the religion of all creatures from the first man to the end of the world. In this sense the Qur'ān calls Abraham and other prophets 'muslim'.[40]

---

36 İlhami Güler, 1998, 'Din, İslam ve Şeriat', (*Dīn, Islam and Shari'ah*) *İslamiyat*, October–December 1998, pp. 55–6.

37 M. Ayoub, 1997, 'Islam and Pluralism', *Encounters* 3/2, p. 114.

38 Ayoub, 'Islam and Pluralism', p. 114.

39 Ayoub, 'Islam and Pluralism', p. 115.

40 Qur'ān, 4:125.

So, according to this explanation the term *islām* in chapter 3 verse 19 should not be understood in a reified sense but as the existential attitude of all believers to God in order to include the teachings of all the prophets under its umbrella, since this verse informs the Prophet Muḥammad to tell his opponents that his way is 'simply one of submitting his being/attention to God and that this is also the path required of them'.[41] To this explanation the term *islām* in this verse is the essence of *al-dīn* which includes the common points of all the prophets. The following famous ḥadīth of the Prophet Muḥammad supports this sort of understanding of the term *islām*. 'Every child is born with an innate capacity for *submission to God*, i.e. islām; it is her/his *parents* that Christianise, Judaise or Magianise her/him, as an animal delivers a perfect baby animal. Do you find it mutilated?'[42]

When we examine this saying of the Prophet Muḥammad deeply we see that it includes two important arguments of religious pluralism. The first is that everybody is born with the potential to believe in God. Hick calls this 'the right to believe'.[43] The second is the function of the accident of birth in choosing one's religion. According to this pluralist argument, the religion we follow depends in the vast majority of cases on where we were born.[44] The second part of the ḥadīth makes this point clear by declaring that being a Muslim or a Christian or a Jew depends on which family the child is brought up in. In Qur'an 30.30 God calls us to follow this *dīn al-fiṭrah* as follows: '. . . set your face steadfastly towards the (one ever-true) faith, turning away from all that is false, in accordance with the natural disposition which God has instilled into man. . .' As we

41 Farid Esack, 1997, *The Qur'an, Liberation & Pluralism: An Islamic Perspective of Interreligious Solidarity Against Oppression*, Oxford: One World, p. 126.

42 Al-Bukhāri, *Sahih al-Bukhari*, Janā'iz, no. 80.

43 John Hick, 1989, *An Interpretation of Religion: Human Response to the Transcendent*, London: Macmillan, pp. 227–9.

44 'Someone born into a Christian family in Italy is much more likely to become a Christian than a Buddhist. If in Pakistan, much more likely to become a Muslim than a Jew. If in Thailand, much more likely to be a Buddhist than a Christian. And so on.' John Hick, 2005, 'The Next Step beyond Dialogue', in Paul F. Knitter (ed.), *The Myth of Religious Superiority*, Maryknoll: Orbis Books, p. 7.

have seen up to now, the diversity of religions is designed by God Himself. For that reason, religious plurality is our destiny and we need to live our lives in accordance with the necessities of this diversity. So, 'the intrinsic principle in Islam is pluralism not exclusivism or inclusivism'.[45]

The term '*muslim*' as the noun form of '*islām*' is employed in the Qur'ān for those who submit to God. It is used not only for those who follow the teaching of the Prophet Muḥammad but also for Abraham,[46] the sons of Jacob,[47] the apostles of Jesus Christ[48] and those who submit to the Creator from the followers of those prophets who came before the Prophet Muḥammad.[49] This is because the Qur'ān teaches that the true muslim is a person who submits and surrenders himself/herself to his Creator by not associating anybody or anything with Him.[50] Additionally, the Qur'ān makes a distinction between the institutionalized religion of the Prophet Muḥammad and *islām* which is the true faith and the virtuous life in the following verse:

> 'The Bedouins say: 'We believe'. Say: 'You do not believe, but say: We submit'; for belief has not yet entered your hearts. If you obey Allah and His Apostle, He will not stint you any of your works . . .'[51]

When we consider this factual reality we can conclude that the terms '*islām*' and '*muslim*' are used in the Qur'ān not in the sense of the established or institutionalized religion of the Muslims but in the sense of submission to the authority of God and obedience to His orders. Thus when Joseph demanded to die as a 'muslim' in his prayer[52] and when Abraham described himself as 'muslim' they did not mean that they were members of the institutionalized religion of the Prophet Muḥammad. But they meant that they submitted to

45 Atay, 1999, *Religious Pluralism and Islam*, p. 219.
46 Qur'ān 3.67.
47 Qur'ān 2.133.
48 Qur'ān 3.52.
49 Qur'ān 22.78.
50 See, Rashid Rıda, *Tafsīr al-Manār*, III, pp. 211–12.
51 Qur'ān 49.14.
52 Qur'an, 12.101.

Allah and obeyed His orders. In conclusion, by the term *islām*, the above-quoted verses of the Qur'ān do not indicate a legal system or the institutionalized religion of the Muslims as we have today, for *islām*, in these verses, is the name of the common religion that Allah has sent through His messengers from the first prophet to the last one. There is no difference among the teachings of the prophets in terms of their beliefs. However, there are some differences on some issues which occurred in accordance with the time and the circumstances of the message. But changeable laws are limited to practical issues of the worldly dimension of the religion. So, it seems to us that the traditional argument which states that the messages of the prophets are different in essence or that one particular religion abrogates the other(s) needs to be reconsidered in the light of the qur'ānic teaching which we have summarized so far, for the Qur'ān points out that '. . . We vouchsafed this divine writ, setting forth the truth, confirming the truth of whatever there still remains of earlier revelations . . .'[53] As we can see from this verse, the reason for God's sending different books (messages) is not to negate each others' orders but to confirm each others' messages.

If this is the case, the question is how Muslims started to use *islām* as the special name of the institutionalized religion of the Prophet Muḥammad by reducing *al-dīn* to institutionalized Islam and reducing Islam to *sharī'a*. When we take into account the process of the construction of established Islam, we can answer this question as follows: In the course of Islamic history Muslim scholars have understood *sharī'a* (which became concrete through the Qur'ān and the Prophet Muḥammad in the beginning of the seventh century) as *al-dīn* and named it as Islam. Thus, *al-dīn*, which has a universal meaning, had been reduced to the qur'ānic *sharī'a*, and the qur'ānic *sharī'a*, too, had been equated with the institutionalized religion of the Prophet Muḥammad (Islam). As a conclusion of these developments, too, *al-dīn*, *Islam* and *sharī'a* have become identical terms that express the same meaning. So, the terms *dīn* and *islām* have been used to express not the common name of the divine message which was sent by Allah from the first prophet Adam to the last prophet Muḥammad but to indicate only the followers of the Prophet Muḥammad. As a result of this development, the verses

53 Qur'ān 5.48.

3.19, 85 and 5.3 have been attributed only to the institutionalized teaching of the Prophet Muḥammad and then as a natural result of this, those who are not following this teaching have been considered infidels.[54]

When we take into account what we have said up to now we can conclude that there is only one faith, and it is called '*islām*', to submit oneself to the will of God. And He revealed this faith to us through His prophets under different names and different structures. This means that a religion whose objective is to call its followers to submit to Allah without associating anybody or anything with Him can be accepted as a different version of this one religion. If this is the case, the following question naturally can start to occupy our mind: What is the possibility of salvation of those who do not follow the teaching of the Prophet Muḥammad?

The Possibility of Salvation of Non-Muslims

A re-reading of the above verses (3.19, 85; 5.3) in light of the general teachings of the Qur'ān and a multifaith context will not support the exclusivist and inclusivist Muslim views that only those who follow the institutionalized religion of the Prophet Muḥammad can be acceptable to God and thus can go to Paradise. It suggests that Muslim theologians ought to develop a Copernican revolution in their own understanding of their faith as John Hick suggested for the Christian faith in the 1970s. This means that Muslims need to put the meaning of the term *islām*, namely, submission and obedience to Allah, at the centre instead of the institutionalized teaching of the Prophet Muḥammad, in order to rescue themselves from absolutizing their own faith by excluding others. Unless they do this, they cannot avoid absolutizing the institutionalized teaching of the Prophet Muḥammad as the only way through which people can be acceptable to God and saved. Furthermore this sort of absolutism explicitly contradicts the following qur'ānic verses, which clearly

54 Mehmet Okuyan & Mustafa Öztürk, 2001, 'Kur'an Verilerine Göre 'Öteki'nin' Konumu (The Status of the Other According to the Qur'anic Accounts)', in Cafer S. Yaran (ed.), *İslam ve Öteki (Islam and the Other)*, İstanbul: Kaknüs, pp. 174–5.

affirm the availability of salvation for those who belong to other religious communities apart from the Muslim community (*umma)*.

> The believers, the Jews, the Christians and the Sabians, whoever believes in Allah and the Last Day and does what is good, shall receive their reward from their Lord. They shall have nothing to fear and they shall not grieve.[55]

> Surely, the believers, the Jews, the Sabians and the Christians – whoever believes in Allah and the Last Day and does good deeds – shall all have nothing to fear and they shall not grieve.[56]

These verses, one revealed at the beginning and the other at the end of the Prophet Muḥammad's Medinan career, clearly inform us that there are three minimum conditions of being acceptable to God: (1) to believe in one God; (2) to believe in the Hereafter; and (3) to do good deeds. So, if someone fulfils these three conditions in his/her life fully, without looking at which religious tradition he/she belongs to, we can say that he/she can go to Paradise. Unfortunately, as Fazlur Rahman underlines, the vast majority of Muslim commentators exercise themselves fruitlessly to avoid having to admit this obvious meaning of these verses. Because of the wholesale approach of these commentators, the obvious meaning of these verses has been either manipulated or reduced to a few people who lived in the time of the Prophet Muḥammad or they have simply been abrogated.[57] M. Ayoub gives the following response to these commentators: When the Prophet arrived at Medina the verse 2.62 was revealed as a guidance to deal with 'Jewish Tribes of Madina and the Christian community of Najran'.[58] Later on, it is 'repeated verbatim in the last but one major chapter to be revealed to the Prophet before his death.'[59] Neither the repetition, nor the timing of the verses is discussed by those who abrogated these verses. Ayoub points out that there are important implications of this fact to weaken the claims

55 Qur'ān 2.62.

56 Qur'ān 5.69.

57 See, Rahman, 'A Muslim Response', p. 75; Rahman, 'The People of the Book and the Diversity of "Religions"', p. 106.

58 Ayoub, 'Islam and Pluralism', p. 113.

59 Ayoub, 'Islam and Pluralism', p. 113.

of abrogation. Suppose the first one, 2.62, was abrogated, then the second one, 5.69, still stands. If it was abrogated already, why was it necessary to repeat it? That the second revelation is close to the end of the Prophethood of Muḥammad makes it very unlikely that it is abrogated. So, as Ayoub concludes, 'neither the words nor the purport of these two identical verses was abrogated.'[60]

Another reason for undertaking this revolution in Muslim theology concerns the qur'ānic doctrine of God. The Qur'ān, in its opening chapter, strongly emphasizes that Allah is not only the Lord of those who follow the institutionalized teaching of the Prophet Muḥammad, but He is the Lord of the Universe.[61] If Allah is the God not only of Muslims or another community but of all mankind, this means that His grace and mercy is not limited only to a particular community but extends to all His creatures without any limitation, since He gives all persons an equal opportunity and capacity within their historical and cultural situation to relate to Himself in such a way that salvation is possible for them. Naturally, this would mean that Islam, the teaching of the Prophet Muḥammad, is not the only religion in which God manifests Himself, since He may disclose Himself in other ways or through other religious figures in other places and traditions.

Reconsideration of Some Absolute Claims

Now, the question is: if Islam, the institutionalized teaching of the Prophet Muḥammad, is not the only way but is one of the ways of salvation, what is the implication of this for the status of the Qur'ān and the Prophet Muḥammad? On this point we would like to discuss whether it is possible for Muslims to reconsider their traditional understanding of the Qur'ān and the finality of the Prophet Muḥammad in order to move away from exclusivism and inclusivism and thus give equal room to the others in the inter-faith dialogue process. While the uniqueness of the Qur'ān and the finality of the Prophet Muḥammad can and must be reconsidered in the light of today's dialogical relations between Muslims and others, these beliefs need not be abandoned nor their value be reduced by Muslims

60 Ayoub, 'Islam and Pluralism', p. 113.

61 Qur'ān 1.1.

in order to create better relations for the sake of dialogue. Within this context, we suggest Muslims do not consider God's revelation to the Prophet Muḥammad as *full, definitive and unsurpassable* but as *universal, decisive and indispensable* messages of God.[62]

God's revelation in the Qur'ān is not full, definitive and unsurpassable. This argument indicates three things. First, Muslims cannot claim that they possess the fullness or totality of divine revelation in the Qur'ān as if it exhausted all the truth that God has to reveal, since theologically speaking no created medium can exhaust the fullness of the Infinite. Second, Muslims cannot consider the Qur'ān as the definitive word of God as if there could not be other norms for the divine truth outside of it. This means that the Qur'ān is the word of God not in the sense that there are not other words of God. Third, Muslims cannot consider God's revelation in the Qur'ān as unsurpassable in the sense that God could not reveal Himself in other ways apart from the Qur'ān at other times. It seems that if Muslims believe that God's revelation to them in the Qur'ān contains the whole truth of God without allowing the possibility of other revelations, this would contradict the qur'ānic world-view which maintains that Allah gave us different laws and ways of conduct through His prophets to encourage us to excel each other in goodness.[63]

God's revelation in the Qur'ān is universal, decisive and indispensable. This argument indicates three things. First, Muslims need to announce that the Qur'ān is a universal revelation and message of God and is not a call just for them only but for all people at all times. For if the Qur'ān shows people how they become acceptable to God by informing and demonstrating how to live and how to attain God's grace, this knowledge cannot be limited only to Muslims but should be made available for all people. This argument indicates that God's message through the Qur'ān is relevant to everyone without restrictions and this could also be true for other religious figures and divine revelations. Second, Muslims should regard the revela-

62 Here I have employed a suggestion made by Paul F. Knitter in relation to the status of Jesus Christ. See, P. Knitter, 'Five Theses on the Uniqueness of Jesus', 1997, in L. Swidler & P. Mojzes (eds.), *The Uniqueness of Jesus Christ: A Dialogue with Paul F. Knitter*, Maryknoll: Orbis Books, pp. 3–16.

63 Qur'ān 5.48.

tion granted in the Qur'ān as decisive because when people follow this revelation, it makes a difference in their lives by transforming them from self-centredness to God-centredness. So, if the qur'ānic revelation is universal and decisive, it should be normative not only for Muslims but also for others as well. Third, Muslims need to continue to announce the Qur'ānic revelation as indispensable in the sense that just as the truth proclaimed by it has enriched and transformed the lives of Muslims, it should also to do the same for the others' life.

So, within the context of these arguments, it seems that in order not to underestimate the dialogical attitude of the Qur'ān and our own established beliefs about the status of the Qur'ān and the Prophet Muḥammad, we need to adopt a mediating position that neither absolutizes nor abandons the uniqueness of the Qur'ānic revelation and the finality of the Prophet Muḥammad. This means that the Qur'ān is definitely the universal, decisive and normative revelation of God and the Prophet Muḥammad is the final prophet for those who follow the qur'ānic teaching, and the way of the Prophet Muḥammad is acceptable to God and thus people who follow the way deserve to go to Paradise. But it is not necessary for those who follow the path of another religion or religious figure in order to be acceptable to God.

However, we must not forget that this sort of understanding should not be regarded as an attempt to undermine the faith of believing Muslims, but should be seen as an attempt to equalize the status of the teaching of the Prophet Muḥammad with the teachings of other prophets while keeping the centrality of this teaching for Muslims. It seems that this position would help Muslims in the process of interreligious dialogue more than others, since it urges them to consider the teachings of the Prophet Muḥammad as the tool for salvation for themselves, and also to be open to acknowledge other teachings as ways of salvation. Also, this stimulates Muslims to approach other world religions with openness and eagerness to learn more of God's ways in the world. As Hick states, in our world of diverse faiths 'we have no reason to restrict ourselves to the spiritual resources of our own tradition'.[64]

64 John Hick, 2005, *The Rainbow of Faiths*, London: SCM Press, p. 139.

Conclusion

As our examination of qur'ānic teachings about others has shown, Allah sends different prophets to different communities or nations but their messages are universal and identical. Within this context, the Prophet Muḥammad was not a founder of a new religion but was the proclaimer and fulfiller of *dīn al-fiṭrah* and his teaching is not the only way but is one among the others as the reassertion of this primordial religion. In the light of this conclusion one can ask which principles Muslims need to take into account in their relationship with others in our world of diverse faiths.

1. *Common humanity should be the first meeting point of Muslims with 'others'*. As is well known, there have always been both believers and unbelievers in the world. In the light of our knowledge of the religious history of mankind we can say that there would not be any time in which all people were believers or unbelievers. It seems that also in the future there will not be a time in which all people will be believers or unbelievers. Because of this undeniable fact, if Muslims want to live with others in harmony and peace they need to be respectful to them as human beings without taking into account whether they are believers or unbelievers.

2. *Everybody has freedom to choose whatever faith s/he wants or not to choose any faith*. In their relationship with others, Muslims should not forget that the Qur'ān clearly underlines that nobody can be forced or put under pressure to choose a religion.[65] It seems that this qur'ānic principle is the clearest expression of the philosophy of modern democracy concerning freedom of religion and conscience. According to this qur'ānic principle nobody can be forced to choose a religion and can be put under pressure because of his/her faith.

3. *In their relationship with non-Muslims, Muslims should aim only to witness and share their own faiths with them without imposing their beliefs on them or putting them under pressure.* They should not forget that guidance is only from Allah and nobody apart from Him can lead people to the right way. When we look at the religious history of mankind we see that Allah has had respect for the free will of His creatures while conducting His divine guidance. According

65 Qur'ān, 2.256.

to qur'ānic teachings, it is quite easy for Him to take control of His creatures and make them believers but He has not done this.[66]

4. *Differences among people are not for conflict and enmity.* The Qur'ān clearly indicates that Allah created mankind not as a single nation but as different nations and societies in accordance with His will so that they come to know one another as they are. As human beings we need to make contact with each other because we cannot live in isolation. Because of this fact, the history of mankind should be considered as being in a constant process of communication. Fulfilment of our humanity can only be achieved in a society in which we have contact with others.[67]

5. *Religious difference and diversity are not to instigate violence and hatred but to urge followers of different faiths to compete with each other in doing good.* The Qur'ān emphasizes that God has made us not as a single nation but as different communities and gave us different ways of life not to fight but to compete with each other in good works in order to attain His will.[68]

6. *Conflict and disagreement are inevitable among different communities because of the diversity and the plurality of religious beliefs, cultures and ethnic identities.* The Qur'ān invites Muslims to argue with those people with whom they disagree not in enmity but in the most kindly manner in order to establish a dialogical environment in which both sides can live in mutual respect and mutual understanding.[69]

7. *When there would be any disagreement and conflict which would lead the sides to fight with each other, the final decision should be left to God.* So, within the context of this principle what we need to do in our discussions with people of other faiths is produce and bring out our arguments without condemning and making negative judgements about beliefs and ways of life. Who is right and who is wrong will be determined by God in the Hereafter.[70]

8. *The principle of reciprocity should be a main criterion through which Muslims need to determine their attitudes towards others.* The Qur'ān urges Muslims to determine their attitudes towards

66 Qur'ān, 10.99.
67 Qur'ān, 49.13.
68 Qur'ān, 5.48.
69 Qur'ān 16.125.
70 Qur'ān 5.48.

others with regard to the others' attitudes towards them. According to the principle of reciprocity, Muslims should treat others just as they treat them.[71]

9. *Muslims should no feel enmity and revenge in their daily relationship with others.* The Qur'ān gave the following warning to those who wanted to take revenge on Meccan pagans after the conquest of Mecca: 'O you who have attained faith! Be ever steadfast in your devotion to God, bearing witness to the truth in all equity; and never let hatred of any one lead you into the sin of deviating from justice . . .'[72]

10. *Muslims should give preference not to orthodoxy but to orthopraxy in their relationship with others.* According to this principle, Muslims should fulfil the necessities of their beliefs and thus present them to others in practice rather than making a priori dogmaticclaims concerning their superiority.

In short, the Qur'ān explicitly calls Muslims to adopt a 'dialogical world-view' which rules out any exclusive claim to the truth and connected with this salvation by Islam, the institutionalized teaching of the Prophet Muḥammad, in their relationship with others. While doing this, the Qur'ān, far from eliminating the differences between various religious traditions, invites Muslims to come together for mutual understanding and mutual discussion. Furthermore, the Qur'ān commands Muslims to regard the diversity of ways of life and cultures as a way of building peace and harmony between different communities. As we have pointed out above, diversity is not meant to bring about the clash of civilizations but rather an alliance of civilizations.

---

71 Qur'ān, 60.8–9.

72 Qur'ān, 5.8.

4. Response to Aydin

JACQUES WAARDENBURG

Mahmut Aydin's paper can render an important service to widen the horizon of a religious community. It offers an alternative to the rather closed attitude which people usually have within the framework of their own religion, whether it is Christianity, Islam, Judaism or any other. They then have hardly any interest in other religions that are held to contrast with their own, the 'true' one. A theology of religions in the plural is then a way to give a place to other religions and assign some value to them. It may evoke an interest in them or in religion in general. It also relativizes a certain inborn naive absolutizing of one's own religion and gives an idea of the human element of all religions, exotic and strange as they may be. Aydin's paper could widen the horizon of Muslim communities.

Moreover, a theology of religions can render a service to a dialogue between religions, at least indirectly. As I see it, 'dialogue' takes place on the level of living people and indicates a kind of communication between them. Dialogue between religious believers is more than an exchange of ideas or experiences between persons or groups. It demands a certain knowledge and understanding of each other's religion and may stimulate the desire to get to know more about it. In such a situation people may become aware why someone is not only an observer of, but also a believer in, a particular religion. A theology of religions in the plural is a way of evaluating religions on the basis of criteria on a theological level. It gives an idea about the way in which someone views the various religions and how he or she constructs coherence between them. The basic question, of course, is that of the criteria of synthesizing and evaluating them. Aydin's paper, for instance, shows how an Islamic theology of religions might look. This not only leads to dialogue with other Muslim scholars but also with scholars of other backgrounds.

The academic study of religions can contribute to this dialogue by providing adherents of different religions with scholarly knowledge about each other's religion. Here we do not deal with evaluations as in a theology of religions but with scholarly factual knowledge. Without such knowledge, however, no evaluation can be made, no theology of religions can be developed, and no informed dialogue can be carried out.

In the Muslim as in the Christian world the presence of believers outside one's own community has been a problem that could lead to apologetics, polemics and various kinds of mission to bring people to one's own belief. Religious communities developed religious arguments to safeguard their religions and defend one's religious identity, for instance in debates between Muslims, Christians and Jews, developed with particular structures which can be analysed in terms of the self-defence of closed communities stressing their excellence. Mahmut Aydin does the opposite: he presents arguments that can be developed by Muslims in favour of opening up, co-operation and dialogue rather than exclusivism, self-defence and separation.

One of the major arguments of Professor Aydin is the distinction between *islām* as a human religious attitude with regard to God and institutionalized Islam as the result of Muḥammad's activities as a prophet. The first can be found already in the case of Abraham and his followers. Mutual recognition of this religious attitude of *islām* favours understanding and co-operation between believers in different communities.

He also draws attention to a particular positive theological trend in the Qur'ān that is suitable for dialogue and co-operation with other believers. This trend is opposed to some other trends that signalize conflicts between doctrines (rejecting non-Islamic ones) or between communities (Muslim and other ones) in particular contexts. Aydin demonstrates the positive trend by means of some striking qur'ānic references. It would certainly be rewarding to consider the historical contexts of these texts, that is, of the positive and negative judgements given in the Qur'ān about other believers.

Let me also add some more critical remarks from the point of view of a historian of religions. Aydin contends that all prophets since Abraham called for monotheism. This may be so, but they proclaimed particular kinds of monotheism, linked not only with one particular god but also with particular religious and ethical prescripts, in particular situations, in a particular social order. We should recognize the great variety of prophets and the variety of responses they gave to various human situations.

Although the prophetic messages had a universal orientation towards what they preferred to call 'God', the religious communities resulting from the work of the prophets were not so universal. Jews, Christians and Muslims were quite particularistic, stressing their special identity at any price, entertaining often tense relations between them which were susceptible to political interests. What the communities made of their religions is a story in itself.

Any theology of religions tends to treat them as ideal spiritual normative entities. Their serious limitation is that they neglect the social realities in which people have been living. The religious communities with their leaders had to face serious social dilemmas and they have been subjected to powerful political and economic forces from outside, beyond their will. How did the religious communities, for instance, respond to political power?

Another point concerns the people that have constituted these religious communities. Centuries ago such communities were more or less autonomous and defined their identity according to religious criteria. They were categorized according to religions but their life depended in fact on very different kinds of factors. For an adequate theology of religions we need to take into account how people interpreted and used their religions, and what these religions meant to them according to their own interpretation.

I like Mahmut Aydin's critical mind. He denounces 'religious patriotism' with extraordinary claims for Islam and he shows that the Qur'ān opposes it. He makes a clear distinction between those jurists, theologians and their followers who claimed, and still do so, that institutionalized Islam is the most perfect revelation (and who were followed by the majority) on the one hand, and on the other hand the few creative thinkers open to the necessities of religious pluralism and a dialogical world-view at the present time. I think he rightly stresses that the Qur'ān rejects all kinds of exclusive and superiority claims for Islam. Such claims depend on (erroneous) absolutist understanding of this religion instead of its demand to submit to the will of God and to do righteous works. So, according to Aydin, Muslims should not make 'the same exclusivist claims against which the Qur'ān so strongly warns Jews and Christians'.[1] I fully agree with his argumentation as to how Muslims soon started to reduce *al-dīn* to institutionalized Islam, and to reduce Islam as a religion to *sharīʿa*. As a result the three terms lost their distinct original meanings. He also lucidly explains how those people who were not following the institutionalized teaching of Muḥammad erroneously 'have been considered infidels'.[2] I further agree with Aydin that Muḥammad's main mission, as he himself saw it, was to follow and complete the religion of Abraham and to confirm all the previous prophets. But he also established a religion that was new to the Arabs and increasingly enjoyed having Jews and Christians among his followers.

Though I admire Aydin's argumentation as to the possibility of salvation of non-Muslims and the necessity to reconsider some absolute claims as to the Qur'ān and Muḥammad, I think that these sensitive issues need further elaboration and I would be grateful if he would be willing to do this in the future. From a historical point of view, I am not convinced that the fundamental messages of all prophets are identical and universal. Historical evidence shows major differences between, for instance, the messages of Jesus and Muḥammad, without pronouncing judgement here. I, for my part, do not agree that 'it does not matter which faith we belong to, it is incumbent on all of us to believe in all the messengers without making any distinction among them.'[3]

Aydin's contribution, as I see it, is an Islamic theological manifesto for dialogue, over against all kinds of self-seclusion, self-aggrandizement and self-absolutization of Islam. It will be welcomed by those striving for openness of faith among human beings. It will also meet resistance among those who are distrustful of open communication, wanting to subordinate it to political and other interests. One of the virtues of this design of an Islamic theology of religions is that it is based on the mutual trust of believers. The author applies a logical argumentation on a strictly theological basis. He accepts revisions of theological positions that have been current in Islamic history. Last but not least, he believes in the good fruits of prophetical messages

1 Cf. Aydin's chapter in this book, p. 41.
2 Cf. Aydin's chapter, p. 47.
3 Cf. Aydin's chapter, p. 39.

in religious communities other than his own. Here we are presented with a valid theology of religions from an Islamic perspective, but it is up to Muslim colleagues to judge this.

5. Response to Waardenburg

MAHMUT AYDIN

Interaction between Islam and the West is a centuries-old phenomenon. But after the September 11 tragedy this interaction has been framed in terms of 'us versus them' and 'Islam versus the West'. Recent events such as terrorist attacks in Spain and London, the cartoon controversy that emerged from Denmark, and Pope Benedict XVI's polemical, ugly and very unfortunate citation about Islam and the Prophet Muḥammad in the Regensburg speech have further exacerbated this confrontational discourse. As a result of this development, rather negative images of Islam and its followers have become widespread all over the Western world. Today when we walk into any bookstore we can come across a stack of titles that are truly frightening, journalistic publications 'revealing' worlds of so-called terrorist intrigue and plots against the West. Within this context, as a Muslim student of inter-religious dialogue, I really appreciate Jacques Waardenburg's chapter, which surveys Muslims' attitudes towards the others from the time of the Prophet to our modern time from a historical point of view. As historians of religions we both begin our investigation of the position of Islam in a world of diverse faiths by emphasizing the need to distinguish between the original religion, its practices and its interpretation by the followers in order to understand the main message concerning other religions more accurately. It seems to me that in a sense we both follow Wilfred Cantwell Smith's distinction between faith and cumulative tradition[1] or Hick's distinction between an inner (spiritual) and outer (institutionalized) aspect of religion.[2]

1 Wilfred Cantwell Smith, 1991, *The Meaning and End of Religion*, Minneapolis: Fortress Press (originally published in 1962), pp. 42–4.

2 John Hick, 2005, 'The Next Step beyond Dialogue', in Paul F. Knitter (ed.), *The Myth of Religious Superiority*, Maryknoll: Orbis Books, pp. 4–5.

However, I have also some questions and objections in relation to Waardenburg's arguments. He argues that in the Meccan period the Prophet Muḥammad called not only pagan Arabs but also other people such as Jews and Christians to accept his teaching. But when we look at the Meccan verses their main message is to invite pagan Arabs to believe in one God and the Hereafter and not to exploit poor people and orphans. In this period the Qur'ān regarded the Jews as good models for pagans in order to lead them to belief in God. Further, Waardenburg claims that after migrating to Medina the Prophet moved from a tolerant to a more hostile attitude to other religions in order to establish an autonomous Muslim community there. However, Waardenburg seems to neglect *the Pact of Medina*, which the Prophet signed with Jews and pagan Arabs who lived in Medina as soon as he arrived there. As Waardenburg knows well, in this Pact all tribes, including the Jews of Medina, were considered as a single community within the context of equal citizenship. Only after the Jews broke this Pact, did the Prophet expel them from Medina. This shows that negative Muslim attitudes towards the religious other such as Jews and later on Christians came about as a result of historical and political developments – as similarly negative attitudes of Jews and Christians towards Muslims. Furthermore, Waardenburg cites the present official situation of Saudi Arabia as evidence of Islamic exclusivism by stating that in Saudi Arabia 'no other faiths than Islam are allowed'.[3] However, this is not true of the whole of Saudi Arabia but relates only to Mecca and Medina where there are restrictions for non-Muslims. In short, the source of this practice is not the teaching of Islam but the political decisions of Muslim leaders including the present Saudi regime.

Second, I would also like to add a remark on Waardenburg's statement that Islam is 'the Arab version of the basic religion God has given to mankind'. In one sense, Waardenburg is right. According to qur'ānic teaching, Islam is not the religion of the Prophet Muḥammad but is the religion of Allah (*dīn al-fitrah / religio naturalis*) which had been proclaimed by all the prophets from Adam to the Prophet Muḥammad. However, some Western scholars are keen to confine Islam by showing that its message was *only* for the Arab pagans. Kenneth Cragg, for example, argues that the main duty of

3 Waardenburg's chapter in this book, p. 20.

the Prophet Muḥammad was to bring pagan Arabs to believe in one God by abandoning all forms of idolatry. However, Cragg and other like-minded scholars seem to overlook that the Prophet's duty was not only to introduce monotheism to Arab pagans but also to correct some wrong beliefs of Jews and Christians as a prophetic corrective.[4]

Third, I have reservations about Waardenburg's attempt to interpret the teaching of the Prophet Muḥammad, or better, the institutionalized religion of Islam, as an exclusive faith by implying that Muḥammad's teaching should be followed in order to be acceptable to God or, in other words, to attain salvation. As I stressed in my paper, it is not only those who follow the teaching of the Prophet Muḥammad but also those who submit themselves to God without associating anything or anybody with God who can go to Paradise. In other words, the teaching of the Prophet Muḥammad and the Qur'ān strongly insist that God's grace and mercy is not limited to a particular community, e.g. to the Muslim community, but extends to all His creatures. In accordance with the universality of His plan of salvation, God gives all His creatures an equal opportunity and capacity, within their historical and cultural situation, to relate to Him in such a way that their salvation is possible. I have difficulties in understanding why Waardenburg, on the one hand, seems to interpret Islam as an exclusivist and absolute faith, and, on the other hand, rightly argues that seeing Islam in that way inevitably creates serious tensions with those who reject it. It seems to me that the main reason for this dilemma is his preference for the historical and cultural formulations of Islam to qur'ānic teachings. However, to be fair to Waardenburg, I do acknowledge that in his paper he generally maintains that it is not Islam as a faith but its interpretations and historical formulations that cause problems for Muslims' relations with other religious traditions. Also, he strongly opposes the perception of Islam as the only 'political' religion and rightly affirms that 'all religions with a particular vision of society, favouring or resisting particular social projects, have been politicized in certain

4 Cf. Hans Küng, 1993, *Christianity and the World Religions: Paths of Dialogue with Islam, Hinduism, and Buddhism*, 2nd edn, Maryknoll: Orbis Books, p. 338.

ways.'[5] I think this argument of Waardenburg is very important to correct the distorted image of Islam as a political religion which justifies and intensifies terrorism and other human evils.

Finally, I would like to express my complete agreement with Waardenburg's suggestion that in our current world, as people of different faiths, we need not only to enter into dialogue with each other but also to study each other's religious and cultural sources in order to enrich and to be enriched by them. For, as John Hick rightly states, 'we have no reason to restrict ourselves to the spiritual resources of our own tradition'[6] in our religiously and culturally pluralistic age.

5 Waardenburg's chapter in this book, p. 25.

6 John Hick, 1995, *The Rainbow of Faiths*, London: SCM Press, p. 139.

Part II

Islam and Judaism

6. A Muslim View of Judaism

MUHAMMAD KALISCH

In the first part of my paper I sketch an overview of the different methodological discourses in traditional Islam and briefly discuss their relevance to an Islamic view of other religions in general and to Judaism in particular. In the second part I suggest how and why one should rethink some of the traditional positions and on this basis I will present my personal theological view.

Methods and Discourses in Traditional Islam and their Relevance to the Islamic View of Other Religions

*Systematic theology (*kalām*)*

Islam, just like every religion, is not a uniform phenomenon. Throughout history many different understandings of Islam have developed. These understandings differ on various questions. However, the most influential understanding of Islam comes from systematic theology which is called *'ilm al-kalām*.[1] *'Ilm al-kalām* itself is divided

1 Beside *'ilm al-kalām*, which I have translated here as systematic theology, there exists in Sunnī Islām a tradition which is called Salafīya or the tradition of the *Ahl al-ḥadīth*. This tradition shares the same basic beliefs as *Sunnī 'ilm al-kalām*, represented in the two schools (Ash'arīya and Māturīdīya), but rejects the methods of *'ilm al-kalām* which according to the Salafīya are alien to true Islam and have been taken from Greek philosophy. A good example for a Salafī creed is the *risāla* of Abū Ja'far aṭ-Ṭaḥāwī. Cf. aṭ-Ṭaḥāwī, Abū Ja'far, 1985, 'Aqīdat aṭ-Ṭaḥāwī (Ehl-i sünnet inanç esasları – Tahavi ve Akaid Risalesi), Ankara: Seha Neşriyat, 1985 (original Arabic text with a Turkish translation by Arif Aytekin). For several reasons (perhaps one of the most significant being the economical power of Saudi Arabia), the Salafiya has become widespread among Sunnī Muslims,

into various schools that differ on the major questions of theology. But regarding our subject, the Islamic view of other religions and especially Judaism, the approach of the different schools does not differ.

What is typical for all systems of *'ilm al-kalām* is that they regard the affiliation to Islam as the indispensable condition for salvation. The root for this belief is how the *mutakallimūn* (the theologians) understood salvation history. From their viewpoint, Muḥammad was the last prophet who brought the last and unchanged message of God. Whenever a new prophet comes, his message is the actual commandment of God which people have to follow. This implies that all mankind now has to follow Muḥammad who is definitively the last messenger of God who brought to mankind God's last and unchanged revelation. Although a Muslim has to accept all prophets, the only valid message for him is the message of Muḥammad. According to the *mutakallimūn* this is due to two reasons: The revelations received prior to Muḥammad have not been preserved without error and change, and there is the theory that in legal matters (not in matters of faith of course) God may change (abrogate) some laws of former communities. But beside these two points, from a traditional *kalām* viewpoint it is sufficient that there was a new messenger sent by God. Not to recognize this messenger and not to believe in him would be an act of disobedience against God in matters of faith and therefore has to be qualified as disbelief.

For all the *mutakallimūn* there was no salvation outside of the one true religion which was Islam. There was a debate among the *mutakallimūn* about the priority of deeds (*a'māl*) or faith (*īmān*) but this debate was restricted to Muslims. The Islamic debate about the state of the grave sinner has always been centred on the Muslim who commits grave sins.[2] That a non-Muslim will go to hell automatically because he has the wrong religion was a common belief among the *mutakallimūn*. Therefore the *mutakallimūn* spent a lot of time defining true religion and how true faith could

---

especially in the Arab world. The Shī'ites have their own systems of *kalām* differing from Sunnī *kalām* on many points.

2 Cf. Al-Sharafī, Aḥmad b. Muḥammad b. Ṣalāḥ, 1995, *'Uddat al-akyās fī sharḥ ma'ānī l-asās*, Ṣan'ā': Dār al-ḥīkma al-yamānīya, vol. 2, pp. 237–384; al-Taftāzānī, Sa'd al-Dīn Mas'ūd b. 'Umar, (without date), *Sharḥ al-'aqā'id*, Istanbul: Salah Bilici Kitabevi, pp. 140–59.

be separated from heresy and disbelief. It was vital to distinguish disbelief from belief because the latter implies eternal punishment in hell. For the traditional viewpoint of *'ilm al-kalām* the Qur'ān is the direct word of God. It is a text formulated by God and given to the prophet Muḥammad by the angel Gabriel (Jibrīl). According to the *mutakallimūn* the text of the Qur'ān remains unchanged and God himself protects it from error and corruption.[3] The *mutakallimūn* believe that before Muḥammad there were other prophets and some of them like Moses (Mūsā), David (Dāwūd) and Jesus ('Īsā) received a book from God, just as Muḥammad did, but these books were corrupted by their communities. Traditional Islamic theology derives a certain concept of salvation history from the Qur'ān which takes the stories about the prophets literally as historical truth, and it sees prophecy as a phenomenon that appeared in earlier periods in the likeness of the model of Muḥammad too. This means that God directly gave messages and books he himself had formulated to certain people he had chosen as his messengers.

Within this context of the *kalām* tradition Judaism is seen as a religion belonging to the category of the *Ahl al-kitāb* (people of the book). *Ahl al-kitāb* is a term taken from the Qur'ān and describes religious groups who have a holy book that according to Muslim beliefs goes back to a prophet. Jews and Christians are accepted as *Ahl al-kitāb* by all Muslim schools of theology and law. The Islamic theological tradition accuses the *Ahl al-kitāb* of having corrupted their books. On the other hand the *Ahl al-kitāb* are clearly separated from the *mushrikūn* (polytheists)[4] in the Qur'ān. The Qur'ān criticizes the Jews in particular for claiming to be special friends

---

3 Sūra 15 verse 9 is often seen as a qur'ānic proof for this claim see sūra 15 verse 9: 'We have, without doubt, sent down the message (*dhikr*); and We will assuredly guard it (from corruption)'. (All translations of the Qur'ān in this article are from Abdullah Yusuf Ali). Abdullah Yusuf Ali here translated the word *dhikr* (literally meaning 'mention' or 'thinking of') as message. The traditional Islamic understanding is that *dhikr* here stands for the Qur'ān.

4 There have been debates among traditional Islamic scholars whether the term polytheists (*mushrikūn*) can be applied to the *Ahl al-Kitāb*. Cf. the commentary of Yūsuf al-Ṯulā'ī on sūra 9, verse 28 in al-Ṯulā'ī, Yūsuf b. 'Uṯmān, 2002, *al-Ṯamārāt al-yāni'a*, Ṣa'da: Maktabat at-turāṯ al-islāmī, vol.3. p. 408 f.

of God[5] but states also that God had preferred (*tafḍīl*) the Banū Isrā'īl (Children of Israel),[6] and it mentions the patriarchs, Moses (Mūsā), Aaron (Hārūn), David (Dāwūd) and Solomon (Sulaymān) as prophets. The Qur'ān and the *kalām* tradition recognize a special relationship between the *Ahl al-kitāb* and the Muslims. Although the Qur'ān clearly states that God had sent messengers to all communities, it deals with the Semitic religious traditions only, and priority is given to mentioning Abraham and Moses. Muslims do not regard Islam as a new religion. For them Islam is the original message that has been sent to all mankind throughout history by many prophets but which has been lost in its full clearness because the former communities have brought some corruption.

*Islamic law (*fiqh*)*

The practical aspects of these theological questions are the subject of Islamic law. Within Islam various traditions of law developed that differed in method and legal rules. The Sunnī schools of law[7] allow a Muslim man to marry women of the *Ahl al-kitāb*[8] and to eat meat that they have slaughtered.[9] The Shī'ite schools[10] tend to be more reserved in these questions. Among the Zaidī Shī'ites there are scholars like al-Hādī and an-Nāṣir who regard marriage with non-Muslims as generally forbidden.[11] Non-Muslim inhabitants of

5 Qur'ān, sūra 62, verse 6: Say: 'O ye that stand on Judaism! If you think that ye are friends to Allah, to the exclusion of (other) men, then express your desire for death, if you are truthful!'

6 Qur'ān, sūra 2, verse 47: 'O Children of Israel! Call to mind the (special) favour which I bestowed upon you, and that I preferred you to all others (for My message).'

7 Ḥanafīya, Mālikīya, Shāfi'īya and Ḥanbalīya. The origin and development of these schools is described by Christopher Melchert, 1997, *The Formation of the Sunnī Schools of Law 9th–10th Centuries C.E.*, Leiden, New York, Köln: Brill.

8 al-Jazīrī, 'Abd al-Raḥmān, 1987, *Kitāb al-fiqh 'alā l-madhāhib al-arba'a*, Istanbul: Çağrı yayınları, vol. 4, p. 75

9 al-Jazīrī, *Kitāb al-fiqh 'alā l-madhāhib al-arba'a*, vol. 2, pp. 21–3.

10 Zaidīya, Iṯnā 'Asharīya and Ismā'ilīya.

11 Ibn al-Murtaḍā, Aḥmad b. Yaḥyā, 1988, *al-Baḥr al-zakhkhār al-jāmi' li-maḏāhib 'ulamā' al-amṣār*, Ṣan'ā': Dār al-ḥikma al-yamānīya, vol. 3, p. 40.

Islamic territory were regarded as *Ahl al-dhimma*. This concept was a progressive concept in medieval times and the Jews in particular had better conditions under Islamic rule than under Christian rule (but the position of Jews here should not be idealized). It must be seen and judged according to the circumstances of the medieval world. Although the basic idea of *dhimma* is that the *ahl -al-dhimma* share the rights and obligations of the Muslims as the books of Islamic law express it (the formulation used by Muslim jurists is: *lahum mā lanā wa-'alayhim mā 'alaynā* = they have the rights we have and they have the obligations we have)[12] and although they were even allowed to work as high officials in the government[13] they clearly were not equal citizens and some of their rights were restricted.[14] The *ahl -al-dhimma* were not totally equal to the Muslims and many Muslim jurists themselves understood the concept of *dhimma* as a concept of Islamic superiority. This idea of Islamic superiority is best expressed in the commentaries on sūra 9, verse 29:

> Fight those who believe not in Allah nor the Last Day nor hold that forbidden which hath been forbidden by Allah and His prophet, nor acknowledge the religion of truth, (even if they are) of the people of the Book, until they pay the jizya with willing submission,[15] and feel themselves subdued (*wa-hum ṣāghirūn*).

The *jizya* was a special tax (which was not very high) for the *Ahl al-dhimma*. And it was really a substitute for not participating in the army, since they were exempt from military participation with the Muslim army. But the really problematical aspect of being a *dhimmī* was the attitude of some jurists towards the phrase *wa-hum ṣāghirūn*. This phrase was understood as an expression of Muslim superiority. Ibn al-Murtaḍā wrote that it is obligatory to disdain the *dhimmīyūn* when they paid the *jizya* (*wa-yalzimu iṣghāruhum 'inda l-'aṭā'*).[16] It is this attitude of superiority that corrupted the general

12 Zaidān, 'Abd al-Karīm, 1988, *Aḥkām al-dhimmīyīn wa-l-musta'minīn fī dār al-islām*, 2nd ed., Beirūt: Mu'assasat al-risāla, p. 61.

13 Cf. al-Māwardī, Abū l-Ḥasan 'Alī b. Muḥammad, 1985, *al-Aḥkām as-sulṭānīya wa-l-wilāyāt ad-dīnīya*, Beirūt: Dār al-kutub al-'ilmīya, p. 31

14 Cf. for example Zaidān, *Aḥkām al-dhimmīyīn*, pp. 62; 82–5.

15 *'an yad*, meaning literally 'from the hand'.

16 Ibn al-Murtaḍā, *al-Baḥr al-zakhkhār*, vol.5, p. 459.

concept of equality in rights and obligations and that led to an understanding that made the *ahl -al-dhimma* second class citizens.

*Islamic philosophy (*ḥikma*)*

Beside systematic theology and law another tradition had emerged within Islam that became known as Islamic philosophy. This tradition was different from *'ilm al-kalām* in origin, method and views. The first Muslim scholar who is known as a Muslim philosopher was al-Kindī, but the real founder of an independent tradition of Islamic philosophy was al-Fārābī. The philosophical tradition in Islam, which is divided into two major branches known as *Mashshā'ūn* (Peripatetics)[17] and *Ishrāqīyūn*,[18] sees itself as a continuation of classical philosophy in the tradition of Aristotle or Plato.

Islamic philosophy was never interested in defining belief, disbelief and heresy. The Muslim philosophers like al-Fārābī, Ibn Sīnā or Suhrawardī all declared their belief in prophecy and revelation[19] but their view about revelation differed from the approach of the

17 The Mashshā'ūn saw themselves as Peripatetics although their philosophy was under the strong influence of Neoplatonism. Some Muslim philosophers mistakenly believed that a book called the 'Theology of Aristotle', which was in fact a translation of parts of the *Enneads* of Plotinus, was a work of Aristotle. Only Ibn Rushḍ (Averroes) attempted to be a pure Aristotelian.

18 This philosophical tradition goes back to Shihāb al-Dīn Yaḥyā al-Suhrawardī who saw himself as the protagonist of an ancient universal wisdom tradition, the major representatives of which in the Greek tradition were Pythagoras and Plato. The philosophical tradition of Suhrawardī is examined in John Walbridge, 1992, *The Science of Mystic Lights – Qutb al-Dīn Shīrāzī and the Illuminationist Tradition in Islamic Philosophy*, Cambridge, MA: Harvard Middle Eastern Monographs; J. Walbridge, 1999, *The Leaven of the Ancients – Suhrawardī and the Heritage of the Greeks*, Albany, NY: SUNY, and John Walbridge, 2001, *The Wisdom of the Mystic East – Suhrawardī and Platonic Orientalism*, Albany, NY: SUNY. The term *ishrāq* means illumination. Suhrawardī believed that true philosophy needs mystical vision and he used the allegory of light for explaining the various degrees of existence.

19 Cf. Al-Fārābī, Abū Naṣr, 2002, *Ārā' Ahl al-madīna al-fāḍila*, 8th ed., Beirūt: Dār al-Mashriq, pp. 114–16; Ibn Sīnā, 1960, *Al-Shifā', al-Ilāhīyāt*, al-Qāhira: al-Hai'a al-'āmma li-shu'ūn al-maṭābi' al-amīrīya, pp. 441–3; al-Suhrawardī, Shihāb al-Dīn Yaḥyā, 1999, *Ḥikmat al-ishrāq*, Provo Utah: Brigham Young University Press, pp. 153–7.

mutakallimūn.[20] For the philosophers it was evident that the message brought by the prophets had an allegorical character and the philosophers were the people who were able to understand the truth through reason alone without need for revelation. The philosophers saw salvation as an individual process by acquiring knowledge through philosophical thinking and by purifying the soul. Therefore, their writings do not discuss matters of orthodoxy and heresy. Although the Muslim philosophers understood themselves as Muslims their writings do not deal with the question of belonging to a certain religion. This is quite logical because their understanding of salvation has nothing to do with a certain religion but with individual understanding and purification of the soul.[21]

*Islamic Gnosis (*ʻirfān*)*

In Islam there is also a tradition of Gnosis (*ʻirfān*) which is based on mystical experience (*kashf*, *mukāshafa*). This is the reason why the Islamic Gnostics are also called *ahl al-dhawq* (People of tasting), because they experience truth. The Gnostics (*ʻurafā'*) basically followed the known schools of Islamic thinking and Islamic law but developed some additional ideas, especially in the field of ontology.[22] Like Gnostics of all religions they interpreted their holy scripture in an allegorical way, just as Philo of Alexandria interpreted Jewish scriptures. Although Islamic Gnostics developed a certain idea of a transcendent unity of religions it seems that most of them did not go so far as to declare affiliation to a certain faith as irrelevant for salvation. In the most important school of Islamic *ʻirfān*, the tradition of Ibn ʻArabī,[23] the problem of God's mercy and punishment

20 On their theory of revelation cf. Herbert A. Davidson, 1992, *Alfarabi, Avicenna, & Averroes on Intellect*, New York, Oxford: Oxford University Press, pp. 116–23.

21 Cf. for example al-Fārābī's discussion about salvation and eternal life in his *Ārā' Ahl al-madīna al-fāḍila* (fn. 19), pp. 131–74 or Suhrawardī's discussion in *Ḥikmat al-ishrāq* (fn.19), pp. 141–63.

22 Mainly the theory known as *waḥdat al-wujūd* (unity of existence).

23 Ibn ʻArabī is known by his followers as al-Shaykh al-akbar. He is the author of a large number of books among which *al-Futūḥāt al-makkīya* and *Fuṣūṣ al-ḥikam* are the most important. His tradition is the most eminent tradition of Sufi thinking in Islam and some of the

was solved by introducing the idea of the apocatastasis.[24] According to this idea hell has an end and the final goal of all creation is general salvation.[25] But even a great Sufi thinker such as ʿAbd al-Karīm al-Jīlī declared in his work *al-insān al-kāmil* that every non-Muslim will go to hell because he follows a religion of damnation (*dīn shaqāwa*).[26] It seems that Jalāl al-Dīn Rūmī, a contemporary of Ibn ʿArabī, had the idea that belonging to a certain faith is irrelevant for salvation. In one of his poems he declares:

> What shall I do, O ye Muslims, for I do not know myself anymore;
> I am neither Christian, nor Jew, nor Zoroastrian, nor Muslim . . .[27]

What must be added is that this poem is not found in the critical edition of the Kullīyāt-i Shams[28] and so its authenticity is doubtful. But even if it is not a poem by Rūmī it demonstrates that at least some of his followers had such ideas, and Annemarie Schimmel writes that, in its whole tenor, it resembles the effusions of slightly later poets in the Persian and Turkish speaking areas.[29] It is also known that in India Hindus were sometimes initiated into Sufism by Chishtī

---

greatest *ʿurafā'* like al-Qashānī, al-Jandī, al-Qūnawī, Muḥammad b. Ḥamza al-Fanārī, ʿAbd al-Karīm al-Jīlī or Dawūd al-Qayṣarī were influenced by his ideas and many scholars wrote commentaries on his Fuṣūṣ.

24 Ibn ʿArabī declares in his *Fuṣūṣ al-ḥikam* that the *ʿurafā'* before him did not regard the apocatastasis as impossible, cf. Ibn ʿArabī, Muḥyīddīn, 2002, *Fuṣūṣ al-ḥikam*, ed. ʿAfīfī, Beirūt: Dār al-kitāb al-ʿarabī, p. 114. The term 'apocatastasis', which I use here comes from the Christian tradition. There is no specific Islamic term for this theological opinion.

25 Cf. Ibn ʿArabī, Muḥyīddīn, (without date), *al-Futūḥāt al-makkīya*, Bairūt: Dār Ṣādir, vol.3, p.25; al-Qaiṣarī, Dawūd, 1423 h., *Maṭlaʿ khuṣūṣ al-kalim fī maʿānī fuṣūṣ al-ḥikam*, Qumm: Mu'assasa muḥibbīn li-ṭ-ṭibāʿa wa-n-nashr, vol.2, p. 46.

26 al-Jīlī, ʿAbdalkarīm, 2000, *al-Insān al-kāmil fī maʿrifat al-awākhir wa-l-awā'il*, Bairūṯ: Mu'assat at-ta'rīkh al-ʿarabī, p. 255.

27 Cited in Annemarie Schimmel, 1993, *The Triumphal Sun – A Study of the Works of Jalāloddīn Rumi*, Albany, NY: SUNY, p. 389.

28 Schimmel, 1993, *The Triumphal Sun*, p. 389; William C. Chittick, 2005, *The Sufi Doctrine of Rumi*, Bloomington: World Wisdom, p. 76.

29 Schimmel, 1993, *The Triumphal Sun*, p. 389.

masters without converting to Islam.[30] But in general it can be said that Islamic Gnosticism tended to embrace the idea of the apocatastasis but not the idea that other religions than Islam lead to direct salvation.

Rethinking the Traditional Approach

In the second part I want to present my own view about the subject which depends on ideas of traditional Muslim philosophy, Muslim Gnosticism and ideas of modern Muslim thinkers like Sayyid Aḥmad Khān and Muḥammad Iqbāl and on the application of these ideas to our modern knowledge about the history of religions and comparative religious studies. My concept of an Islamic view of Judaism is only a special application of my general concept of an Islamic theology of religions. I start from the traditional Zaidite and *mu'tazilite* viewpoint that reason (*'aql*) is superior to revelation.[31] If we take this statement seriously then our modern knowledge about the history of religions and comparative religious studies forces us to rethink many traditional Islamic theological concepts and to find new solutions. Here again the tradition of Islamic philosophy as well as Islamic Gnosticism can be very helpful.

The nature of revelation and the genesis of the Qur'ān

Modern archaeological research has shown to us that the stories told in the Bible and the Qur'ān are not history.[32] Personally I think that the approach which is known as biblical minimalism represented by scholars as Niels Peter Lemche,[33] Thomas Thompson[34] and Philip

30 Carl W. Ernst, 1997, *Sufism*, Boston–London: Shambala Publications, p. 222.

31 Cf. al-Qāsim b. Ibrāhīm, 2001, *Uṣūl al-'adl wa-l-tawḥīd* in: Majmū' kutub wa-rasā'il al-Imām al-Qāsim b. Ibrāhīm al-Rassī, vol.1, Ṣan'ā': Dār al-ḥikma al-yamānīya, p. 631.

32 The results of modern archaeology are summarized by Israel Finkelstein and Neil Asher Silberman, 2002, *The Bible Unearthed: Archaeology's New Vision of Ancient Israel and the Origin of Its Sacred Texts*, New York: Free Press.

33 Cf. Niels Peter Lemche, 1998, *The Israelites in History and Tradition*, London: SPCK.

34 Cf. Thomas Thompson, 2000, *The Mythic Past: Biblical Archaeology and the Myth of Israel*, New York: Basic Books.

Davies[35] is the best approach to deal with all such problems. This approach is purely rationalistic and takes the facts as they are. In my opinion the obvious result of modern research is that the patriarchs, Moses and even David and Solomon are not historical persons. They never existed. Even if one holds that there was a historical Moses or a historical David one would have to admit that the real historical person behind the legend and the myth is totally unknown to us and this means nothing else than that the Moses or David of the Bible or the Qur'ān never existed. If there was a historical person (and I think there was not) this person is totally unknown for us and irrelevant for Jewish, Christian and Muslim faith. The Hebrew Bible is a product of the Hellenistic period, possibly of the Persian period.[36] It contains salvation history and theology, not historical truth. This is also relevant for Islam which shares many myths with the Hebrew Bible, and the Qur'ān makes use of them for its own construction of salvation history. From the viewpoint of reason we must treat holy texts on an equal footing regarding our methods of research. It cannot make any difference whether we examine the Hebrew Bible, the Gospels, the Qur'ān or the Enuma Elish of Babylonia or the Tao Te Ching of the Chinese.

If we take a look at human spirituality and its history, it becomes clear that God doesn't write books. The holy books of mankind are the products of human spiritual experience and we cannot exclude the Qur'ān from this realization. Spiritual experience can be traced back to God in an allegorical sense because human spirituality comes from a source which is given to man by God, but it remains a subjective human experience. This means that the Qur'ān is the spiritual experience of Muḥammad and like the Bible it constructs salvation history and does not tell us anything about real history. According to my view the latter is not the intention of the Qur'ān. The Qur'ān does not show any interest in times and places, and like other holy texts it uses the method of allegory and myth for explaining spiritual truth and does not even want to teach us history in the modern sense of the word.

---

35 Cf. Philip R. Davies, 1995, *In Search of Ancient Israel*, Sheffield: Sheffield Academic Press.

36 On this problem see Lester L. Grabbe (ed.), 2001, *Did Moses Speak Attic? – Jewish Historiography and Scripture in the Hellenistic Period*, Sheffield: Sheffield Academic Press.

The idea that the Qur'ān is the direct word of God is a product of theological tradition and not the only possible way to understand what the Qur'ān itself states about the nature of revelation. The Qur'ān identifies the angel Gabriel with the *rūḥ* (spirit) (also *rūḥ al-qudus* = holy spirit, or *al-rūḥ al-amīn* = the trustworthy spirit).[37] But *rūḥ* (spirit) is an element given by God to every human being[38] and so revelation is the product of the *rūḥ* of Muḥammad. In Muslim philosophy revelation was seen as the product of the active intellect (*al-'aql al-fa''āl*) which is identified with Gabriel. This is the tenth and last intellect in a chain of emanations from God and from this active intellect the world of generation and corruption emanated.[39] Here we have a model of revelation which sees revelation as a natural process, and in my view this is in line with the qur'ānic understanding.

Now, although I am rather convinced that there was a historical Muḥammad,[40] I am also convinced that we can't know much about his life. The first two centuries of Muslim history can only be reconstructed by sources from the third and the fourth century of Muslim history.

The *sīra*, literature (the biography of Muḥammad) is a piece of

---

37 Qur'ān, sūra 2, verses 97–98: 'Say: Whoever is an enemy to Gabriel – for he brings down the (revelation) to thy heart by Allah's will, a confirmation of what went before, and guidance and glad tidings for those who believe – Whoever is an enemy to Allah and His angels and messengers, to Gabriel and Michael – Lo! Allah is an enemy to those who reject faith.'

Qur'ān sūra 26, verses 192–193: 'Verily, this is a revelation from the Lord of the worlds: with it came down the spirit of faith and truth.'

Qur'ān sūra 40, verse 15: 'Raised high above ranks (or degrees), (He is) the Lord of the Throne (of authority): by His command doth he send the spirit (of inspiration) to any of his servants He pleases, that it may worn (men) of the Day of Mutual meeting.'

38 Qur'ān sūra 32, verse 9: 'But He fashioned him in due proportion, and breathed into him something of His spirit.'

39 For Ibn Sīnā's theory of the ten intellects see Ian Richard Netton, 1994, *Allah Transcendent – Studies in the Structure and Semiotics of Islamic Philosophy, Theology and Cosmology*, Richmond: Routledge, p. 165.

40 The arguments given in Yehuda Nevo and Judith Koren, 2003, *Crossroads to Islam*, Amherst: Prometheus Books, against his historicity do not convince me, but they indeed show us that the Muslim account of history cannot be correct.

literal fiction written much later after his death reflecting the theological views of second century AH Muslims.[41] Whether it contains an iota of historical truth at all can be questioned seriously. Was the *hijra* (Muḥammad's emigration from Mecca to Medina) a historical event because there is no miracle in the story and it does not sound implausible? Or has Muḥammad a *hijra* because Moses and the exodus story play such an important role in the Qur'ān,[42] and because Moses was the model for Muḥammad and therefore his biographers created an exodus for him? In 1977 Michael Cook and Patricia Crone opened a debate about the reliability of the traditional Muslim account of the development of Islam and this debate continues until today.[43]

Muḥammad, according to my view, was a historical person but a historical person whose biography is unknown and therefore the Muḥammad of Muslim faith is a mythical person too. Islamic faith as we know it today is a product of the first two centuries of Islam, those two centuries about which we get our information mostly from later sources only.[44] What we can see clearly is that for the first Muslims Muḥammad did not play that outstanding and important role that he played from the end of the second century AH onwards. Although we have earlier inscriptions from the first Islamic century it seems that the first mention of Muḥammad appears in the year 71 AH, eventually 66 AH on coins.[45] In the same way the Islamic sources reflect the fact that for the earlier Muslim generations the term *sunna* was not connected exclusively with the *sunna* of the prophet but referred to the general praxis of a certain generation of Muslims

---

41 The earliest biography of Muḥammad is that of Ibn Isḥāq which survived only partially.

42 Moses is the most mentioned prophet in the Qur'ān. He occurs more often than Abraham.

43 Cf. Michael Cook and Patricia Cone, 1977, *Hagarism: The Making of the Islamic World*, Cambridge: Cambridge University Press; see also Patricia Crone, 1987, *Meccan Trade and the Rise of Islam*, Princeton: Princeton University Press, and John Wansbrough, 2006, *The Sectarian Milieu: Content and Composition of Islamic Salvation History*, Amherst: Prometheus Books.

44 We have some sources dated earlier but here the question of pseudepigraphy or later interpolations and manipulations arise.

45 Cf. Nevo and Koren, 2003, *Crossroads*, pp. 247–54; 297–336.

or a local praxis of Muslims. *Sunna* at the beginning was a term similar to *ijmāʿ* (consensus).[46] Only from the time of al-Shāfiʿī[47] did the concept of imitating Muḥammad become dominant, and I think it is no coincidence that the first biography of the prophet appeared in the second century AH at a time when the idea of referring to the prophet came into being. It is quite obvious that Muḥammad was not a paradigm for the believer in the first century of Islam. So the question remains. What was Islam at that time? Both archaeological evidence and non-Islamic contemporary sources from the first two centuries of Islam,[48] as well as the contradictions in the Muslim tradition itself, make it clear that the traditional Islamic account of early Islamic history is salvation history and not history.

Regarding the Qur'ān, in the present stage of my research, I think that it is still probable that this text was collected relatively early and contains the spiritual experience of Muḥammad. It is also probable that the text remained unchanged although it is impossible to prove this and it is not impossible that something was added to or removed from the text. An argument for an early collection of the Qur'ān is the fact that Muslims could agree on one version.[49] Although different schools and sects differ on the interpretation of the text, they all accept the same text and do not raise doubts about the authenticity. They prefer to make complicated argumentations regarding verses that do not fit into their views. This can be explained best by assuming that the text had an authority that it gained because it was collected early and agreed upon. It is difficult to see a political authority in the Umayyad and ʿAbbāsid period that would have been able to

46 Cf. John Burton, 1994, *An Introduction to the Hadith*, Edinburgh: Edinburgh University Press, pp. 148–77.

47 Muḥammad b. Idrīs al-Shāfiʿī (150–204/767–820) was an eminent scholar of Islamic Law to whom the school named Shāfiʿīya is traced back. Today some scholars debate whether the works ascribed to him were really written by him or whether they are products of later times, cf. Melchert, 1997, *Formation* (fn. 7), p. 68.

48 Of course the non-Muslim sources are not more historically trustworthy than the Muslim sources. One should not wait for finding historical truth in them. But some information can be derived from them. It is interesting to see what they know – or do not know – about Islam and Muslims.

49 This version differs only in minor reading variants (*qirā'āt*) and even regarding the *qirā'āt* one of them, regarded as the reading of ʿĀṣim reported by Ḥafṣ, became practically dominant.

implement a commonly accepted version against the will of different sects. That discussions about alternative versions of the Qur'ān existed is clear from the Islamic material, especially Shī'ite sources,[50] and if the commonly accepted version had not had extremely high authority different versions of the Qur'ān would have resulted.

The question of salvation

Another argument for an early dating of the Qur'ānic text is the appearance of theological ideas in it, which were opposed by later theological thought. In sūra 2, verse 62 we read:

> Those who believe (in the Qur'ān), and those who follow the Jewish (scriptures). and the Christians and the Sabians; any who believe in Allah and the Last Day, and work righteousness, shall have their reward with their Lord: on them shall be no fear, nor shall they grieve.

And in sūra 5, verse 69 we read again:

> Those who believe (in the Qur'ān), those who follow the Jewish (scriptures) and the Sabians and the Christians; any who believe in Allah and the Last Day, and work righteousness, on them shall be no fear, nor shall they grieve.

These two verses clearly contradict the later Islamic theological position that there is no salvation outside Islam. All the commentators of these verses tried their best to harmonize Islamic theology with these qur'ānic verses by presenting absurd constructions,[51] and the reader clearly feels how strange the idea expressed in these verses appeared

50 Cf. Reiner Brunner, 2001, *Die Schia und die Koranfälschung* (Abhandlungen für die Kunde des Morgenlandes, Band LIII.1), Würzburg: Ergon.

51 Cf. for example al-Zamakhsharī, Jārallāh Maḥmūd b. 'Umar, 1987, *al-Kashshāf 'an ḥaqā'iq ghawāmiḍ at-tanzīl wa-'uyūn al-aqāwīl fī wujūh at-ta'wīl*, 3rd ed., al-Qāhira-Beirūt: Dār ar-rayyān li-t-turāṯ – Dār al-kitāb al-'arabī, vol.1, p. 146, or al-Qurṭubī, Abū 'Abdallāh Muḥammad b. Aḥmad, 1985, *al-Jāmi' li-aḥkām al-qur'ān*, Beirūt: Dār iḥyā' at-turāṯ al-'arabī, vol.1, pp. 432–6, who even reports a tradition according to which Ibn 'Abbās made the claim that verse 62 of sūra 2 is *mansūkh* (abrogated).

to the later commentators. In these qur'ānic verses exclusive salvation through one religion is obviously rejected and Judaism is one of the religions specifically mentioned as a way to salvation, although the specificity of Judaism is not important because the qur'ānic text makes three conditions: belief in God, working righteousness and belief in the Hereafter. In the last century some modern commentators like Abdullah Yusuf Ali understood the text as it was mentioned in the Qur'ān[52] and some Muslim authors rejected the idea of exclusive salvation.[53]

There are other verses in the Qur'ān that call Christians and Jews to leave certain ideas, to reform themselves or to co-operate with Islam, but not to abandon Christianity or Judaism and become Muslims. A good example is sūra 5 verse 77:

> Say: 'Oh People of the Book! Exceed not in your religion the bounds (of what is proper), trespassing beyond the truth, nor follow the vain desires of people who went wrong in times gone by, – who misled many, and strayed (themselves) from the even way.'

Or sūra 3, verse 64:

> Say: 'Oh people of the Book! Come to common terms as between us and you: That we worship none but Allah, that we associate no partners with Him, that we erect not, from among ourselves, Lords and patrons other than Allah'. If then they turn back, say ye: 'Bear witness that we (at least) are Muslims (bowing to Allah's will).'

Therefore I do not think that Muḥammad had the idea that everyone should become his follower and enter his faith. The Qur'ān aims to reform certain concepts of Judaism and Christianity and heavily attacks polytheism but it has no concept of exclusive salvation.

---

52 'Abdullah Yūsuf 'Alī, 1989, *The Meaning of The Holy Qur'ān*, Beltsville: Amana Publications. See his commentary on sūra 2, verse 62, note 77, and on sūra 5, verse 72, note 779.

53 Some examples are mentioned by Kamāl, Yūsuf, 1990, *al-'Aṣrīyūn Mu'tazilat al-yawm*, 2nd ed., al-Manṣūra: Dār al-wafā' li-l-ṭibā'a wa-n-nashr wa-l-tawzī', pp. 30–40.

Interestingly the document known as the constitution of Medina as cited in the *Sīra* of Ibn Hishām refers to Muslims and Jews as one *umma* (community).[54] It is also wrong to read the terms *kāfir/kufr* and *mu'min/īmān* as unbeliever/unbelief and believer/belief in the meaning of accepting the Qur'ān as the revelation of God and Muḥammad as the messenger of God. These are definitions of the words given to them by later Islamic tradition. In the Qur'ān they have nothing to do with adherence to a certain faith. The Qur'ān also contains no concept of an infallibility of Muḥammad or any other prophet. The prophets in the Qur'ān are portrayed as pious persons but as fallible human beings with normal human weakness (cf. Moses or Jonas). Also the Qur'ān does not call on people to imitate Muḥammad on all points. He is called an *uswa ḥasana* (beautiful pattern) but this was not understood by the first generation as a command to imitate him on all details. Islamic tradition itself contains a lot of material about how the first generation acted independently. It is also interesting to see that many early Islamic inscriptions request pardon for him.[55] This shows us that there was no early Islamic concept of *'iṣma* (infallibility) of the prophet.

Conclusion

The Muslim view of Judaism, I think, has two aspects. The first aspect is the general view of other religions in Islam. In my opinion religions are human affairs. God doesn't care about whether one is a Jew, a Muslim, a Buddhist or a Shamanist and so on (cf. Qur'ān 2.62). What is important is to struggle for the truth, but no human being can ever reach all truth and can ever be free from subjective ideas. Every human understanding is subjective understanding. That does not mean that it is not possible for human beings to understand objective truth but the fact remains that every human understanding has a subjective component and therefore is subjective understanding. Wherever is real freedom of thought, there will inevitably be a diversity of opinions. Everyone can only be responsible for what he can understand (cf. Qur'ān 2.286: 'On no soul doth Allah place

54 Ibn Hishām, 2004, *al-Sīra al-nabawīya*, 4th ed., Beirūt: Dār al-ma'rifa, p. 452.

55 Nevo and Koren, 2003, *Crossroads*, p. 199.

a burden greater than it can bear'). And it also makes no sense for anyone to believe in something that he or she does not understand. The vast majority of traditional Muslim theologians hold the view that *taqlīd* (blind imitation without personal verification) in matters of *uṣūl* (principles of religion) is forbidden.[56] If one takes this view seriously it means nothing else than that no one is allowed to believe in anything except what s/he can personally verify. Of course in medieval times Muslim scholars did not apply the consequence of their view that *taqlīd* in matters of *uṣūl* is forbidden. They interpreted this principle in such a way that everyone had to find the well known theological truth by his/her own verification. So they stated that there is a truth everyone has to reach – if not, s/he is a heretic or an unbeliever. But those who define this truth are themselves human beings who found this truth by their own verification. Every religious and philosophical understanding whether based on a holy scripture or on pure reason is the result of subjective human reflection. To determine that there is a certain truth that everyone has to accept means nothing else than to regard the subjective opinions of human beings as binding for other human beings, and this is nonsense. A view is meaningless for those who accepted it by blind faith without personal verification and understanding.

The second aspect is that Islam has a special relationship with Judaism. There are obvious parallels between the two religions, and however Islam emerged in history it is clear that Judaism and most probably Judaeo-Christianity played an important role in its development. Studying the origins and the development of Judaism means also to study an important background of Islam and the Qur'ān.

---

56 Cf. Al-Sharafī, Aḥmad b. Muḥammad b. Ṣalāḥ, 1991, *Sharḥ al-asās al-kabīr – Shifā' ṣudūr al-nās bi-sharḥ al-asās*, Ṣan'ā': Dār al-ḥikma al-yamānīya, vol. 1, p. 206; al-Muẓaffar, Muḥammad Riḍā, (without date), *'Aqā'id al-Imāmīya*, Tehran: Ketābkhāne-ye bozorg-e eslāmī, p. 31f.; al-Shaukānī, Muḥammad b. 'Alī, (without date), *Irshād al-fuḥūl*, Beirūt: Dār al-ma'rifa, p. 266.

7. A Jewish View of Islam

ALON GOSHEN-GOTTSTEIN

The strength of a broadly sketched presentation is also its weakness. A wide view of such broad phenomena as Judaism and Islam perforce essentializes them, while overlooking many details and much nuance that are essential to a balanced picture of the two entities, their historical relations and the possibilities that may be held for their common future. Nevertheless, such a broad sketch also allows us to recognize the main currents of the past, challenges of the present and possibilities for the future. The following generalizations should therefore be taken as just that, along with the hope that these general reflections will withstand the test of finer scrutiny, while suggesting directions for future research and reflections. I would like to express the hope that whatever nuancing this paper invites, particularly regarding the refinement of statements concerning Islam as these emerge from the observations of a Jewish scholar whose knowledge of Muslim sources is perforce second hand, should be motivated by the spirit of unapologetic examination of self and other in which I myself have tried to write. The present overview seeks to point to complicated and menacing realities, without masking their complexities. I look forward to the overall notions being engaged with the spirit, both critical and constructive, with which these thoughts are offered.[1]

---

1 The present essay sounds a very different note, though it ultimately remains complementary, to a paper co-authored by myself along with Paul Ballanfat and Paul Fenton, 'Judaism and Islam: Directions for Dialogue, Collaboration and Mutual Recognition', in preparation for the First Congress of Imams and Rabbis that I helped organize in January 2005, and which is available through the Elijah Interfaith Institute. That essay sought to create a historical and conceptual common ground between religious leaders of two traditions often considered as being at war with one another.

Elective Monotheisms – A Conceptual Overview

As a way of bringing together a series of distinct, though clearly interrelated, observations regarding Islam from a Jewish perspective, I would like to suggest a conceptual framework that allows us to grasp the commonality as well as the difference between the two traditions. These traditions are often referred to as Abrahamic, as though the figure of Abraham provided the conceptual, or genealogical, common ground between Muslims and Jews.[2] I prefer to adopt the usage of Martin Jaffee, who coined the term 'elective monotheisms' to describe the two traditions, as well as Christianity.[3] As Jaffee rightly suggests, simply pointing to the belief in a common God, or even to other theological principles that Judaism and Islam share in common, is to mask the complexity of the issues and the real differences between the religions. On the vertical level the two religions do indeed point to a belief in a common God. However, this God enters the arena of history and engages humanity through his word. The act of revealing his word, choosing a community to whom his word is entrusted and which therefore becomes his community proper and the passage through history with the sense of unique revelation and relationship, until the eventual messianic vindication of the one chosen community – these are all constitutive components of elective monotheism. Consequently, an honest mutual assessment must take all these components into account. Accordingly, the present observations will be grouped according to the key elements that make both Judaism and Islam elective monotheisms, and that suggest where their major agreements and disagreements lie. These include God, revelation, the religious community (the community that God chooses and to which he reveals

---

The irenic note sounded by that paper is an example of the kind of constructive direction recommended by the present paper. However, the appeal to history and commonality, while useful for the occasion and while possessing educational and psychological merit, is also fraught with difficulties, as the present essay suggests.

2 For a critique of this designation, see A. Goshen-Gottstein, 2002, 'Abraham and "Abrahamic Religions" in Contemporary Interreligious Discourse: Reflections of an Implicated Jewish Bystander', *Studies in Interreligious Dialogue* 12, pp. 165–83.

3 See Martin Jaffee, 2001, 'One God, One Revelation One People: On the Symbolic Structure of Elective Monotheism', *JAAR* 69:4, pp. 753–75.

himself), history (the passage of the two communities along the axis of time and the interweaving of their relations) and the messianic end (the tension and the quest for the ultimate vindication of the truth and meaning of the commitment of the religious community).

God

It is important to acknowledge the theological common ground of Judaism and Islam, a common ground which may provide the ultimate foundation for Jewish–Muslim relations and whose significance must be reaffirmed despite all the complexities that make 'elective monotheism' more than simply monotheism. Judaism and Islam recognize and worship the same God. This has been the general tendency of Jewish authorities towards Islam throughout the ages.[4] The ruling of Maimonides, according to which Muslims are not to be considered idolaters, because they believe in true monotheism, has become a default position in a Jewish assessment of the Muslim recognition of God.[5] The recognition of the common God also opened the door to a great deal of theological and spiritual exchange between Jews and Muslims throughout the generations. Particularly noteworthy are the spiritual exchanges that characterize Maimonides' own descendants, as they forged a unique Jewish-Sufi spiritual synthesis, in which a particular spirituality and a variety of customs and forms of worship were integrated into Jewish praxis.[6] None of this could have taken place without the fundamen-

4 The affirmation has not by any means been universal. Some of the exceptions to this general recognition will be noted below. See Marc Shapiro, 1993, 'Islam and the Halakha', *Judaism* 42, pp. 332–43. It is fair to suggest that underlying the lack of recognition of the identity of the God worshipped by Judaism and Islam, particularly as expressed by various authorities who considered Islam to be a form of *Avoda Zara*, a form of foreign, hence prohibited, worship of God, are identity politics, as these get played out in the historical relations of the two communities. For a particularly clear articulation of this relationship see the halachic discussion of Rabbi Eliezer Waldenberg, *Ziz Eliezer*, vol. 14, responsum 91.

5 See Maimonides, *Laws of Yein Nesech* 11,7.

6 See Paul Fenton, 1998, 'Abraham Maimonides (1187–1237): Founding a Mystical Dynasty', in M. Idel and M.Ostow (eds), *Jewish Mystical Leaders and Leadership in the 13th Century*, Northvale: Jason Aronson, pp. 148ff.

tal acknowledgement of the identity of the God recognized by the two traditions. It is therefore a commonplace that Judaism considers itself closer to Islam than it does to Christianity. In other words, when a theological, rather than a cultural, perspective is chosen, Judaism and Islam share a fundamental understanding of the one God, which is free of the complexities that characterize Jewish–Christian relations.

Revelation

The profound differences between Judaism and Islam arise as we move from God understood philosophically to the relations God forges and the revelations he gives. In theory one could reconcile multiple revelations, assuming different intended audiences. While this position was not common, we have at least one precedent of a Jewish philosopher who was willing to acknowledge the validity of the Qur'ān's revelation, as long as its intended audience was not the Jewish people, for whom the Torah remains the final revelation. Thus, R. Nethanel Alfayumi, a twelfth-century Jewish philosopher, who has been described in this regard as a Jewish Isma'īlī, allows for the possibility of the Qur'ān's validity for a Muslim audience.[7] Needless to say, the Qur'ān itself has a variety of references that recognize the fact of a previous revelation in the Torah. Thus, if other social, political and historical circumstances had prevailed, this position might have enjoyed greater currency. Circumstances were different, however, and they are best illustrated through the reasoning offered for why Islam should be considered *Avoda Zara*, an alien worship, even though it affirms belief in the same God. There are, as is well known, three prohibitions that must not be transgressed and for which the law prescribes choosing death over

---

7 See Steven Wasserstrom, 'Mutual Acknowledgements: Modes of Recognition Between Muslim and Jew', 1992, *Islam and Judaism, 1400 years of Shared Values*, ed. Steven Wasserstrom, Portland: Institute for Judaic Studies in the Pacific Northwest, p. 63 f. Al Fayumi's position was echoed recently, though without reference to him, by British Chief Rabbi Jonathan Sacks in the first edition of his *The Dignity of Difference* (London: Continuum, 2002), p. 55. This formulation is one of the points of the work to have drawn the ire of his critics, leading to its reformulation in the second edition of the work.

committing those transgressions.[8] One of those is idolatry, the worship of other gods, *Avoda Zara*. If the God of Islam is the same as the God of Judaism, how should one act under conditions of religious persecution? If God alone were considered, it would seem that conversion to Islam should be the recommended course of action. This conclusion was unacceptable to legal authorities who addressed the political realities of religious persecution. Rabbi David ben Zimra (sixteenth century) arguing in favour of martyrdom, shifts the basis of the discussion from the understanding of God to revelation.[9] Were we only to consider God from the theological and philosophical perspectives, the entire Torah would be undermined. The Torah is a way of life, an entire religious system communicated by God to his people. One should prefer death to conversion to another religion, even if it recognizes the same God, because such conversion undermines the ability to live out the relationship mandated by God. Under historical circumstances of forced conversion and religious competition, the option that recognizes the validity of other forms of revelation finds no fertile ground to grow.[10]

Even though on a certain level Islam recognizes Jewish Scriptures, in many significant ways it fails to do so in a way that is satisfactory to Jewish religious, as well as historical, sensibilities. Unlike Christianity, Islam does not consider itself the next chapter of the same story. Rather, it is a variant telling of many components of Judaism's foundational story. Consequently, it does not own the Jewish Scriptures as such. This diminishes the kind of friction that developed from the scriptural takeover of the Jewish Bible by the Church. But it also introduces friction on another, possibly more profound, level. Christians have always recognized Jewish Scriptures, leading them to value Jewish learning and the tradition of interpretation entrusted to the Rabbis. This has led to millennia of study of Jewish sources by Christian students, always aware of the direct rela-

8 Maimonides, *Laws of Foundations of the Torah* 5,2.

9 Shut Radbaz 4,92, citing the earlier authority of the *Ritva*.

10 Steven Wasserstrom (cf. fn. 7) makes the point that symbiosis could take place because it served mutual needs. Theological positions are also couched within social realities. Neither cultural models nor theological positions grow in a historical vacuum. The climate of interreligious dialogue could in theory provide a soil upon which this hitherto marginal view could gain greater currency.

tionship between Judaism and Christianity. By contrast, Muslims do not consider themselves fundamentally indebted to Jewish tradition. They are in possession of the full revelation, making any need for the study of Jewish tradition and the related acknowledgement of a historical relationship superfluous. Whatever interest the modern historian may have in tracing the Jewish sources of Muslim teachings, to the Muslim believer such historical dependence is meaningless. God's revelation is not in need of historical precedent or formative materials. The discrepancies between the Jewish and the Muslim telling of related narratives is reconciled through what may be considered the earliest form of biblical criticism – the elaborate Muslim criticism of the contents of the biblical narrative as morally inferior and as spiritually impossible, leading to a recognition of a gap between the theory of revelation and the actual product that is said to contain it. The Jewish Scriptures are thus viewed as having been impaired and falsified by human hands. To all intents and purposes there is no need to learn from Jews and their concrete Scriptures are not appreciated as words of revelation.[11]

Recognition can take many forms. Upon closer scrutiny one realizes that Jewish–Muslim relations are fraught with various degrees of lack of recognition of historical continuity.[12] The most contemporary expression of this tendency is the widespread attempt to deny any relationship between the historical Jerusalem Temple and the Haram al-Sharif. Erasure of memory and denial of continuity cast the two religions as increasingly distinct from one another, thereby undermining the historical basis of continuity that could in theory have served a constructive role in the relations between the two religions.

Issues of memory and continuity concern self-image and under-

---

11 There may be alternative ways of understanding these early charges of falsification, that may be more harmonious with the present desire to ameliorate inter-group relations. See the paper composed by Paul Ballanfat, Paul Fenton and myself, 'Judaism and Islam: Directions for Dialogue, Collaboration and Mutual Recognition' (The Elijah Interfaith Institute, 2004), pp. 14–15.

12 The ambivalence toward the *Isra'iliyat*, traditions that made it to Muslim sources from Jewish origins, is an additional instance of this ambivalence. Attempts to expunge these traditions are instances of conscious erasure of memory.

standing. What is at stake is not historical fact, but the construction of identity and the relationship to the other. These in turn draw upon different cultural modes of relating to the past. The different uses of history reveal significant cultural differences, on account of which Jews and Muslims often lack a common language. The Jewish appeal to history is, in principle, more open to a critical perspective, while many Muslim spokesmen would deny a meaningful role to historical enquiry and its critical methods as far as these can contribute a historical depth dimension to Jewish–Muslim relations. Consequently, resolving tensions over memory and image is dependent to a large extent on finding the conceptual and methodological common ground that would allow Jews and Muslims to share a discourse in light of which issues of history, continuity and identity could be explored.

There is one final point I would like to add in relation to Scripture and its implications for shaping the view of the other. Reuven Firestone has made a significant point regarding the long-term implications of the qur'ānic representations of Muḥammad's complex relations with the Jews and of some of the difficult statements made in that context.[13] Appealing to the historical method, it is understandable that under the pressure of particular historical circumstances various statements of a derogatory nature were made. However, once these statements take on metaphysical significance, their destructive potential is brought to light. If the Qur'ān is God's word of truth from all eternity, it is harder to relativize negative statements concerning the Jews and to see them as merely products of a given historical moment. The text's metaphysical status can in theory lead to the negative essentialization of the other.[14]

---

13 Reuven Firestone, 2005, 'Jewish-Muslim Relations', in N. de Lange, M. Freud-Kandel (eds), *Modern Judaism, An Oxford Guide*, Oxford: OUP, pp. 438–49, p. 440.

14 In principle, the concern is mutual, and could be equally applied to Jewish descriptions of Ishmael or non-Jews in general. However, the dynamics of tradition are different. Negative views of Muslims are not found in Judaism's most fundamental text, but in later strata that are less authoritative. Nevertheless, it is clear that ultimately both communities must tackle traditional religious sources that portray the other in a negative light.

The People – Receiving Revelation and Moving through History

The next component in Jaffee's scheme to be considered relates to the choice of community that receives the divine revelation and traverses history with it. More is at stake here than the simple, though fundamental, difference regarding the identity of the chosen community – whether it is the people of Israel or the Muslim Umma. Under this rubric we would do well to consider the matrix of Muslim–Jewish relations throughout the long periods in which Jews were subjects of Muslims. Relations between the groups reveal fundamental theological understandings.

Islam understood its political victory as theological victory as well. It is this close juxtaposition of political history and theological triumph that provides the backdrop for much of the theological difficulty that Islam faces with the change of historical tides. As Jewish–Muslim relations are coloured by the historical changes in power relations, one must be aware of the significant role that the political dimension plays in defining inter-group relations.

From a completely theoretical perspective, one could develop a Jewish model of Islam that would legitimize Islam's mission in the world, as a religious community. Just as one could contemplate notions of multiple revelations, one could also contemplate complex relations between different communities, chosen to fulfil different parts of God's plan for humanity. To the extent that Judaism is bound up with its ethnic identity and to the degree that it is perceived as non-missionary and not seeking to convert the world to its form of belief, a convenient division of labour could be conceived in relation to Islam. Islam could be the outreach arm of the monotheistic and spiritual vision of Judaism.[15] However, such a view would require a level of mutual recognition the two traditions lack; and the power relations between them, as well as their different approaches to their respective and intertwined histories, play an important role in frustrating such mutual recognition.

---

15 Of course, this is just as true of Christianity. Indeed, very often Christianity and Islam are considered together in attempting to provide a place for them within the overall Jewish economy of history and salvation. See Maimonides, *Laws of Kings* 11,4.

Judaism has lived in the shadow of Islam since the latter's birth. At certain historical moments as much as 95 per cent of the Jewish people lived in a Muslim context. The status of Jews in Muslim societies was governed by the rules of the *dhimmī*. These rules provide protection and security while at the same time also expressing subjugation and humiliation. The *jizya* tax imposed upon the *dhimmī* is a sign of subjugation that seeks to establish the clearly inferior status of the *dhimmī*, seeking to humiliate them, even as they are offered protection.

The status of Jews as *dhimmī* left them vulnerable to a series of injunctions that were applied in different degrees at different periods of history. These included the obligation to wear distinguishing clothes, the prohibition on building tall houses, the obligation to give right of way to Muslims, the prohibition against riding horses, against bearing testimony against a Muslim and more. The vicissitudes of history saw these rules enforced to different degrees, but they remained on the books, and hence always applicable in potential. It only took a change in the course of history and of how the Jews were perceived in a given society for what was purely theoretical to become operative.

Thus, Jewish life in the shadow of Islam is characterized by great complexities, if we will – ambivalences. One often speaks of the Golden Age of Jewry under Muslim rule in medieval Spain.[16] For all its splendour, we must not over-idealize it, nor ignore the darker side of that splendour. The testimony of Maimonides, in many ways a symbol of the height of Jewish integration within prevailing Muslim culture and a sign of the Golden Age, is telling. Maimonides writes, following the persecutions of the Almohads:

> on account of the vast number of our sins, God has hurled us in the midst of this people, the Arabs,[17] who have persecuted

16 On the Golden Age as a historical construct and the role it played in the contemporary quest for Jewish emancipation, in the hands of Jewish historians, see Norman Stillman, 2000, 'The Judeo-Islamic Historical Encounter – Visions and Revisions', in Tudor Parfitt (ed.), *Israel and Ishmael*, Richmond: Curzon Press, pp. 1–12. See further Michel Abitbol, 'Jews and Arabs in Colonial North Africa', Parfitt (ed.), *Israel and Ishmael*, pp. 124ff.

17 The distinction between Arabs and Muslims is, of course, completely

> us severely, and passed baneful and discriminatory legislation against us . . . Never did a nation molest, degrade, debase and hate us as much as they.[18]

As historians have observed, the decline of the historical fate of the community as a whole leads to a deterioration of the status of the Jews within it.[19] And yet, even during the finest of moments, Jewish living under Muslim rule, it seems fair to suggest that Jews never really felt at home. They were aware of being out of their natural place, out of their natural society, guests – often fairly treated, regularly abused – in a foreign society. Historians paint diverging pictures of Jewish life in the shadow of Islam. Some seek to portray Jewish–Muslim relations along the 'Golden Age' model; others highlight persecution as the governing narrative. Both portrayals seem to be ideologically invested. The truth seems to lie somewhere in between. One thing may be safely stated, nevertheless: Difficult as the relations may have been at various points in time, Jews still seem to have overall fared better under the shadow of Islam than they did under the shadow of Christianity. However, what allowed for the toleration, and at times integration, of Jews into Muslim society was the very recognition of Muslim superiority and supremacy. This has one significant implication: even in the finer moments of Jewish life in the shadow of Islam the relationship was not only unequal; it was non-reciprocal. Jews became part of surrounding Arab or Muslim culture. They learned the languages and arts and partook of other cultural expressions. Muslims did not make a similar effort to learn, appreciate or become conversant with Jewish culture. Thus, we have a precedent in history for successful toleration and cultural absorption, not for mutual respect, dignity and coexistence, in the sense mandated by contemporary reality.

It is precisely here that we can identify the secret of the success of the past. Jews took part in a surrounding culture; they did not join up or make compromises with a neighbouring religion. That the

---

irrelevant, if we seek an appreciation of the historical reality and, more importantly, of the subjective experiences of Jews living under Muslim rule.

18 Abraham Halkin, 1993, 'The Epistle to Yemen', in Abraham Halkin and David Hartman, *Epistles of Maimonides: Crisis and Leadership*, Philadelphia: Jewish Publication Society, p. 126.

19 See Firestone, 2005, 'Jewish-Muslim Relations', p. 442.

culture was thoroughly religious in character is a given. However, what made Jewish participation in broader society possible is the common cultural context. This culture no longer exists. One may evoke the memory of Al-Andalus or appreciate the heights of Ottoman culture and the place that Jews found within that culture. However, those cultures are no longer in existence and the contemporary cultural background that drives the quest for present day understanding between religious groups is very different.

In important ways, therefore, the past cannot serve as a guide to the future. The culture it provided as common background no longer exists, and the network of political and power relations that defined and governed Jewish–Muslim relations has since changed. The present day places before us the challenge of establishing Jewish–Muslim relations in a culturally and politically different context from the one under which the finest moments of Jewish–Muslim coexistence took place. To understand the complications of the present moment, we need to turn to the next element in Jaffee's scheme – the quest for the messianic future.

Looking to the Future

The model that reigned in Jewish–Muslim relations for centuries underwent radical changes as a consequence of political changes that have taken place since the nineteenth century. The growing influence of Europe in Arab societies and the move of Jews away from a Muslim social and cultural context are processes that had been under way well before the Zionist movement came along. However, it is clear that the single most dramatic force that reshaped Jewish–Muslim relations was the Zionist movement, and in time the founding of the state of Israel.

Zionism opened a new chapter in Jewish–Muslim relations, one that to a significant extent makes a return to earlier models impossible. On the one hand, the status of the *dhimmī* is no longer maintained, within a geographic region that at least some consider to be Muslim territory. Jews who came to Israel from Arab countries in fact exchanged their *dhimmī* status for a more powerful and autonomous status, provided by the state of Israel. On the other hand, the prevalent identification of Zionism with the West and with Western colonialism plays into a Muslim narrative that pits Muslim culture and history against those forces. Israel is thus viewed within a matrix of power relations and conflicts that touches upon fundamental perceptions of Muslim identity and dignity.

Islam has a strong territorial dimension. Geographical territories are defined in ways that establish their Muslim affiliation. Concern with politics, government and territory plays into how the particular territory of Israel is viewed by many Muslims. Consequently, the changes brought about by the establishment of the state of Israel touch some very fundamental concerns of Muslim law and world-view. This is not to suggest that there is no way that a Muslim world-view can accept a Jewish state. However, it is certainly not the popular or default position, and a good deal of goodwill and constructive work would have to go into such acceptance. For the most part such goodwill has been lacking. From the political angle, the present (2006) Palestinian government, scores of Muslim radicals and governments such as the Iranian government all share a view of the state of Israel that is nurtured by the sense of violation of traditional Muslim norms, and that sees the only hope for the future in the return to those norms, in other words in undoing the Jewish state and replacing it with a Muslim regime.

I do not wish to be understood as claiming that the Israeli–Arab conflict is fundamentally a religious one. Nevertheless, even if at its historical roots it is a national conflict, the close association of religion and politics and the ways in which religion spills over into all facets of life make a neat division between the religious and the political impossible. Consequently, we witness the conflict being viewed increasingly in religious terms. Along with the Islamization of the conflict we can also observe a shift in its fundamental parameters. If several decades ago the conflict was with the Israelis, it is increasingly spilling over into a conflict with the Jews. This accounts for the apparently significant penetration of Christian anti-Semitic materials, including the notorious *Protocols of the Elders of Zion*, into the Muslim world. Muslim anti-Semitism has become one of the most prominent forms of anti-Semitism in the world today.

All these developments can be explained in terms of political developments as these impact upon the psyche and the traditions of the players in the seemingly endless drama in the Middle East. However, we may also consider a more principled dimension of the events of the past century. Jaffee points to the eschatological moment as the point in time towards which competing elective monotheisms march, at which point they expect their vision and world-view will be vindicated, proving who is the ultimate chosen community of God. If so, messianism is not simply a detail of a religious world-view. It is a climax of an entire religious structure, what gives it meaning and direction, its ultimate point of fulfilment along the axis of time. Now, Zionism is at one and the same time a political movement and a messianic movement. It draws upon ancient messianic dreams and for many of its followers it is part of the realization of a messianic vision. This, of course, raises the stakes regarding acceptance and rejection of Zionism, within the broader matrix of a competing religious system. Furthermore, the messianic element is not exclusive to Judaism. It plays an important role in some forms of Islam, including those currently making their mark in the contemporary political arena. Messianic dimensions seem to loom particularly large in the world-view informing the decisions and actions of the present Iranian regime.

All this may point us to the source of the irrational element that plagues the Israel–Arab conflict. I believe there is no other conflict upon earth that has lasted for so long, that captures the imagination of the entire human family in such a powerful way and that still seems as far as ever from adequate resolution. All these elements open us to a consideration of something beyond the purely historical conflict of competing national groups. The messianic dimension of the conflict could perhaps account for the particular charge and the great complexity of the Jewish–Arab conflict. Thus, underlying the conflict, even if not always fully consciously, is a battle about the story and the legitimacy of the competing religious world-views. If history is the ultimate testing ground of elective monotheisms, then the state of Israel may be considered the conclusive test for these religions.

Regardless of how important the following tradition may or may not be in the broader economy of Muslim sources, it may point to an important dimension that fuels present day conflict. There is a Muslim eschatological tradition that affirms that on the Day of Judgement, a battle will take place with the Jews, who will then be destroyed.[20] As Moshe Sharon points out, the Jews were never so

20 See Moshe Sharon, 1989, *Judaism, Christianity and Islam: Interaction and Conflict*, Johannesburg: Sacks, p. 103.

powerful politically as to justify the creation of such a tradition. It would therefore seem that only a deep theological rivalry, whose resolution awaits the eschaton, can lead to such a radical formulation.

The upshot of the radical changes in political perspective, coupled with messianic overtones, is that the present chapter in Jewish–Muslim relations redefines the relations between the two religions. It is fair to say that almost everything positive that was created in the centuries of Jewish living in the shadow of Islam has been erased.

It is interesting to conclude this section by revisiting, yet again, the issue of the definition of Islam as *Avoda Zara*. When considered from the eschatological perspective, viewed through the particular political context of the state of Israel, a surprising position is encountered. One of the great halachic authorities, writing shortly after the Six Day War, considers Islam's role on the political ground and points to continuing Arab hatred of Israel. It is not conceivable that Islam possesses true knowledge of God, argues Rabbi Halberstam of Kloisenburg. Its political position and the alliances it makes with Israel-hating Christians (who for him are obvious idolaters) prove that Islam is *Avoda Zara*.[21] Islam's spiritual value is thus tested not by its theological affirmations but by the actions that it exhibits, particularly as these concern God's people Israel.

Assessing the Present Moment – Our Challenge

We seem to be at a moment of climax as far as the historical process is concerned. If our elective monotheisms traverse history awaiting their final vindication, the present moment in time brings unprecedented pressure to bear upon the realities common to Jews and Muslims, as well as Christians. Even if the present moment in time is not viewed as the final messianic showdown, it must be acknowledged as unique in the intensity of feelings, the enormity of challenge and the profound potential for destruction for all involved, not only in the Middle East but throughout the world. It seems there is no going back. We cannot return to the lost Golden Age, whether it ever existed or not. We seem to be pushed deeper and deeper into the inevitable conflict, and the ensuing conflagration. The move-

21 Rabbi Yekutiel Halberstan, *Yisrael Sava*, vol. 4, no. 48.

ment toward the future thus brings to light all the uncontrollable forces and conflicts that are contained within the religions. We may, then, be headed towards the inevitable conflagration.

There may be, nevertheless, an alternative to the passive waiting for the unleashing of the deep forces contained within our religions in a grand showdown. Much depends on who it is we are talking to and how much power those who are willing to talk with each other actually have within their respective religions. We must at least do our best to cultivate those understandings of religion that will provide an alternative to the vision of the clash of religions coming to a head. It is worth noting, in this context, that as for the basic paradigm of competing claims made by different elective monotheisms, the situation between Judaism and Christianity is no different from that of Judaism and Islam. In relation to most forms of Christianity we have found the way of living in the present time without messianic expectations spilling over in destructive ways into contemporary reality. The deep tensions inherent in the existence of parallel elective monotheisms thus need not be translated into concrete conflict. Other factors exacerbate these profound tensions. These factors could in theory be addressed. This is our task.

We can identify several dimensions to the growing tensions between Judaism and Islam. The conflict, to the degree that one may speak of a conflict between the religions, has *national*, *cultural* and *religious* dimensions. It is fed by the conflicting territorial claims of two nationalities. It is sustained by different cultural attitudes. The differences in cultural attitudes relate not only to the world-view at large but also to how tradition(s) are to be understood in light of historical thinking and critical thinking in general. Attitudinal differences stemming from different degrees of adaptation of critical self-awareness often frustrate attempts at dialogue and understanding between Jews and Muslims. Finally, the conflict is religious, inasmuch as an appeal to religion underlies the attitudes that inform treatment of the various aspects of Jewish–Muslim relations. The challenge is how to construct, or lift up, those aspects of Judaism and Islam, those Judaisms and Islams, if we will, that can play a positive and constructive role in alleviating the conflict that the deep structures of religion could lead to, if not appropriately diffused.

Work can be done in all three areas. I do believe that there is a good chance that if the appropriate work is done by the right people, it can stem the tide of violence that we seem to be headed towards. It is, of course, only a chance, inasmuch as what is at stake is not only a conflict between the religions, but a battle within each of the religions regarding the form it takes and the self understanding of its practitioners in relation to contemporary reality. The chances may not be high. Yet, we cannot assume the responsibility of not trying. The consequences are too grave.

Meeting the Challenge of the Moment – Ways not Taken

Alleviating conflicts between Jews and Muslims is an important contemporary concern and one can point to any number of initiatives that seek to address this important challenge. In light of the above analysis, I would like to suggest that some of the ways that are most commonly taken in this context are, in fact, ill suited to the task. Perhaps the most common strategy is the appeal to the past. Jews often point to the Jewish roots of Muslim faith; Muslims often point to the positive statements found in the Qur'ān in relation to Jews, usually ignoring the other side of the complex picture that emerges from the Qur'ān. An appeal to the Golden Age of Jewish life under the shadow of Islam is often made, in an attempt to remind us that the two religions can indeed coexist in fruitful and mutually sustaining ways.

All these strategies seek to provide an alternative to present and potential conflict. That which is considered to have been historically positive is thus called upon to address the difficulties of the moment. The implied understanding is that that which is positive, and which is being highlighted, is the essential and fundamental reality. Therefore it ought to govern relations between the religions. The various negative phenomena that one seeks to combat are in some way secondary aberrations, whose influence can be checked if only we recollect the fundamentally harmonious relationship that characterizes the two religions.

I find these moves to be very problematic. Any irenic presentation of history is by definition one-sided. It fails to address the problematic dimension of Jewish–Muslim relations, leaving the untreated area as a festering wound that will continue to impact relations if untreated. Jewish–Muslim relations have been complex from the earliest historical foundations of Muḥammad's relations with the

Jews. There will therefore always remain alternative voices, ghosts in our religious closets, that will continue to haunt us. The complexity of the Jewish experience in the shadow of Islam can similarly not be ignored, if we seek to take stock of the good as well as the problematic sides of our history as part of addressing the future.

A related strategy is the attempt to highlight the commonalities both religions have. In this context one can construct entire catalogues of similarities and commonalities the two traditions share. However, listing similarities ignores the deeper issue: can these similarities be extricated from the structures within which they are contained?[22] If the similarities are fully enshrined within the broader context of the two religions, then the irenic potential of the similarities becomes insignificant, in view of the more powerful forces of competition and of potential conflict that drive both traditions. In fact, similarities may be found between any two religious systems, regardless of the particulars of time, space and their relationship to one another. Identifying similarities may not be enough to stem the tides of conflict.

Highlighting commonalities, just like highlighting positive precedents, is only meaningful in the framework of a broader effort to construct religions in a particular way. Such an effort involves making self-conscious decisions regarding how one understands one's own religion as well as that of the other. It is an educational-constructive process, rather than a naive appeal to one element in the broader descriptive canvas. If we are to succeed, a prior commitment to such a constructive process must be made. History can only be appealed to as part of a self-conscious reconstruction of identity, in light of which relations may be restructured. It is my contention that until such reconstruction has taken place, we are better off leaving history aside. Appealing to history implicates us in the very matrix of conflict and complexity that has characterized Jewish–Muslim relations since their inception. If history is part of the inevitable collision course, as competing monotheisms await their ultimate vindication, we may fare better by putting aside history altogether and seeking

22 Put more theoretically, one must consider to what extent pointing to similarities grows out of the study of religions in a neutral, scientific manner, or to what extent it is an ideologically motivated statement, and as such an oversimplification of more complex realities.

other ways in which the two religious communities can best coexist. In my estimation, in the overall scheme of things, the negative heritage of history far outweighs the model moments to which we can appeal. One is therefore better off attempting to construct Jewish–Muslim relations as one would construct Jewish–Hindu relations. That is, the two religious communities ought to come together on the platform of mutual concerns for coexistence, peace and contribution to the world. Initially our respective and interdependent stories ought to be left behind, as we seek to contribute to peaceful coexistence. Let us come to know one another as parallel religious communities, leaving aside the baggage we carry through history. The baggage will wait for us. We can pick that load up again when we have successfully constructed the kind of Judaism and the kind of Islam that we would like to bring to each other and to the world.

Meeting the Challenge of the Moment – Areas of Focus

This chapter issues a call to self-conscious construction of identity within a relationship: constructing Jewish and Muslim identities in ways that support the Jewish–Muslim relationship, and by so doing contributing to the peace of the world at large. Such self-conscious construction grows out of an assessment of the needs of a particular moment in time. This point in time calls for an attitude that circumvents much of history, and seeks to construct an alternative vision to that of an inevitable collision. I would like to suggest several areas that deserve future work, as part of such self-conscious construction. Each of these areas can make an important contribution to a new construction of Jewish–Muslim relations. The four areas are culture, knowledge, values and theology.[23]

Culture

We have already noted that one component of the conflict is a cultural divide, through which Jews and Muslims (that is, stereotypical Jews and Muslims) relate to the world, to their history, to Scripture and to society at large in very different ways. The present challenge

---

23 One might almost present these four areas as alternatives to the four areas that feed conflict – sovereignty, territory, self-image and memory.

grows out of what in UNESCO terminology is dubbed 'creating a culture of peace'. What, then, are the prerequisites for the creation of such a culture, common to Jews and Muslims? Can a medieval construction of these religions contribute to such a culture of peace, or can it only grow on a modernist, or postmodern, platform? Jewish–Muslim relations in the Middle Ages were characterized as a symbiosis. This symbiosis fell apart because the culture that sustained it ceased to exist. In today's world a different kind of symbiosis is emerging, one in which all religions seek to partake in a culture that can sustain the global village. This broader context provides an opportunity for Judaism and Islam to construct their identities in ways that support the broader needs of the contemporary culture of peace.

There seem to be some distinct components to the present cultural moment. Globalization, the quest for common values and for peace are central. Knowledge, communication and new ways of expressing the age-old quest for truth are additional components of a present-day cultural outlook. Historical knowledge and critical thinking, in particular self-critical, are additional important components of contemporary culture. They are also much needed tools in combating the potential for violence inherent in our religions. The implications of interiorizing a more complex and self-aware perspective on our religions is the adoption of a particular religious identity that is at one and the same time also a broader human identity. They also point to adopting a religious identity that can patiently await the end time, while postponing some questions of ultimate significance in favour of peaceful living in the here and now. It seems the common living of Jews and Muslims in the west is facilitating the construction of the kind of complex identities called for by the present situation.

Knowledge

Prominent characteristics of contemporary society are the availability of knowledge, its easy dissemination and the breadth of interest in knowledge, facilitated by technology and communication. Knowledge must be the basis of any cultural development, including advances in inter-religious relations and in the self-understanding of religious groups. Knowledge has always played an important role in inter-religious relations. The successes of the Golden Age of Jewish–Muslim relations have much to do with a shared knowledge base, in the fields of language, philosophy and more. However, there has been great asymmetry in knowledge within Jewish–Muslim relations. We have already remarked that while Jews knew Arab culture, Arabs did not show parallel interest in Jewish culture. That the Qur'ān as text, rather than as revelation, is not considered a sequel to the Bible meant that the quest for learning the original revelation that characterized Jewish–Christian relations was absent from Jewish–Muslim relations. Even in contemporary times we find asymmetry in knowledge. Jews have been at the forefront of the modern academic study of Islam. The reverse cannot be said.

The present-day situation cannot tolerate partial or exclusive knowledge. Forms of knowledge that have been hitherto guarded and secret are becoming increasingly open and available.[24] The global situation challenges us all in similar ways. If part of the challenge concerns forging new relations between members of faith communities, this must also be translated to interest in and exchanges of knowledge. It is important that Jews and Muslims learn about each other at all levels. On the popular level this means ensuring proper knowledge replace stereotypes. On the academic level this means ensuring a high quality academic study of the other religion in major academic centres worldwide. Once again, the academic setting in the West provides a welcome context for establishing new paradigms of mutual learning between Jews and Muslims. The very few individuals in Arab-speaking universities who have gained proficiency in Judaism also testify to the potential that academia holds for balanced spreading of knowledge between Jews and Muslims. Intellectuals have an important responsibility. The lack of reciprocity that has traditionally characterized interest in knowledge and its sharing within Jewish–Muslim relations must give way to a broader and more reciprocal perspective. This task will probably be best achieved with the help of the academy.

---

24 An interesting instance of this from a different religious tradition concerns the effects of the internet on the dissemination of teaching that had hitherto been guarded and protected in one form of Hinduism, the Madhva tradition. See Deepak Sarma, 2005, *Epistemologies and the Limitations of Philosophical Inquiry: Doctrine in Madhva Vedanta,* London: Routledge Curzon, pp. 66–7.

Values

Religions have different dimensions and these can be variously highlighted and presented in different cultural contexts. Highlighting the truth value of religions can easily lead to awareness of the conflicts inherent in competing truth claims. One notes, partly in an attempt to avoid such conflicts and partly in an attempt to harness religions to meet the common challenges of contemporary society, the increasing emphasis upon religions as sources of values, and more particularly of common values. If, as suggested above, earlier expressions of Jewish–Muslim symbiosis grew out of a situation of common needs, one may ask what are the contemporary needs and what response can they draw forth from our religions.[25] Turning to religions as sources of values indicates a value crisis in today's world and the recognition that religions are repositories of key values of living. If Jews and Muslims partake, to some degree or other, of the crisis of modern living,[26] this provides a context for a new and broader kind of symbiosis, in which Jews and Muslims, along with others, reach to their traditions to provide guidance for the contemporary needs of society. The appeal to values allows us to put aside the range of history-related issues that weigh down upon Jewish–Muslim relations. A search for common values and their contemporary relevance can be conducted between religious traditions that have no common past. Approaching our religions in this light allows us to look to their spiritual depth and present contribution, rather than to their complicated historical past and conflicting future visions.

Nevertheless, the quest for values, or common values, may not be as straightforward as one initially imagines. Our traditions possess many common values, and they make repeated appeals to those values. Truth, love, peace and justice are but some of the most cur-

---

25 I shall leave out of the discussion the more political dimension of joining forces in combating hate and xenophobia, as these are expressed through anti-Semitism and Islamophobia. While this may provide potential meeting ground and space for collaboration, often Jews and Muslims are caught on opposing sides of these issues, thereby fuelling these very attitudes towards the other.

26 See on this issue the collection of articles published by the Elijah Interfaith Institute, *The Crisis of the Holy*, 2005.

rent values to which we find repeated appeal in the public discourses of our religions, educational as well as political. But what do these values actually mean? Often, it seems that we use the same words with very different understandings. Justice is a particular case in point. The regular appeal on the Muslim side to justice as a self-evident value in light of which various political moves should be made contrasts with the Jewish understanding of what is implied in justice, in light of a particular history of Israeli–Arab relations. Core values can easily degenerate into slogans.

This does not invalidate the search for common values. But it does suggest that the process is complex and must be founded upon serious and open discussion. It involves study, mutual listening, discernment and a scrutiny of the past, even if this is focused on ideals and their realization, rather than on historical relations between groups. Not only individual values must be considered but also the dynamic of clustering values together and the process of making choices between conflicting values. These complexities are as relevant to the possible joint contribution of Jews and Muslims to contemporary society's concerns at large as they are to helping advance their own wounded relationship. It therefore stands to reason that identifying values and suggesting commonalities is to a large extent itself a constructive, rather than descriptive, enterprise, and is therefore an important component of how we seek to construct our religious self-understanding in the broader contemporary context.[27] In some way or another all appeals to values and to the past are attempts at constructing a common base of values, through appeal to our past. However, the unexamined appeal is clumsy, inasmuch as it is one-sided and therefore lacks credibility. We must thus avoid a naive appeal to values, just as we must avoid a naive appeal to history.

---

27 It may bear stating that such a construction is a religious project, and belongs properly to the field of theology. It should not be confused with attempts to shift the basis of encounter from religion to secular or other contemporary values. The recognition that religions must construct or readdress their theologies in light of the changes and needs of contemporary realities informs the projects that I have initiated through the Elijah Interfaith Institute. We have gathered both Jewish and Muslim scholars to engage in work on the construction of contemporary theologies of other religions. This ongoing enterprise is part of the Institute's broader vision that seeks to stimulate fresh theological reflection among all religions.

Both involve conscious constructions in light of our traditions and their resources.

The quest for values and the move away from history lead us to a consideration of the appropriate context for carrying out such conversations. It is often assumed that 'Abrahamic' religions have a particular conversation that is unique to them and should therefore also be exclusive to them. While this position can be defended, and while there is room for work to be carried out in any bilateral inter-religious relationship, I would argue in favour of the work on values being carried out in a multilateral inter-religious context. I note with approval that the present volume does in fact seek to address Islam through a broader multilateral context, as it is broken down into its individual bilateral relationships. If we seek to contribute to the human family as a whole, living in the global village, this may be best done by sidestepping the historical charge that any individual relationship is fraught with and by lifting up the message of meaning and value that can speak to all, and that should be articulated in the presence of all. The new global situation is the cultural context that issues a call to religions to restate their message. This call is issued in a context that already transcends the relations between individual religions.[28] It therefore also holds the promise of helping specific relationships transcend the limitations of their historical relationships.

Theology

It is time to return to our starting point – God. So much has divided us, when we consider the broader structures of competing elective monotheisms. Yet, what unites us is the recognition of the common God. At the end of the day we must ask what is most important in our religious lives. I think we strive towards making God the

28 One might add that, as Reuven Firestone (cf. fn. 13) has pointed out, present-day tensions between Jews and Muslims are fuelled by a broader global perspective. Relations of the Muslim world and the West, economic considerations, trends of emigration and globalization all come to a head in the context of Jewish–Muslim relations, particularly as these focus upon Israeli–Palestinian relations. As Karen Armstong has recently claimed, the Israeli–Palestinian issue has become a symbol for all sides, far surpassing its objective importance. Hence the charge associated with it.

most important thing, more than religion itself. Making religion with its particularities and choices, even those God-given choices, more important than the recognition of the one God, source of all, allows our egos and identities to take over. It is, in some sense, idolatrous.[29] Return to God is a return to the source that could allow us to rediscover each other. This is very different from making a statement concerning the common faith of Jews and Muslims. Return to God involves reaching the spiritual insight that truly makes God the centre of our religions, rather than anything we have made of them.[30] To construct our religions is not simply a theological or intellectual exercise. It is a call for spiritual regeneration that would allow us to grow to the fullness of vision promised by our traditions. It is my faith that in that fullness we can also find the resources for living together.

Conclusion

I have argued that if we are to get past the present historical difficulties in Jewish–Muslim relations we must step for a moment outside history and outside our historical memories. Living our relationship under the scrutiny of history, viewed differently by the two groups, places us on a collision course. The present moment calls for a self-conscious construction of our religious identities in light of contemporary challenges. This is a theological project, through which values, relations and self-understanding must be constructed anew. It ultimately involves spiritual regeneration and reaching out to the heights of our religions' spiritual visions. We must first step outside

29 See the powerful conclusion to Vincent Cornell's essay, 'Islam: Theological Hostility and the Problem of Difference', in *Religion, Society and the Other: Hostility, Hospitality and the Hope of Human Flourishing*, The Elijah Interfaith Institute, 2003, p. 92 (forthcoming also with Fordham University Press).

30 On the turning of Islam into a programme of social reform, and the loss of theology and mysticism in much of contemporary Islam, see Vincent Cornell, 2005, 'The Crisis of the Holy: Islam', in: *The Crisis of the Holy*, The Elijah Interfaith Institute, pp. 120 ff. These issues arise in different ways in a Jewish context, given that Jewish self-understanding is both national and religious. See my 'Judaism: The Battle for Survival', The Struggle for Compassion, Chapter 2 in *Religion, Society and the Other* (cf. fn. 29).

historical memory and of the parameters of our bilateral relations in order to gain new perspective. From that perspective we can then revisit our histories, choosing to integrate their testimony in a self-conscious way in how we construct our memory and identity. This is a complex task. It suggests that important work lies ahead for academics, educators, and men of spiritual vision. It may prove to be beyond our abilities. But if the alternative is heading towards further violence and conflict, do we have the right not to try?

8. Response to Goshen-Gottstein

MUHAMMAD KALISCH

Judaism and Islam have much in common. Muslim scholars have no doubt that Jews and Muslims worship the same God. From an Islamic viewpoint this is logical because there is only one God, so everyone who worships the one God worships the same God even if there might be theological differences on certain questions about his essence or attributes. Furthermore Islam accepts the Torah as revealed Holy Scripture but claims that it has been corrupted. From this viewpoint Islam too, like Christianity, sees itself as a continuation of the same story, but Alon Goshen-Gottstein is right in pointing out that there is a significant difference in Jewish–Muslim relationship in comparison with the Jewish–Christian relationship. Although Christianity also has important theological differences with Judaism – and these differences in my view are greater than the theological differences with Islam (see, for example, the common Jewish and Muslim doubt about whether Christianity is really monotheistic because of the Trinity) – it accepts the Hebrew Bible as Holy Scripture and claims it as valid for Christianity. The reason for this is that Christianity in its present forms dates back to early Catholicism which was under the influence of Judaeo-Christianity. It rejected Jewish law and opened Christianity to the gentiles, but it admitted the Hebrew Bible. If other forms of early Christianity like Marcionism had become the dominating form of Christianity the break with Judaism would have been total, and would have included the rejection of the Hebrew Bible. But this was not the case and therefore the Hebrew Bible became the common Holy Scripture of the two religions. However, the fact that the Christians accepted the Hebrew Bible as their own Holy Scripture did not make the Christian attitude to the Jews any friendlier. It had quite the opposite effect. Christian scholars used the Hebrew Bible against the Jews and tried to show themselves as its true owners and the Jews as illegitimate usurpers.

Most Muslims were never interested in studying other Holy Scriptures. Even today most Muslim scholars just look into the Hebrew Bible, the New Testament or any other Holy Scripture to produce apologetic arguments that Islam is the true religion and that other Holy Scriptures have been corrupted. Today many Jewish and Christian scholars deal with their Holy Scriptures from the perspective of historical-critical scholarship. When today Muslim scholars deal with the results of modern Christian and Jewish scholarship in biblical studies, they usually tend to take only what fits into their world-view and unfortunately do not care very much about the other insights of the historical-critical approach.

For both religions, Judaism and Islam, the role of sacred law is very important. This is another element where Christianity and Judaism differ. I think that the whole structure of both religions, Judaism and Islam, is very similar, despite many differences in special theological matters and legal rules. Within Islam there has always been a debate among Muslim scholars – which in the last century gained particular importance – about the flexibility of Islamic law: To what extent are Muslim scholars allowed to leave the literal text of Qur'ān and Sunna (the normative paradigm of the prophet as it is transmitted in Muslim sources)? The answer to this question, namely, the methodological approach in the *uṣūl al-fiqh* (methodology of Islamic law), decides whether Islamic law is compatible with democracy, human rights, pluralism and a constitutional state. Certainly even the classic mainstream interpretation of Islamic law contains many norms that do not conflict with these principles (at the time of its genesis Islamic law was modern and brought considerable progress) but there are also certain norms which do in fact collide with them.

Alon Goshen-Gottstein mentions the state of Israel, which is indeed an important factor today in Jewish–Muslim relations. I think that the Israeli–Arab conflict is basically not a religious one, but political, although there are those on both sides who see it as a religious one. From the beginning of the conflict Christian Palestinians played an important role but in the last 20 years the conflict became more and more interpreted as a Jewish–Islamic conflict. The Jews are not only a religious group but also an ethnic group, and not all Jewish citizens of Israel believe in Judaism. There are atheists and agnostics who are Jews because they are ethnic Jews.

The Jewish side has a long history of persecution, culminating in the holocaust and therefore the state of Israel as a Jewish state is an important point for many Jews, having a religious dimension too. For the Jews, Israel appears as a homeland that gives them security. The Arabs and Muslims, however, do not understand why they should pay the bill for the European and especially the German persecution of Jews. From a religious dimension, many Jews regard Israel as a country promised to them by God and for the Muslims there is at least the religious idea that they, as the *umma* of God's last prophet, should control the holy city of Jerusalem. This religious dimension can only be solved when Jews and Muslims adopt a rational approach to their religious traditions that enables them to look critically at their own religion and themselves. The existence of Israel and the Arab–Israeli conflict has led to the appearance of strong anti-Semitism in the Arab world which is a sad and deplorable fact.

This short response does not permit a full discussion, but on the other hand it is impossible to write about Jewish–Islamic relations without addressing the issue of the state of Israel. I think that the Arab–Israeli conflict needs two confessions for finding its solution: One confession made by the Jewish side and one confession made by the Muslim side. The Jews need to confess that the history of Israel started with injustice and expulsion. The Jewish side and its Western allies until today behave in a way where the interests of Israel are seen as naturally given rights, and Israel acts even by violating international law. This is an important psychological factor because the Arab and Muslim interests are clearly seen as secondary or not relevant at all. This is a situation the Muslim world can never accept because accepting such a state of affairs is tantamount to considering themselves as second-class human beings.

The Muslims need to confess that Israel is a fact. Whatever one thinks about the beginnings of Israel, this state now exists and people live there who were born there and see it as their only homeland. All borders on this planet are the product of violence and there simply is no such thing as a natural or God-given place for certain people or religious communities. Israel now has become an established fact. It makes no sense to try to turn back time, for this would only produce new injustice. The Muslim side has to guarantee the existence of Israel and should seek for co-operation with it. Israel is a highly developed country and we as Muslims should regard the Jewish presence as an enrichment and a chance and not as a detrimental factor. We should be allies, not enemies and treat each other as equal. If Judaism and Islam are not able to stop violence, killing and bloodshed then there must be something wrong with such an understanding of Judaism and Islam. That's the obvious judgement of reason.

With a view to the future, I do not think that people need Jewish or Muslim states. What people really need are states that apply the declaration of human rights and that protect human dignity and freedom and bring justice to people. In such states it doesn't matter whether the majority is Jewish, Muslim, Christian or atheist because all their citizens are equal, share the same rights and therefore all have the freedom to practise their religion or world-view. In a world of globalization the mix of religions in many societies will grow more and more. For Islam my vision of its theological development in matters of sacred law is that a dynamic and flexible understanding of Islamic law should prevail, one that integrates the concepts of human rights, democracy, pluralism and a constitutional state as a part of its contemporary sacred law.

I think it is the duty of contemporary theology to get over religion. What I mean by this phrase is not to abolish religion. The different religions of this world all have their rich inheritance which is important for mankind. Judaism, Islam and other religions have contributed many positive elements to the development of mankind. But an honest view of history also demonstrates that concepts such as the superiority of one religion, or that God writes books, have been the cause of immense violence, torture and stultifying brainwashing. To my mind, as explained in my chapter, all human understanding is subjective understanding. If a person or a group of persons claims that their own understanding of truth gives them the right to persecute, torture or kill others this is indeed nothing else but the highest form of polytheism because whoever does so puts himself, puts his ego, in the place of God. The history of monotheism is filled with examples where people worshipped their own ego in the name of monotheism.

All religions are products of a certain historical context and human spiritual experience. There are many points in all traditional religions which today can no longer be accepted by reason. Religions are only starting points. If one takes the traditional Islamic doctrine seriously that *taqlīd* (blind imitation) is forbidden, then the only consequence must be that every human being has to search independently for truth and to find his or her own religion. Traditional religion is a crutch. This crutch is useful but when one has philosophy and science it is no longer needed. This does not mean that the heritage of the religions becomes meaningless. Most probably a person that grew up in the Islamic tradition will make use of the Islamic spiritual tradition of prayer and fasting for his/her spiritual practice, and will mostly deal with Islamic sources although this must not necessarily be the case. As long as a person takes a spiritual path the traditional religions (whether Judaism, Islam or other religions) have much to offer. What is important is to make use of these traditions by individual critical examination and rethinking them with reason.

9. Response to Kalisch

ALON GOSHEN-GOTTSTEIN

Muhammad Kalisch's contribution is an extremely thoughtful piece of historical and theological reflection. It attempts to tackle the fundamentals of Muslim self-understanding in light of critical thinking in the fields of history, philology and above all comparative religious studies. Much as Muslims have classically done, it takes the state of scientific knowledge of the time and applies it to our religious understanding. In so doing, Kalisch makes a potentially very significant contribution to the understanding between religions, opening up new avenues for reflection and mutual understanding.

Methodologically, one of Kalisch's greatest contributions is his willingness to apply the same critical yardsticks to his consideration of all religions, his own included. Thus, the imbalanced treatment of Scriptures, according to which your (in this case – my) Scriptures are corrupted, while mine are perfect, is replaced by an even-handed critical view of all Scriptures as the outcome of complicated historical and psychological processes. The even-handed approach further leads Kalisch to search for traces of the possibility of salvation outside of Islam, regardless of religious affiliation. Despite slim findings, he is willing to adopt such a position, based on his own understanding of the workings of the Spirit, as supported by the contemporary study of religion. Finally, Kalisch intimates briefly at the end of his essay that the adoption of modern critical methods would also lead us to a different assessment of Jewish–Muslim relations, inasmuch as Judaism's formative role in the development of Islam would emerge from unbiased study of the subject. Kalisch thus constructs his theology on the foundations of contemporary scientific knowledge, be it historical, textual, psychological or what religious studies bring to our awareness. Thus, rather than construct a religious world-view that is based a priori upon truth claims as received and interpreted by tradition, contemporary scientific understanding plays a formative role in shaping religious understanding, which is understood and interpreted in its light, with radical consequences.

While these efforts are truly laudable, they raise some serious questions, both regarding the possible reception of Kalisch's ideas within his own community and regarding their import within a Jewish–Muslim conversation. I am convinced that we need the example of thinkers like Kalisch to suggest alternative understandings of religion and to bring about a change in attitudes to religion, both one's own and that of the other. However, the degree to which Kalisch has internalized contemporary critical thinking and made it the cornerstone of his own theology leads me to wonder how much this approach can be accepted within the Muslim community. If I understand correctly, it grows to a large extent from his own Zaidi tradition, which is itself hardly representative of the major schools of Muslim thought. Moreover, the extreme conclusions he has reached might place him beyond Muslim consensus, thereby making this important voice irrelevant. I therefore wonder to what extent milder strategies that seek to accomplish the same goals might not find a better reception. Alternative understandings of classical thorny issues might provide ways of dealing with them, that do not necessitate undermining the foundations of Muslim faith. Thus, the charge of scriptural falsification is dealt with as part of a reconfiguration of the meaning of Scripture and revelation that leaves little of the traditional understanding of revelation. It becomes irrelevant inasmuch as both Judaism and Islam are called to abandon their traditional understanding of revelation. The problem is indeed solved, but in a way that does a kind of violence to tradition, or to most people's understanding of it. Few traditional believers will accept this solution, I suspect. The alternative understandings of the falsification of Scripture to which Paul Ballanfat pointed, noted in my paper, would seem to achieve the same goal while meeting with far less resistance. The same goes for the benefits of Kalisch's theory as regards opening the gates of salvation for members of other religions. Given his understanding of salvation, one can no longer claim exclusive salvation for Muslim believers. But he himself has demonstrated there were seeds of such an understanding in traditional sources. To achieve this goal one would therefore not have to go as far as Kalisch has in reconfiguring traditional understandings of revelation.

Kalisch is a very advanced thinker, who tries to integrate a variety of methods into his new and impressive construction of Islam. However, it may be that precisely this attempt to tackle so many fronts and the daring way in which he undertakes this, would make it harder for his ideas to be received. I wonder whether employing one or some, rather than all, of his daring strategies at a time might not take his intended audience farther. Thus, the assumption that traditions should be dealt with in an even-handed manner could lead to the application of similar criteria for the study of the Bible and the Qur'ān, independently of the critical reflections on the mechanics of revelation and the creation of Scripture. Addressing the early historical evolution of the Qur'ān and pointing to the possibilities of its own textual vulnerability would undermine the basis of the Muslim claim for scriptural superiority, without entering into the more radical statements regarding the mechanics of revelation. Similarly, integrating the fruit of the (Jewish-led) research on the historical influence of Judaism upon Muḥammad within a Muslim worldview, to which Kalisch alludes in his concluding paragraph, would force us to rethink revelation in relation to human and historical circumstances, without completely undermining traditional notions of revelation.

Ultimately, the question of the reception of Kalisch's ideas is an internal Muslim affair. Why, then, my unease with the brave position offered by him? Because it makes the implicit demand for reciprocity, based on the supposed scientific foundations upon which it is based. If all historical knowledge found in Scripture is brought to naught and if revelation is itself only an act of translation of human religious experience, then I too would be asked to acknowledge in relation to my own tradition what Muhammad Kalisch affirms in relation to his own. And, I must confess, I am not willing to do so. The historical and critical issues with which Kalisch grapples are also relevant for the Jewish tradition, which has been the subject of critical reflection long before such reflection was applied to Islam. However, I do not have the full faith in contemporary scientific method (historical, psychological, etc.) that Kalisch does. I believe Moses existed, that there is real meaning to the giving of the Torah and that even if the historical reality of the events depicted in Scripture is different from how they are portrayed in Scripture, there is some historical sense to them. I am willing to think of religious truth in senses other than literal historical truth, and I am willing to apply such alternative understandings where there is serious evidence that it is called for. However, I would avoid the wholesale rejection of a dimension of faith that has been formative to all our traditions – the recognition of the historical validity of scriptural descriptions. The inter-religious situation may offer reasons for supplanting this traditional understanding, in view of the competing truth claims made by religions. But before going so far, we should consider using to the full the arsenal of options that are already available within our traditions.

Finally, I am put ill at ease with Kalisch's position because it leads to, perhaps even represents, religious relativism. It is fairly easy to engage in inter-religious relations from a relativistic perspective, according to which all religions do the same thing and are therefore of equal value in achieving the one common goal of all religions. One of the great challenges of inter-religious dialogue is how to engage in it without subscribing to a relativistic view. This does not mean upholding a triumphalist view of one's religion. Rather, it constitutes a call to stating its uniqueness and its unique contribution to humanity and its religious history. One of our great challenges is to strike a desired balance between holding on to our unique (if not exclusive) faith claims while recognizing (some) validity and effectiveness of other religious paths. Implicit in Kalisch's understanding of revelation is a relativism that goes beyond the limits of my own comfort. Thus, my concerns about the reception of Kalisch's ideas reflect my own concerns regarding the implicit demand for reciprocity contained in his position.

The misgivings I express regarding Kalisch's theological views should not detract from an appreciation of the importance of his thoughts. Even if his thinking has taken him beyond what I or most of my Muslim colleagues are comfortable with, he has challenged us in important ways and suggested stimulating ways of tackling issues. At the very least, his readers owe him an equally courageous account of how they would tackle those same issues in less radical ways. Forcing us to take these issues seriously is in itself an accomplishment for which we must thank him.

Part III

Islam and Christianity

10. A Muslim View of Christianity

ATAULLAH SIDDIQUI

The relationship between Muslims and Christianity covers a wide variety of approaches to explain various kinds of contact, conflict and co-operation between the followers of the two faiths. The readings of the respective Scriptures in the prevailing sociopolitical conditions and their impact at different stages of history have shaped our own understanding of the 'other'. They have conditioned our minds, informed our choices, prioritized our relations and dictated our directions. Today the relation between the two faiths is under enormous strain. The challenge is not only in 'decoding' the Scriptures and their past interpretations but also in the moulding of future relations. However to survey this bumpy ride of the two faiths in history is not the purpose of this chapter. Rather I would like to highlight certain events from the past to show how the prevailing sociopolitical conditions had bearings on the understanding of the 'other'.

Certain Empathy of Christians

It was the sixth year of the Prophet's ministry, and the tide of Persian conquest was on the rise. The Christian Byzantine army was fast losing its territory. It had lost Antioch, Aleppo and Damascus, and finally lost Jerusalem (614–15) to the Persians. The city was burned, the Christian inhabitants were massacred and the 'true cross', on which the Christians believed Jesus was crucified, was taken away to Persia. The Persian army seemed to be unstoppable; they went on to conquer Egypt and part of North Africa. The Byzantine defeat seemed to be final and unrecoverable.

This event had an impact in a distant Arabia. The tormentors of the Prophet in Mecca were happy, rejoicing in the Persian victory. They saw themselves as being closer to them both in spiritual practices and in temperament. The sympathy of the nascent Muslim community was not with the Persians, but with the Christians. This small band of Muslim converts, who would have been rejoicing with the fellow Meccan pagans only few years ago, were comfortable to take sides with the Christians. Their affinity with them was natural, as they saw themselves as part of a monotheistic faith and the inheritors of the Judaeo-Christian traditions. The defeat of the Byzantines was a painful event for them. In the midst of all this, to consider a victory by the Byzantines over the Persians was not only unthinkable and foolish, but an open invitation to ridicule. To have sympathy is one thing, to express it another, but to predict that in the very near future they are going to be victorious was sheer madness. This is exactly what happened. Prophet Muḥammad recited the verses that he had received in revelation through Gabriel and predicted that the Romans (Byzantines) will 'soon be victorious' and 'the believers', meaning Muslims, 'will rejoice' in their victory (30.2–3). This close affinity with the Christians was maintained throughout the Prophet's life. It was the Christians' altruistic behaviour towards fellow human beings that was so much praised by the Muslim community. The Qur'ān highlights such noble examples of Christian behaviour. Just to mention two:

> And nearest among them in love
> To the Believers wilt thou
> Find those who say,
> 'We are Christians':
> Because amongst these are
> Men devoted to learning
> And men who have renounced
> The world, and they
> Are not arrogant. (5.82)

> O ye believe!
> Be ye helpers of God:
> As said Jesus the son of Mary
> To the Disciples, 'Who will be
> My helpers to (the work of) God.'
> Said the Disciples,
> 'We are God's helpers!' (61.14)

The other example of empathy is related to Abyssinia. Small groups of persecuted Muslims in Mecca were advised by the Prophet to leave their city and migrate to Abyssinia. The Prophet highlighted the generosity of the Christian king and said: there rules a king in whose realm no one is wronged. It is a land of righteousness. Go there and remain at that place until God provides conditions favourable for return. In the seventh month of the fifth year of the Prophet's ministry, eleven men and five women left for Abyssinia, a country governed by Nejashi (Negus). These refugees were received warmly, the host community provided all the help necessary and they were at peace. However, the Quraysh from Mecca followed them and asked the king to extradite them. The refugees were denounced as criminals and enemies of society. The good king had the wisdom bring them both – accuser and accused – to attend his court and explain. There is good account of the debate that took place in the court of Nejashi. The end result was that the refugees were allowed to stay in Abyssinia. Over the next 13 years a stream of refugees visited the country – some left again, others stayed longer – but their numbers were not more than 300. Some of them married and had family and business there; others even decided to adopt the religion of the host society. But unfortunately we do not have a detailed account of their 'settlement'. Subsequent historiography of Muslims paid more attention to expansion and legal discourse and this tiny precious corner of Muslim history was not preserved for posterity.

Another opportunity arose to persuade the king. Two years after the migration of the Prophet to Medina, the warlords of Mecca attacked the city but lost the battle. The travel difficulties and the uncertain social conditions of the two cities prevented some Muslims from joining the Medinan society from Abyssinia. Fresh from defeat, the Quraysh again planned to ask Nejashi to hand over the remaining refugees to them, probably to use them at a later stage as a bargaining tool against the Prophet. When the Prophet came to know about the intentions of the Quraysh, he decided to send an envoy to the king, and chose 'Amar ibn Umaīyah aḍ-Ḍamarīy – a Christian. One may say that this was political pragmatism on the part of the Prophet; however, what is significant here is that people who were not Muslims also played a significant role in building a Muslim society. By their affiliation to other faiths they were not disqualified from being part of the wider Muslim society.

One day the Prophet received the sad news that the king of Abyssinia had died. The Prophet said to the Companions, 'Your brother has died, let us pray for him.' It is recorded that he offered *ṣalāt al-janāza*, a special prayer for the deceased offered exclusively to a Muslim, to King Nejahsi. Ibn Taymiyya (d.1328), a famous jurist and theologian, asked the question: did the king implement the *shari'a*? Obviously not, his people were Christians. Nor did he offer five daily prayers, obligatory for every Muslim, or fast in the month of Ramadan, another obligatory act of worship. He says obviously not, because had he done any of these things, he would have been dismissed.[1]

This great belief, that they were not outsiders to the prophetic tradition of Jesus and Moses, continued throughout the Prophet's ministry. This has been seen as part of a wider vision of God's plan. The relationship was further cemented in two fundamental human needs – sustenance and procreation – where in matters of food and family life a Christian does not have to give up his or her belief.

Certain Aversion of Christians

While great cultural exchanges were taking place between Islamic and Latin Christian traditions, especially the philosophical debates and ideas personified in people like Ibn Sina (Avicenna) (d.1037) and Ibn Rushd (Averroes) (d.1198), the Crusades and the Mongol invasion of Baghdad in 1250 changed everything. The reasonably friendly mutual approaches on theological issues increasingly turned into mutual suspicions and hostilities. When Muslim territories were attacked by the Mongols, some minorities (including Muslim fringe sects) who lived in these territories sided with the Mongols, and conspired against the Muslim authorities. The theology of Ibn Taymiyya was predominantly occupied with such events. He regarded the *dhimmī* – the minority in a Muslim country including the fringe sects within the Muslim society – as not trustworthy, and the whole question of how to absorb them became the priority. The provocations from them were centred on the figure of the Prophet Muhammad; they were well aware of the consequences

1 I am indebted to Professor Nejatullah Siddiqi who pointed this out to me.

of their actions, and the Muslim *'ulamā'* were also aware of the fact that they could not give up that centre ground of orthodoxy which they considered crucial for the future survival of the community. Ibn Taymiyya's approach to Christianity has to be understood not only against this background but also regarding his concerns that the way Islam was presented to the Christians was as irrelevant and superfluous. Islam was proposed as a religion intended for Arabs only, the Arabic Qur'ān as only relevant to those who speak that language, and Prophet Muḥammad's mission was also limited to the ignorant and boisterous communities of Arabs. Ibn Taymiyya saw this as a challenge that could weaken the confidence of Muslims, especially in the sectarian climate that existed and the erosion of religions that was taking place. He responded to Paul of Antioch's (the Bishop of Sidon) *Letter to a Muslim* by writing *Al-Jawāb al-Ṣaḥīḥ*.[2] He defended the Muslim position on such ideas as the nature and mission of Prophet Muḥammad, the corruption of the Scripture, the question of *ḥulūl* – indwelling of God in Christ, and the *ittiḥād* – or the union of God with a creature.

The centrality of the Prophet Muḥammad to Islam and Islam's world-view is decisive. This is what Ibn Taymiyya was defending in his time. In 1293, a Christian cleric, 'Asaf al-Naṣrānī, was accused of insulting the Prophet. He sought protection from one of the powerful families of Damascus, but Ibn Taymiyya brought the case before the governor. His opinion on such issues was that anyone defaming the Prophet or any prophet *must* be executed whether a Muslim or not. This punishment was not something a judge could commute or reduce in severity, rather, in his view, it was an obligatory punishment where judges have no alternative. Such strong emphasis was largely motivated by his strong desire to protect his community.

Though he was very critical of Christian beliefs, nonetheless Ibn Taymiyya was a man of principles. He was adamant that rights that are given to the minorities within a Muslim domain must be granted to them at all cost. This was vindicated when Damascus fell to the Mongols and both Christians and Muslims were imprisoned. The Mongols left a governor in charge of the city. Ibn Taymiyya negoti-

2 Partly translated by Michel Thomas, 1984, *A Muslim Theologian's Response to Christianity*, New York: Carvan Books.

ated the release of all prisoners of war, but because the Mongols agreed to release only the Muslim prisoners and not the Christians, this was unacceptable to him and he declined to leave without them.

We find that similar strong refutation of Christianity and the emphasis on the prophecy of the Prophet Muḥammad is further highlighted in the writings of Ibn Qāyyim al-Jawziyya (d.1350). He uses Judaeo-Christian Scriptures to demonstrate that the prophecy and the Prophethood of Muḥammad are not only foretold in those Scriptures, but his advent in fact compounded the essence of the teaching of all other prophets before him. He argues his position on the Prophet's coming on the basis of the Qur'ān (61.6). As the advent of Jesus was the confirmation of the Jewish Scripture, so was the advent of the Prophet Muḥammad the confirmation of Christian Scriptures. What is interesting in his writing is that he traces the fulfilment of the prophecy of Muḥammad in the story of Abraham and Hagar, well before Jesus and Moses, and strongly places the Islamic traditions there, to the effect that the rejection of the Prophet Muḥammad also means the rejection of Jesus and the traditions of Moses.

Ibn Qāyyim lived at a time when strife, suspicion and betrayal were common, and his approach to Christianity was influenced by the circumstances of his time. Features of dialogue and understanding were the last thing on his mind. His views on the people of the book and their status in a Muslim society were further evidence of how much he was conditioned by the sociopolitical situation of his time. In his book *Aḥkām ahl al-Dhimma* he not only demanded that the people of the book should pay *jizya* (a poll tax), but also demanded that their dresses and homes should be marked distinctly and their freedoms should be restricted.

The fall of Granada in 1492 served a further blow to a positive Christian–Muslim understanding. Though according to the terms of agreement the Christian ruler promised to respect the freedom of Muslim subjects in their religious affairs, that matter of freedom was interpreted differently within the kingdom. The Archbishop of Granada, Hernando de Talavera (d.1502) advocated a missionary approach, hoping Muslims would accept the truth of Christianity and gradually be baptized and incorporated into the Christian society. On the other hand, the Archbishop of Toledo Francisco Jime'nez de Cisneros (d.1517) had a different idea. He preferred a campaign of forced conversion of Muslims. In 1499 the campaign began in earnest in Toledo, Alcala and Granada, where Muslims were forcefully converted to Christianity. Mosques were turned into churches, the land and properties of *awqāf* (religious trusts) were confiscated and the destruction of Islamic books, with the help of crowds, was carried out. Muslims faced assimilation and inquisition. Against this background they had two choices: either, to have a kind of double allegiance which would help them to be Muslim at home but Christian outside; or, to oppose and revolt against the forced assimilation. Both approaches were tried but those who adopted a double standard were gradually merged into a Christian society with few remnants of their faith, while the others were expelled forcefully during 1609–10 to Turkey, Tunisia and other Muslim countries via France and sea routes. Their numbers were almost 300,000.

This resulted in anti-Christian polemics and suspicion of Latin Christianity. There was urgency among Muslims to establish the superiority of Prophet Muḥammad over Jesus; the idea of Muḥammad as a messiah, as described in *Gospel of Barnabas*, began to circulate. Islam was seen as a doctrine of purity without superstition, and the expulsion of Muslims compared to the expulsion of the Jews from Egypt. As the Jews were part of that expulsion experience, they found some sympathy and a common narrative in biblical and qur'ānic texts.

Certain Hesitation of Christians

The colonial era brought new approaches and perspectives on Christianity in particular, and Christian–Muslim relations in general. On the one hand the Muslims responded to the increasing polemical approach to Islam, and on the other they tried to interpret the meaning of Christian revelation, particularly the Gospels, in the context where they found themselves. The centre of such activities was focused largely in South Asia.

European powers brought a new era for Muslim countries. They faced a politically superior body, equipped not only with new technologies and as a consequence a new economic power, but also a 'new' world order. For Muslims the 'new' world order was full of contradiction. On the one hand it was dominantly God-centred, but on the other was almost anti-religious. Christianity was the main vehicle of religious idiom; philosophy and secularization was another vehicle that devalued religious beliefs and convictions. The Muslim religious leadership at this juncture had two priorities. First, the reform or *iṣlāḥ* of the community in order to protect it from growing Christian/secular influences and second, to challenge European polemicists who saw in their religion an amalgam of Christian heresy and animism. These two broad issues preoccupied Muslim leadership up to the first quarter of the twentieth century. The *'ulamā'* (Islamic scholars) became the vanguard of community reform, especially in the areas of education and the preparing of Muslims to challenge European influences and the Christian mission in particular. Public polemical debates became an important tool in reasserting 'Islamic identity' and reforming the community. The need to do so was generated largely by Christian missionaries, especially people like Karl Pfander (d.1865) whose legacy continues to vibrate even today. It was not so much *what* the Europeans and missionaries said, but *how* they said it and how they approached things. *'Ulamā'*, such as Rahmatullah Kairanwi (d.1890), responded to Pfander's book *Mīzān al-ḥaqq* ('Balance of Truth') by publishing *Izḥār al-ḥaqq* ('Demonstration of Truth'). Their contents were overwhelmingly to 'establish' the 'authenticity' of the Bible and Jesus and, therefore, the 'falsity' of Islam. The *'ulamā'* adopted a similar approach in relation to Christians in India.

The polemical approaches to Christianity for Muslims were largely a mechanism to protect and generate confidence in the community, particularly among the young. Such approaches have survived ever since among Muslims with the same justification, and prevented them, to a large extent, from seeing the 'other' as they see themselves. The late Ahmad Deedat (d.2005) of South Africa was a towering figure who influenced a generation of Muslims towards this approach to Christianity. Fundamentalist Christians too have consistently relied on a polemical approach to Islam, and have hardly engaged with Muslims in a meaningful way to see them as they see themselves. This polemical spiral is playing havoc in cyberspace.

The Indian Rebellion of 1857 had a great impact on young Sayyid Aḥmad Khān (d.1898), and all his efforts were centred on education and the intellectual development of the Muslim community. He began to look at other faiths, and particularly Christianity which he faced through British colonizers. His book *Tabyīn al-kalām fī tafsir al-tawrat wal-injīl ʻala millat al-islām* (ʻTheological clarification on the subject of the exegesis of the Old and New Testament destined to the community of Islam') appeared in English as *The Mohamedan Commentary on the Holy Bible* (published privately in 1862–5). The purpose seems to be making the Bible known to Muslims without being polemical or apologetic. This book largely deals with the authenticity, corruption and abrogation issues of the Bible and also provides a commentary on the first part of Genesis and part of the Gospel of Matthew. The way Khān deals with the issue of revelation appears like this: he differentiates between the *waḥy* given to the Prophet Muḥammad and the *waḥy* given to the prophets before him. The Qur'ān, he states, is literally dictated and Allah is the One who dictated it, hence the miracle of the language. The prophets before Muḥammad, by contrast, received only the contents of the revelation that they rendered into their own language. In some cases 'special text' (*matn khāṣṣ*) was revealed, therefore not all words are divine. In such cases the prophets of that nation made 'elaboration' (*riwāya*). Against this background Khān examines the nature of the Bible. This is considered an 'inspired' text and authentic. Differences that occur in the biblical text are not the result of 'wilful corruption', but are there because of mistakes that occurred in the transmission of the message. At the time this position on such an issue could be considered as a major shift of understanding of the Bible. He recognized religious values in Christian Scriptures, but he was also preoccupied with Western scholarship and their critique of the Prophet Muḥammad, particularly the Prophet's biography written by Sir William Muir (d.1905), *The Life of Mahomet*. Khān was outraged and decided to respond to Muir, and he did this while he was in England. He hired people to translate material from Latin, German and other European languages, and developed an elaborate scheme for a biography of the Prophet that would be a fitting reply. In the process he became penniless. Finally he published *A Series of Essays on the Life of Mohammad*, which remained incomplete. During his stay in England he visited universities such as Oxford and Cambridge and some private schools, which gave him the idea to create an educational centre for Muslims, and he established the Muhammadan Anglo-Oriental College, which later became the Aligarh Muslim University. Later Shiblī Nu'mānī (d.1914) took up the task of writing a biography of the Prophet. He emphasized the need to search deep into Muslim resources and highlighted that there were, within Muslim history, those who could match and even surpass the western thinkers and leaders. He wanted to reform and rebuild the crumbling Muslim society, especially the youth, and wrote *Al-Farooq*, *Al-Ma'mūn* and *Al-Ghazālī*.

The Napoleonic invasion of Egypt created the same upheaval which was witnessed in India. Muḥammad 'Abduh's (d.1905) approach was to rediscover the Muslims' own strength within their Islamic sources. He adopted a method that could establish the superiority of Islam vis-à-vis Christianity and Western political power, and prepared Muslims to assert themselves with vigour and self-respect both within and outside the community. He saw in humanity a dialectic progression and Islam as a synthesis of all. He emphasized that in 'Childhood, man needed stern discipline which equated with the Law of Moses. During adolescence, man relied on feelings, the compassion being the Age of Christianity. But in maturity, when man relied on Reason and Science then his recourse was the Age of Islam.' The underlying emphasis among all three, Nu'mānī, 'Abduh and Sayyid Aḥmad Khān, seems to be that Christians should not find another reason to demoralize Muslims. In 'Abduh's disciple, Rashīd Riḍā (d.1935), we find a combative approach to Christianity where he was eager to establish the 'authenticity' of Islam and sought to 'expose' Christianity's weakness. He serialized the translation of the *Gospel of Barnabas* into Arabic in his journal *Al-Manār*.

Certain Connection with Christians

The increasing secularization in Muslim countries, erosion of political rights and accountability of the rulers, created a kind of discourse vacuum. The Muslim intellectuals and masses mistrusted their rulers as well as the Western powers, whom they held responsible for such a situation. For their political and economic gain, Muslims thought, the Western powers would prefer to work with the dictatorial regimes in hostility to the masses.

The *'ulamā'* in particular viewed increasing Western influences in Muslim countries as a vehicle of 'corruption', 'evil' and 'moral decadence'. Against this background the call for dialogue by the churches, especially from the West, was a breath of fresh air. Muslims saw the churches as an ally in their struggle against increasing secularization of their society, as well as injustice in the world and particularly against the Palestinians. They saw the dialogue between the two faith communities as a dialogue of 'common cause'. In Bhamdoun, Lebanon in April 1954 they participated in the Convocation. Western-educated Muslims, the *'ulamā'* and others all participated enthusiastically in this dialogue. The creation of the State of Israel, in 1948, resulted in the displacement of hundreds of thousands of Palestinians. A large number of these took refuge in neighbouring countries such as Jordan, Syria and Lebanon, and the Bhamdoun dialogue obviously felt the pressure and concerns of the participants. The Muslims hoped that through such dialogue they would be able to win the hearts and minds of the Western churches, if not Western governments. As there were a significant number of Christians among these refugees, they hoped that Western churches would be more willing to co-operate with Muslims on the issue of justice. Muṣṭafā al-Sibā'ī (d.1964), one of the dialogue participants, identified three causes that disenchanted people with Western democracies and attracted them instead towards communism:

> 1) 'Corrupt social systems, especially in the Muslim East . . . the corrupt systems of government; the failure of rulers to enforce the laws of justice . . .'
> 2) 'The hostile opposition of the Western democracies to the peoples of the East in their aspirations for independence and liberation.'
> 3) 'The support Zionism was able to get from the Western democracies and through which it was able to establish itself in the heart of the Arab home'.[3]

Two days later, at the same dialogue he highlighted the reasons behind his participation:

> [The] purpose for which I came to this Convocation is that my country and my nation have some problems, and . . . the nearest people to us in our beliefs and moral values are those others who believe in a divine religion . . . we should come to an understanding on these problems as friends. I presumed that I might be able,

3 *The Proceedings of the First Muslim-Christian Convocation* (Bhamdoun, Lebanon, 22–27 April 1954), New York: Continuing Committee on Muslim–Christian Cooperation, 1955, p. 68.

> together with my colleagues, to convince this distinguished group of religious and cultural leaders of Europe and America to understand our problems.[4]

This dialogue makes it very clear that Muslims expected an existential relationship, that is they were not especially concerned about theological issues. The emphasis was more on the *people of faith* rather than the *faith of the people*. The theme of justice for the Palestinian vibrated in subsequent Christian–Muslim dialogues and created at times some embarrassing moments.

The 1970s saw the rise of *Shari'a*/Human Rights controversies, and against this background the Muslims increasingly saw Christians, both in Asia and Africa and in European and North American countries, as siding with secular forces, allying themselves with those who wanted to see Muslim countries become modern-secular rather than Islamic. This fear was paramount and in some cases it was reflected in dialogue. Furthermore, in this process the Christian mission was seen as an arm of the secularization process. Conversion to Christianity was not simply a conversion of faith but also of a culture and to the world-view of the Europeans.

To address such critical issues and especially 'The Christian Mission and Islamic *Dawah*', in 1976, was the theme of the Chambésy Dialogue organised by the World Council of Churches. The presentations were essentially intellectual. One thing one does to begin to notice in this Dialogue is the way in which the issue of religious freedom was addressed and perhaps handled in clearer terms. The Muslims were constantly challenged during this decade about how 'Islam does not give religious freedom' and does not allow a Muslim to become Christian. In this Dialogue, we find, however, a unanimity amongst the Muslims that as long as a person is convinced and wants to change his/her religion, and unfair means are not employed to entice a person to switch his/her faith, then both Muslims and Christians should accept this as the basic right of anyone. It is significant that the final statement documents in clear terms that the

> conference upholds the principles of religious freedom recognising that the Muslims as well as the Christians must enjoy the full liberty to convince and be convinced, and to practice their faith

4 *Proceedings of the First Muslim-Christian Convocation*, p. 98.

and order their religious life in accordance with their own religious laws and principles . . .'[5]

More recently some serious but controversial theological issues have been raised, especially in relation to qur'ānic instruction on Christianity. Mahmoud Ayoub, for example, suggests that Muslim theologians need to revisit the whole Islamic Christology. He encourages Muslims to look afresh at Jesus' 'redemptive role in human history'. The Qur'ān clearly denies the death of Jesus on the cross, as atonement for sinful humanity; however, he points out that the actual death is not denied. Here he suggests Muslim theologians need to examine what role the earlier converts to Islam from Christianity had played.

The Qur'ān uses the term Islam in two senses, argues Ayoub, Islam as an institutionalized religion and *islām* as the framework of *true faith* (*imān*) and *righteous living* (*iḥsān*). He argues that 'neither the Qur'ān nor the [traditions] of the Prophet demand of the Jews and Christians that they give up their religious identity and become Muslims, unless they freely choose to do so.' He has also explored some new dimensions of the qur'ānic usage of the word *ibn* and *walad*. The word *ibn* in the Qur'ān signifies 'filial relationship' which he regards as a metaphorical relationship: 'son through a relationship of love and adoption'. *Walad* signifies a more intense relationship of 'offspring'. This is where he finds the qur'ānic commentators took the word *walad* and produced a whole genre of qur'ānic literature that argues the Christian concept of Divine sonship.[6] But he also puts the blame on early Christian theologians providing that meaning, from which the Muslim theologians took *walad* for *ibn*. The root of this meaning he finds lies in medieval Christian literature, and particularly in the writings of Theodore Abū Qurra (d. *c.*820).

5 See the 'Statement of the Conference' published in the *International Review of Mission* Vol. LXV No. 260 October, 1976, pp. 457–60. Also in *Christian Mission and Islamic Dawah*, 1982, Leicester: The Islamic Foundation.

6 Mahmoud Ayoub, 1995, 'Jesus the Son of God: A Study of the Terms *Ibn* and *Walad* in the Qur'an and *Tafsīr* Tradition' in Y. Y. Haddad and W. Z. Haddad (eds) *Christian-Muslim Encounters*, Gainesville: University Press of Florida pp. 65–81.

Certain Concerns for the Future

Today a large number of Muslims feel that they are politically and economically under siege. After the Bosnian crisis, the Gulf crisis, Iraq, Afghanistan, Bali, Madrid, 9/11 and the London bombings, Muslims do not know which way to turn. They see the accusing fingers pointing at them and their response is largely to look inward. They see blatant double standards applied to them. In many Muslim minds, Christianity and the West are the same, and an attack on Muslim countries by the West is also seen as an attack by Christians. This perception is further compounded by the American evangelists' and Christian Zionists' interpretation of the events in the Middle East. In a situation like this it is natural to look into a religious tendency that provides more 'comfort' zones for them.

Given the socio-economic situation of Muslims and Christians, which also includes the Western political powers, what impact might it have on future relations between the two communities? The investment of mistrust will have a far-reaching influence on the coming generations of Muslims and Christians, especially in the Muslim world. We can only hope that the large protest rallies against the war(s) and the increasing engagement of Muslims and Christians in European and North American countries (as well as other parts of the Muslim world) may reduce the impact; however, there is no guarantee that it will bear the desired result. The 1950s engagement between the two communities that perceived a common threat, like communism, is replaced by the perception that a partner in dialogue is a suspect of crime. Kevin Philips argues that American evangelical, fundamentalist, and Pentecostal churches, in turn, have become 'the new flag-bearers of crusades against Islam's "evil ones". . . . The anti-Muslim comments of prominent leaders of the Christian right . . . [and their] antagonism to Islam replacing hatred of the Soviet Union.'[7] Today's encounters between the two religions may generate tomorrow's theology of hate. The future Muslim interpretation of Christianity will rely more on today's politics and less on the spiritual and hospitable aspects of Islamic traditions. This in my view will be a serious handicap to any sensible understanding of Christianity. The trend among Christians that is hostile and aggres-

7 Kevin Phillips, 2006, *American Theocracy*, New York: Viking, p. 259.

sive to Islam and Muslims is only a part of Christian understanding, which may not feel comfortable engaging in a meaningful dialogue with Muslims. Such a branch of Christianity may never break free of their self-induced spectre of Islam to become closer to Muslims. However, there is another part of Christianity that advocates love, charity, devotion and a sense of justice, to which Muslims need to connect, with respect and in dignity. To connect with this formidable force is a challenge for Muslims. The first part of that challenge is to see Christians as they are – their spirituality, charity and devotion needs to be explored through the prism of Christian self-understanding.

There are a few major areas of perception between the two communities that I believe need to be addressed. Here, as Muslim perspectives, I would like to highlight four such areas.

Recognizing the 'otherness of the other' is the first step towards meeting the 'others' as they see themselves. Stereotyping others has been a major challenge for both communities. While Islam has a view of Christian beliefs at times diametrically opposite to the Christian viewpoint, this should not prevent us seeing Christians as they understand their own beliefs. Despite the fact that Islam had strong criticism of the Cross and salvation history, it sympathized and saw Christians within the wider fold of faith as very close to Islam.

Second, our use of Scriptures is another issue that I believe needs revisiting. The comparison of the Qur'ān vis-à-vis the New Testament has created a polemical atmosphere that generated more strain than anything else. The Qur'ān is the communication of God to humanity, and how that communication should be acted upon is shown by the Prophet Muḥammad. How the Prophet lived and practised the message of the Qur'ān was recorded by his Companions, known as *sunnah* of the Prophet and available in *ḥadīth* literature. The New Testament is about Jesus and how he lived and practised his life with his disciples, while the Qur'ān is not 'about' the Prophet Muḥammad, rather Muḥammad was about the Qur'ān. Here is a major difference of approach to our Scriptures, which in turn provides a different approach to faith and righteous living.

Third, there is the deficit of history. The Second Vatican Council's declaration *Nostra Aetate* (no. 3) advocates that both Christians and Muslims should forget the past, and urges that 'sincere efforts be made to achieve mutual understanding . . .' The spirit behind this plea is a noble one. In both communities the memory of history is very selective. We tend to compare the ideals enshrined in our Scriptures, and our good practices of the past, with others' flawed behaviour containing human weaknesses. We have a propensity to disregard our own weaknesses and standards that fall short of our own ideals. The lack of openness to admit our own mistakes remains a big challenge for both communities. This leads me to another important factor: the churches towards the end of the last millennium began a move asking forgiveness from Muslims for the Crusades. But Muslims are in a strange situation where they feel that this generation of Muslims cannot take responsibility for past generations. *They* were responsible for their own actions and *this* generation is responsible for its own. The past may affect the two communities today; however, what we do today will have an impact on coming generations.

This leads us to another crucial point, and that is dialogue. In any number of dialogues between the two communities, and this is my fourth point, we have managed to conduct great monologues. We are willing to talk, but not willing to listen to what the other party is saying. We presume in our dialogue that what has been conveyed in our encounter is understood. Usually what happens is that we *hear* what we want to and conveniently *ignore* what is unpalatable. But the dialogue, if it has any future, must have the capacity to go beyond nicety and cross-communication, and be ready for *co-action* and even *co-witness* in a modern world.

11. A Christian View of Islam

MARTIN BAUSCHKE

Christianity is considered to be the 'religion of love' and Islam to be the 'religion of peace'. However both religions often enough during their history appeared not only in loving but also in unloving ways, not only by peacemaking but also by causing strife, and this not just within their own ranks but also in the way they faced one another. Nevertheless it is by no means the case that the entire common history of both Christians and Muslims was solely confrontational. There were and are times of peaceful coexistence, which were and are so unspectacular that we hardly or never hear of them in history books and newspapers.

Long periods of time, in Christian and Muslim history, resemble family conflicts. Obviously those closest to one another can fight best with each other; for they know exactly where and how they can hurt the other best. This is the reason why conflicts among siblings or with neighbours are worse than those between strangers, who happen to clash with one another. For this reason civil wars are more brutal than wars between different countries. Similarly one could say that precisely because Christians and Muslims are close to one another, being religious (or rather monotheistic) brothers, so much worse were the dreadful wounds they inflicted upon each other. And by 'dreadful wounds' I do not only mean wounds from which blood flows, but also mutual theological injuries.

In what follows, I will briefly review the major Christian images of Islam in the past, and subsequently develop my own interpretation of Islam.

The Christian Views of Islam: Review of a Common History

The Christian View of Islam does not exist, for Christianity is as diverse as Islam. Concretely there are very different ideas of Muḥammad, of the Qur'ān and of 'Allah' that Christians developed throughout history. I distinguish *five different types of Christian views of Islam* (but there are certainly more):

Islam as a Christian heresy

Christianity was afraid of Islam right from the beginning because the very fact that there was another prophet *post Christum,* another Word of God after the New Testament, a new world religion after the Christian Church, was frightening. This put the Christian self-image – as the climax and ultimate point of God's revelation – radically into question. So, what can one do with a feared opponent? One ridicules him, one tries to deprive him of his dignity. This is exactly the strategy the teachers of the Church used. Thus the idea Christians had of Islam was distorted right from the beginning, and still is so frequently to this very day: marked by ignorance and prejudices.

For more than 1,000 years the judgement of John of Damascus (d.750[1]), was seen as valid: Islam is no authentic religion, but only a Christian heresy, a diabolic distortion of Christianity. Muḥammad was no real prophet, but a Christian heretic, a misguided monk and impostor from the Arab desert.[2] This interpretation of Islam was so widespread that Dante (d.1321) in his 'Divine Comedy' (*La Divina Commedia*) naturally placed Muḥammad in hell along with the Christian heretics.[3] The existence of Islam meant – psychologically speaking – a narcissistic offence to exclusivistic Christian self-assurance. Islam was only bearable while being *theologically marginalized.* Islam had been deprived of its claims. It could only be a Christian heresy. Muḥammad could only be a pseudo-prophet on behalf of an Arab false god called 'Allah'. The Qur'ān could only be a book full of lies, blasphemies and pseudo-revelations. For hun-

1 The years in the text are following the Western calculation of time.
2 Johannes Damascenus, *De haeresibus*, chapter 100.
3 *Inferno*, chapter 28.

dreds of years Islam was known to the Christian occident through a demonized and, at the same time, ridiculous caricature.

Further images of Islam, which were valid from the Middle Ages up to the modern times, are:

- Being merely a Christian heresy, Muḥammad, and the Qur'ān, had not brought forward any new ideas, no progress such as Christianity (according to the same claim) had achieved in relation to Judaism and Jesus in comparison with Moses.
- It was believed that Muḥammad was worshipped in the way Christ is in Christianity. This later marked, in missionary circles, the invention of the term 'Mohammedans' modelled on the term 'Christians'.
- Muḥammad not only lets himself be worshipped as God, but abandons himself to indulgence and to all sorts of sexual vices, which the large number of his wives demonstrates.
- Islam is a violent religion, which right from the start – therefore with the deeds of Muḥammad as commander – is spread by the use of 'fire and sword' and through 'Holy Wars'.

The fact that these Christian views have not yet become extinct, but on the contrary are virtually resuscitated, is shown by the controversial Muḥammad caricatures, as well as by the lecture given by Pope Benedict XVI (in September 2006 in Regensburg, Germany). Measuring the spectacular worldwide consequences since the propagation of the first Crusade by Pope Urban II, 900 years ago, there has been no speech in the history of Christianity like that lecture of Benedict XVI. The Pope quoted the fourteenth-century Byzantine Emperor Manuel II Palaiologos: 'Show me what new ideas Muḥammad has brought forward, and you shall only find bad and inhumane things, such as that he dictated that the faith he preaches of, is to be propagated by the sword.' It is hard to believe: 'Pope contra Muhammad' is no slogan from the age of the Crusades but from the present. It is the title of the 18 September issue No. 38/2006, of the German magazine *Der Spiegel*.

Islam as a hostile empire and the Antichrist

The theological depreciation of Islam goes, during the Middle Ages, along with a kind of upgrading of Islam as a military power, as a political threat. *Theologically,* Islam, being not more than a heresy, seemed to be ridiculous, but *militarily*, as a hostile empire, it was terrifying. In 1095 Pope Urban II (beatified in 1881), appealed in Clermont for the first Crusade against Islam. The Crusades deepened the abyss between Christianity and Islam. Bernard of Clairvaux (d.1153 and beatified in 1174), nominated by the Pope as chief ideologist, staged, on his own account, another crusade 50 years later, with a sermon-campaign. The failure of this second crusade – measured by the number of the dead – can be compared with the catastrophes of Napoleon's and Hitler's Russian campaigns. Through the Crusades and the Reconquista in Spain (until 1492), a fair-minded and differentiated view of Islam in the Christian West, and a fair and differentiated view of Christianity in the Arab–Islamic world had almost, with very few exceptions, become impossible.

Regarding the Protestant churches, Martin Luther's assessment of Islam, in particular, had a lasting impact on the Protestant attitude towards Muslims.[4] Luther believed the Qur'ān to be the propagation of a religion of law and not of faith. While John of Damascus considered Islam to be the 'precursor (Gr. *pródromos*) of the Antichrist', Luther went a step further and identified Islam with the Antichrist itself. For Luther, Islam was as bad as the Roman Papacy: both were the devil's work and, in his opinion, the sign of the imminent last days: 'the Pope is the soul of the Antichrist, the Turk is the flesh of the Antichrist.'[5] To this very day, the anti-Islamic, and by the way also the anti-Jewish works of Luther, are hardly discussed critically in Protestant theology.[6]

---

4 When the Ottomans stood at the gates of Vienna, his books *Vom Kriege wider die Türken* ('Of War against the Turks') and *Heerpredigt wider die Türken* ('Army Sermon against the Turks') were published (1529). In these, Luther gave each Christian soldier a good conscience; whoever fought against the Turks thus also fought against the 'enemy and blasphemer of Jesus Christ'. To shed the blood of a Turk was a deed obliging to God.

5 Weimar Edition (WA) *Tischreden*, Vol. 1, 135, No. 330: 'Ego omnino puto papatum esse Antichristum, aut si quis vult addere Turcam, papa est spiritus Antichristi, et Turca est caro Antichristi.'

6 See Ludwig Hagemann, 1998, *Martin Luther und der Islam,* Altenberge: Verlag für Christlich-Islamische Schrifttum; C.U. Wolf, 1941, 'Luther and Mohammedanism', *Muslim Word* 31, pp. 161–77.

Islam as a concern of mission and a spiritual enemy

In the eighteenth and nineteenth centuries there was a systematic Christian 'Mohamedan Mission'. The missionary confrontation with Islam was seen as the 'final battle between the Cross and the Crescent', carried out mainly in the Middle East and in India. Karl Barth, for many the greatest Christian theologian of the twentieth century, joined in the old anti-Islamic slogans, when he wrote: 'The God of Mohammed is an idol like all the other false gods.'[7] Today the medieval rhetoric about Islam as an anti-Christian, satanic power is still alive, primarily in some fundamentalist, charismatic and evangelical churches and parishes. Since the 1990s Islam has become their favourite bogeyman and they revel in conspiracy theories.

For example, at the Southern Baptist Convention, the largest Protestant denomination in the USA with its 16 million members, anti-Islamic agitation has been, ever since 9/11, highly distinctive. A range of well-known pastors participate in it, such as Jerry Vines, Jerry Falwell and Franklin Graham. For them, Christianity and Islam, Jesus and Muḥammad are 'perpetual enemies', because they represent different gods. 'Allah' is only a mask of Satan or of the Meccan moon god 'Hubal'. Christian extremists declared the zone between the tenth and the fortieth degrees of latitude – the core areas of Islam – the 'spiritual battlefield of the 21st century'. Islam is not only a concern anymore, but also a direct rival of the Christian mission – especially in Africa. Here Christian and Islamic fundamentalist preachers are fighting in a missionary duel, thus contributing to the destabilization of whole countries and nations.

Islam as a matter of academic studies

It was not until the Enlightenment, which shone brighter outside the Church than within, that some positive light was thrown on Islam. In the eighteenth and nineteenth centuries a number of scholars made an effort to re-evaluate Islam, the Qur'ān and Muḥammad, and to clear them from prejudices and clichés. For the first time in history, Islam was recognized as a civilizing intellectual power,

7 Karl Barth, 1938, *Gotteserkenntnis und Gottesdienst nach reformatorischer Lehre,* Zollikon: Evangelischer Verlag, p. 57.

and was seriously studied academically. Noted names are, for instance:

- the Dutchman Adrian Reland (d.1718), Professor of Oriental Languages in Utrecht (*De Religione Muhammadica*, 1705),
- the English historian Edward Gibbon (d.1794),
- the Scotsman Thomas Carlyle (d.1881),
- and in Germany, Lessing (d.1781), Goethe (d.1832) and Friedrich Rückert (d.1866), whose translation of the Qur'ān is, to this day, the most beautiful in the German language.

These scholars, poets and thinkers have contributed to *un-demonize Islam* and to appreciate Muḥammad as a 'donor of law', as a prophetical 'hero' and a statesman. In particular, they showed that Muḥammad was no impostor, but that he acted in subjective truthfulness and credibility as a prophet. This enlightened esteem of Islam is only partially a Christian success, for the above-mentioned scholars were not really people of the Church – but perhaps had understood the spirit of Christ better than the Church itself. Modern Western studies of Islam emerged from these beginnings, and developed their own particular views and projections of Islam.[8]

Islam as a partner of dialogue

Not all Christians encountered Islam with contempt, hate and violence. Among the few voices who already during the Middle Ages pleaded for the motto 'religious dialogue instead of religious wars', were four scholars, who were the most important proponents of peaceful communication between Christians and Muslims of their times:

1. Petrus Venerabilis, the Abbot of Cluny (d.1156). He pleaded for a struggle with Islam by the word and not the sword of God. Due to his influence, the *first translation ever of the Qur'ān in Europe* was made by the Englishman Robert of Ketton and published in 1143 – more than 500 years after Muḥammad's death. This quite bad and manipulated Latin translation remained for the following five centuries the most widespread till the much better

8 I am reminded of the 'Orientalism' debate that was initiated by Edward Said's book *Orientalism* (New York: Pantheon 1978).

translation, also into Latin, by Ludovicus Marracci (d.1700) appeared.[9]

2 Francis of Assisi, who travelled to Egypt to the Palace of Sultan Malik al-Kamil I (d.1238), and also preached to him.
3 Ramon Lull, a Franciscan monk and mystic from Spain (d.1316), who as a pacifist missionary – in line with his *via disputationis*, namely, convincing the other through arguments – had various discussions with Muslims.
4 Cardinal Nicolaus from Kues (Cusanus, d.1464), who like Ramon Lull dreamt of nationwide peace among religions. In view of the conquest of Constantinople by the Ottomans, Nicolaus argued in his work *De pace fidei* (1453) for a Council of Religions. He held that Judaism, Christianity and Islam coincide in their fundamental truths, but differ in their manifold rites and customs. In his *Cribratio Alkorani* ('Sight of the Qur'ān', 1461) the Cardinal dealt especially with the Qur'ān (the Latin translation of Ketton) and its Christology. He was better able to understand the Qur'ān from its own point of view (*pia interpretatio*) than Martin Luther in his 'eisegesis'[10] of the Qur'ān a hundred years later, who understood the Qur'ān – especially concerning Jesus – from a dogmatic Christian point of view (*interpretatio christiana*).

Following these 'Church fathers' of dialogue with Islam, the contemporary dialogue with Islam is mainly the domain of the Roman Catholic Church. The most influential theologians after World War Two were Louis Massignon (d.1962), Georges Anawati (d.1994), and Kenneth Cragg (Anglican Church). With *Nostra Aetate*, the declaration of the Second Vatican Council on the relation towards non-Christian religions, proclaimed in 1965, a Copernican turn of Christianity regarding Islam was initiated. For the first time ever, Islam is officially recognized as a respectable and, to some degree, theologically equal partner in dialogue, as one who shares theologically some common ground with the Church. The theological depreciation of Islam, which from the time of John of Damascus was common for 1200 years, had now been to a large extent withdrawn.

---

9 *Alcorani Textus Universus [. . .] ex arabico idiomate in latinum translatus [. . .] auctore Ludovico Marraccio* (Padua: 1698).

10 That is, reading his views into the Qur'ān in contrast to an 'exegesis' which attempts to spell out what is in the text.

The key phrases of *Nostra Aetate* concerning Islam (No. 3) read as follows:

> The church has also a high regard for the Muslims. They worship God who is one, living and subsistent, merciful and almighty, the Creator of heaven and earth, who has also spoken to humanity. They endeavor to submit themselves without reserve to the hidden decrees of God, just as Abraham submitted himself to God's plan, to whose faith Muslims eagerly link their own. Although not acknowledging him as God, they venerate Jesus as a prophet; his virgin Mother they also honor, and even at times devoutly invoke. Further, they await the day of judgement and reward of God following the resurrection of the dead. For this reason they highly esteem an upright life and worship God, especially by way of prayer, alms-deeds and fasting.
>
> Over the centuries many quarrels and dissensions have arisen between Christians and Muslims. The sacred council now pleads with all to forget the past, and urges that a sincere effort be made to achieve mutual understanding . . .[11]

Although not mentioning Muḥammad and the Qur'ān, and not conceding Islam to be theologically on the very same level as the Church, this declaration was a turning-point for Roman Catholic relations with Islam.[12] The exclusivistic paradigm was abandoned: Islam was seen as a possible path of salvation and, to some extent, as communicating a true knowledge of God – measured, of course, against the supposed complete truth of the Christian faith (inclusivistic paradigm). Ever since 1967 the Pope has sent his annual greetings on the occasion of the feast of fast-breaking at the end of Ramadan. During his long Pontificate John Paul II (1978–2005) made many friends in the Islamic world. He was a Pope of great gestures: the first Pope

---

11 *Nostra Aetate 3. Vatican Council II. The Basic Sixteen Documents*, ed. by Austin Flannery, 1996, Northport: Costello Publishing, Dublin: Dominican Publications, p. 571.

12 Cf. also the *Dogmatic Constitution on the Church* ('Lumen Gentium', 1964), No. 16: 'the plan of salvation also includes those who acknowledge the Creator, first among whom are the Muslims: they profess to hold the faith of Abraham, and together with us they adore the one, merciful God, who will judge humanity on the last day.' 'Lumen Gentium', p. 21f.

in history who entered a Mosque (on 5 May 2001 in Damascus), a Pope who was not afraid to kiss the Qur'ān in public – these are symbolic gestures which bring about more than scholarly words.[13] A serious dialogue between the Ecumenical Council of Churches and Islam began in 1969.[14] Although Christian–Muslim dialogue has become a kind of regular process today, its impact on public opinion is rather limited. As current scientific studies about the image of Islam in schoolbooks and the media confirm, a negative image of Islam is still fairly widespread.[15]

My Christian View of Islam: Pillars of Understanding

What we need today is a confidence-building and peacemaking Christian theology of Islam and, correspondingly, an analogous Islamic theology of Christianity, where in both cases Christianity and Islam are – and must be seen – right from the start at *equal theological eye level.* In other words: we need a Christian theology in which Muslims, even if they believe in God differently, are nevertheless seen as legitimate and thus can feel secure from Christian supercessionist claims. When will Christians and Muslims finally discover what unites them as monotheistic brothers? The 'flowers' of mutual esteem and trust in one another might germinate and blossom on the ground of a common faith and of similar beliefs. With that common basis and dealing with each other on the same eye level – with these 'flowers' in our hands instead of weapons –, it is easier to discuss our mistakes, misunderstandings and conflicts. In this spirit we need new bridge-builders between Christianity and Islam.

---

13 Compared with John Paul II, the beginning of the Pontificate of his successor Benedict XVI – the 'Professor Dr Pope' (*Der Spiegel* no. 16, April 2006) – is quite disappointing in view of the Roman Catholic dialogue with Islam. Only Benedict XVI's visit to Turkey (autumn 2006) poured some oil on the troubled water of his Regensburg lecture. Apparently the Pope has now realized that the dialogue between Christians and Muslims does not only need 'head' but also plenty of 'heart'.

14 *Meeting in Faith. Twenty Years of Christian-Muslim Conversations*, compiled by Stuart E. Brown, Geneva: World Council of Churches, 1989.

15 See e.g. *Muslims in Europe: Discrimination and Islamophobia*, European Monitoring Center of Racism and Xenophobia (EUMC), 2006.

For me, the five pillars of understanding – in the double sense of communication and agreement – with Islam are:

1 The One God
2 Abraham as an example of faith
3 Jesus and Muḥammad as brothers
4 Common ethic
5 Common prayer.

First pillar: the one God

A dialogue between Christians and Muslims is only sustainable if it is acknowledged that the God of the Christians and the God of the Muslims is one and the same God. It is not only the above-quoted passages of *Nostra Aetate* and *Lumen Gentium* of the Second Vatican Council that confess that both Christians and Muslims 'adore the one, merciful God' but already the Qur'ān says so: 'our God and your God is One, and unto Him we surrender' (Sūra 29.46).[16] Therefore Muslims confess that there is no mere God of the Muslims ('Allah') but that there is just One God being the 'Lord of the Worlds' (Sūra 1.2) and being the God of the Christians (and the Jews) as well. Indeed, there is a great number of common statements of faith concerning that one God. Both Christians and Muslims believe in him/her

- as the living and eternal One;
- as the creator and conserver, as the king and the light of the world;
- as the loving power from whose hands we come and to whom we shall return;
- as the transcendent, hidden and secret One (*deus absconditus*); and at the same time
- as the self-revealer (*deus revelatus*), who has been speaking through the mouth and wonders of the prophets and the signs and wonders of the creation;
- as the merciful and helpful One towards human beings; and finally

16 All quotations from the Qur'ān, if not indicated otherwise, refer to *The Meaning of The Glorious Qur'ān* by Mohammed Marmaduke Pickthall (Kuala Lumpur, 2001).

- as the One who guides and fulfils history, who raises from the dead and is going to sit on the throne of judgement.

No matter what we call him/her (God, Allah, Higher Being, Father, Mother, the Merciful, etc.), it is the same one God, in whom Christians and Muslims (together with the Jews) believe, even if we might have different images of God or experiences with God. But these different images of God do not constitute different gods (as the fundamentalists in both religions maintain), for we find different images of, or experiences with, God already *within* each religion. The plurality of different images of God is a characteristic even of the Bible and the Qur'ān. A God who would be partial, that is, only the God of Christians (against the Muslims) or, conversely, only the God of Muslims (against the Christians), would remain an idol – a distorted image of the living God, created by human beings in order to serve their particular interests as a group, functionalized and thus misused to support and justify their exclusivistic collective sentiments. Of course, there is no objective proof of God being one and the same in both religions, no more than there is proof of the sheer existence of this God. To speak of the one and same God is no abstract, theoretical point of view, rather a tangible, common experience of faith of those who practise Christian–Muslim dialogue.

Second pillar: Abraham as an example of faith

Judaism, Christianity and Islam, the three monotheistic religions, are also called the 'Abrahamic religions' because of the important role that Abraham plays in each one of them. There are many initiatives of dialogue between Jews, Christians and Muslims that call themselves 'Abrahamic'.[17] Abraham – together with his wives Sara and Hagar – is a wonderful model of faith in and devotion to the one God. Abraham is the archetype of that kind of human being, who amidst an idol-worshipping environment is seeking for the God who deserves his ultimate trust. Such a search justifies his exodus-existence. Abraham is a wanderer between the worlds, religions and

17 E.g. Abrahamic Houses, Abrahamic Feasts, national and international Abrahamic Fora, etc. See Martin Bauschke, 2001, *Internationale Recherche von Institutionen zum trilateralen Dialog von Juden, Christen und Muslimen (Trialog und Zivilgesellschaft, Bd. 1)*, Berlin: Maecenata-Verlag.

cultures on his way to find God and to follow his/her promises. If we, as Christians in dialogue with Muslims, orientate ourselves on the example of Abraham, then we might also find the courage for another 'Exodus' or 'Hijra', to come irreversibly out of the cage of exclusivistic truth and salvation claims on both sides.

Something similar to the above discussion concerning the same one God perceived in different images, can be said about Abraham: the same example, but with different accentuations. Emphasizing common convictions does not exclude, but includes setting different priorities. Thus the three religions, including Judaism, each conceptualize a special profile for this patriarch. Jews mainly emphasize Abraham's unconditional obedience, his allegiance to the point of 'Isaac's binding' (Genesis 22). Christians refer especially, according to Paul, to the ultimate trust Abraham has in God's promise (Galatians 3.6ff). Muslims see in Ibrahim (Abraham) above all a *Hanif*[18] (e.g. Sūra 2.135) who recognized and avowed the one and only God, even before Jews, Christians or Muslims ever existed (Sūra 21.51ff; 37.83ff); Ibrahim who restored und purified the Ka'ba in Mecca (Sūra 2.125ff). Such different accentuations don't need to speak against the nature of sister religions. The common basis is stressed by the Holy Scriptures themselves. In the Bible and in the Qur'ān, Abraham is denominated with the same honorary title 'friend of God' (Isaiah 41.8f; James 2.23; Sūra 4.125). This means for Christians and Muslims the chance to encounter one another in the spirit of Abraham, in a kind and friendly – even hospitable – way.

Third pillar: Jesus and Muḥammad as brothers

Dialogue between Christians and Muslims is sustainable only if it is acknowledged that God wanted both religions as authentic ways to salvation. God revealed himself to both, Jesus and Muḥammad! The Eternal Word of God – as Christians believe – became *flesh*

18 According to Muhammad Asad, 1993, *The Message of the QUR'ĀN*, Gibraltar: Dar al-Andalus, p. 28, footnote No. 110 to Sūra 2:135) the term *hanif* describes the unitarian God-seekers of pre-Islamic times: 'Already in pre-Islamic times, this term had a definitely monotheistic connotation, and was used to describe a man who turned away from sin and worldliness and from all dubious beliefs, especially idol-worship.'

in Jesus Christ (*incarnation*) and – as Muslims believe – it became *book* as Qur'ān (*inlibration*). Our way to God is leading us across the way to the hearts of our believing brothers and sisters. For me, as a Christian, Jesus is 'the way (to God), the truth and the life' (cf. John 14.6). Nevertheless I am conceding that the Qur'ān is the way to God, the truth and life for Muslims. And it is my hope that Muslims can make an analogous concession from their point of view. I am not looking for one-way statements but for reciprocal ones, and not merely for reciprocal tolerance but rather reciprocal acceptance; this is the consequence of the *intellectual Golden Rule:* granting the other the same right to be assured of his/her faith as to myself, independently of whether the other belongs to the same or another denomination or religion as I do.[19]

If Christianity and Islam are equal ways to God, then Jesus and Muḥammad shall become the two younger brothers of Moses, and the Bible and the Qur'ān shall become the second and third testaments of God, added to the first testament, the Torah. Personally I consider the discussion about Jesus to be a pillar of dialogue. For other than in Jewish–Christian dialogue, it can create a *Christological bridge* in Christian–Islamic dialogue. For Jews, Jesus does not play the same important role as for Muslims. Christians and Muslims believe in Jesus, although in different ways. The Qur'ān is – apart from the New Testament – the only Holy Scripture of a world religion in which Jesus plays an important role. This is what makes Christian–Islamic dialogue special, for only in this case is it based, from both sides, on their Holy Scriptures.

Jesus, Mary's son, figures prominently in the Qur'ān. Jesus does not only separate Christians from Muslims, but also unites them. A number of statements can be made about Jesus that find support from both Christians and Muslims. Of course there are also points on which Christians and Muslims cannot (and perhaps will never) agree, for example, the question of whether Jesus died on the cross, as Christians believe, or was saved from death, as many Muslims

19 Cf. John Hick, 1989, *An Interpretation of Religion*, London: Macmillan, p. 234: 'Nor can we reasonably claim that our own form of religious experience, together with that of the tradition of which we are a part, is veridical whilst the others are not. . . . In acknowledging this we are obeying the intellectual Golden Rule of granting to others a premise on which we rely ourselves.'

hold. However, after both sides have, for centuries, mainly gone about matters in controversial and polemic ways, mostly stressing the dogmatic difference of their opinions, nowadays in our multicultural society, it is time for both sides to discuss Jesus in such a way that a consensus which might be reached in some respects comes to the foreground.[20]

A Christological consensus between Christians and Muslims would be, first of all,

1 *theocentric*, emphasizing that Jesus, as a matter of fact (or biblical testimony), subordinated himself to the one God, as his Jewish 'ancestors' did, that he perceived himself as a 'servant' of God and mankind (Mark 10.45; Luke 22.27) and that he consistently differentiated himself from God, who is the only One to be called 'good' (Mark 10.18). Further, a Christological link between Christians and Muslims ought to be
2 *prophetical*, describing Jesus as God's prophet and teacher of wisdom. A Christian–Muslim Christology could have
3 a *charismatic* accentuation in which Jesus is described as a miracle healer, as a charismatic figure who is doing his powerful deeds and signs with the help of the Holy Spirit (Matthew 12.28; Sūra 2.87; 2.253; 5.110). And finally, a Christological consensus between Christians and Muslims should be accentuated
4 *metaphorically*, speaking of Jesus as the 'Son of God' in symbolic language, not in any literal or ontological sense – but in the way Jesus himself used the title, for example, in the Sermon on the Mount: 'Blessed are those who strive for peace – for they shall be called sons of God' (Matthew 5.9). A short passage later Jesus says (Matthew 5.44f): 'Love your enemies! Pray for those who persecute you! In that way you will be acting as true sons of your Father in heaven.' The term 'Son of God' is primarily an ethical not a physical or metaphysical title. It is a democratic and not an elitist title. Already some Muslim theologians, belonging to the Mu'tazilites in the ninth and tenth centuries, saw the analogy (Arab. *qiyās*) between the expression 'Son of God' for Jesus, the expression 'first born son' for Israel (Exodus 4.22) and the title 'friend of God' for Abraham in the Qur'ān (Sūra 4.125).

20 Cf. Martin Bauschke, 2001, *Jesus im Koran,* Köln/Weimar/Wien: Böhlau Verlag.

There are liberal Muslim scholars of the past (for example, Ibn Qutayba, Sayyid Ahmad Khan) and in present times (for example, Mahmoud Ayoub, Ahmad von Denffer) who can accept the 'Son of God' title in this metaphorical sense.

Thus the dialogue about Jesus can inspire and enable Christians and Muslims to move forward to our common work of making peace. Suggesting and elaborating a 'Christological bridge' between Christians and Muslims means we should not discuss the title 'Son of God' merely from a dogmatic point of view (Christo-*Logy*), but we should come to an ethical competition (*imitatio Christi* as Christo-*Practice*). Do Christians and Muslims stand the test of being peacemakers and calling one another true 'sons and daughters of God'? Dogmatical correctness alone will not help but rather doing the will of God, as Jesus himself says at the end of the Sermon on the Mount (Matthew 7.21).[21] Confessing 'the Lord' includes and means first of all the 'compassion and mercy in the hearts of those who are following Jesus' (Sūra 57.27).

But dialogue is not only about Jesus. To me, as a Christian, it is of particular importance to converse also about Muḥammad. First of all, we need to counteract the traditional demonizing of Muḥammad through showing respect towards this younger brother of Christ.[22] Then it is necessary to accept the theological challenge of Muḥammad's mission and acknowledge the dignity of the Qur'ān as a revelation from God. I belong to those Christian theologians[23] who go beyond the mere phenomenological description of Muḥammad as a 'prophet', and who also call for *a theological*

21 Cf. Sūra 49.13: 'O mankind! We created you from a single (pair) of a male and a female, and made you into nations and tribes, that ye may know each other. Verily the most honoured of you in the sight of God is (he who is) the most righteous of you.' (Quotation from *The Holy Qur'ān. Text*, translation and commentary by Abdullah Yusuf Ali, Beirut 1968.)

22 Cf. the *ḥadith* (saying of Muḥammad), narrated by Abu Hurayra: 'Both in this world and in the Hereafter, I am the nearest of all the people to 'Isa (Jesus), the son of Maryam (Mary). The Prophets are paternal brothers; their mothers are different, but their religion is one.' Quotation from *Summarized Sahih Al-Bukhari Arab-English* (Riyadh, 1996), p. 680, No. 1437.

23 E.g. Martin Forward, Notker Füglister, John Hick, Bertold Klappert, Hans Küng, Reinhard Leuze, Paul Schwarzenau, Wilfred Cantwell Smith, Perry Schmidt-Leukel and Keith Ward.

recognition of Muḥammad as God's Prophet. God in his/her sovereignty may reveal him-/herself somewhere else, through someone else rather than just through Moses or Jesus Christ, even if this new approach to mankind might disappoint and cross some of the expectations and self-conceptions of Jews and Christians.

When we speak about the prophethood of Muḥammad, we are ultimately speaking about the *Qur'ān as an authentic Word of God.* 'The Call of the Minaret' (Kenneth Cragg, 1956) is to be taken as seriously by Christians as the call of the gospel of Jesus by Muslims. Within the tradition of Abraham I believe in a continuous revelation of God: it is manifold and also full of tensions and contradictions. But revelation has always been this way, *within* the Torah, *within* the Bible and *within* the Qur'ān. I understand the mission of Jesus and of Muḥammad, the revelation of the Word of God as incarnation and as inlibration as being *complementary* – such as light in physics, which behaves both as a wave and as a particle. Jesus and Muḥammad are not doubles, but brothers with similarities and differences. Jesus' short public mission (up to three years) is complemented by the long mission of Muḥammad (20 years). The kingdom of God is 'not of this world' (John 18.36) – nevertheless it is right in the centre of the world too. To follow God's will in life is not only a question of individual spirituality (*praxis pietatis*) but also a social, political and legal challenge for establishing societies with a just order. God does not only call believers out of the world *(ecclesia),* but rather places them as a viceroy *(khalifa)* into the world (Sūra 2.30). The wandering preacher from Nazareth is complemented by the mediator, politician and commander from Mecca. Jesus, the suffering and murdered righteous in Jerusalem, is complemented by Muḥammad, the suffering righteous in Mecca and in the end the victorious prophet in Medina. From our human point of view the merciful God sometimes seems to be powerless (the cross of Golgotha) and sometimes to be powerful (the purification of the Temple and the destruction of the idols in the Ka'ba[24]) when we look at what his/her messengers are doing or suffering.

24 The purification of the house of God to become a place of prayer instead of merchandise is the powerful mission of many prophets, according to the Qur'ān prefigured by Ibrahim (Sūra 2.125ff) and followed by Jesus in Jerusalem and by Muḥammad in Mecca.

Fourth pillar: common ethic

Beyond the question as to what theologically connects Christians and Muslims in their religious statements, another question arises which is possibly more important: What connects them ethically? It is a fact that both religions have common ideas about what their norms and values are. Both the gospel and the Qur'ān stand in the ethical tradition of the Ten Commandments of the Torah. We find a common *prophetical core ethic,* rooted in Judaism, which unites, despite the differences, Jews, Christians and Muslims. It has a double accentuation – like the two foci of an ellipse: God and the neighbour. This common ethic is theonomic and social. The Abrahamic religions share the following directives:

1. respect for God alone (not to serve idols)
2. respect for parents
3. respect for life (not to kill)
4. respect for love and body (not to abuse sexuality)
5. respect for property (not to steal)
6. respect for the word (not to lie).

Moreover, Christianity and Islam – and many other religions – show a tendency to unite the numerous directives into one most significant commandment – known as the *Golden Rule,* which is testified in various forms throughout the world: 'What you do not wish done to yourself, do not do to others.' Jesus, in his Sermon on the Mount, accentuates the Golden Rule in its positive form (Matthew 7.12; Luke 6.31): 'In everything, do for others as you would have them do for you; for this is the law and the prophets.' An-Nawawi's collection of 40 *Aḥadīth qudsī* contains the saying of Muḥammad: 'No one of you is a true believer until he desires for his brother that which he desires for himself.' The Golden Rule is the core of our ethical world heritage and at the same time the basis for humane behaviour, also among such secular Christians and Muslims, who define their ethic in an autonomic way as self-commitment and not as divine (heteronomic) commandments 'from above'.

Fifth pillar: common prayer

The encounter between Christians and Muslims has an eminent spiritual dimension. Common prayer meetings are increasing worldwide, including Jews where possible. The overlapping of the calendar – Chanukkah, Advent and Ramadan – in past years intensified this new development. There are many occasions for common prayer meetings: services at school, inter-faith weddings or pastoral care in hospital, prison and army. Christian–Muslim prayers for peace, in particular, form an important starting-point for dialogue, and at the same time counter the fundamentalist agitation in both religions.

When I am pleading for friendship and hospitality in the spirit of Abraham, here it becomes concrete: *our common prayer is a form of spiritual hospitality.* It is the offer to Christians and Muslims to be taken into the world of prayer of another Abrahamic religion, and in this way to experience God in a different manner, whether it might be surprisingly familiar or rather strange. Offering spiritual hospitality to one another means that we are taking the risk of making new experiences with the one God through praying together. Christians and Muslims can offer their prayers not only to God but also as a gift to one another, saying them separately or together – without ceasing to be Christians or Muslims. A hero is normally someone who defeats his enemy. A greater hero might be the one who makes, without weapons, his enemy his friend. But the greatest hero seems to be the one who prays together with his friend. I believe that the more Christians and Muslims pray together, the more we shall become a blessing to the world and a source of reconciliation among peoples.

I like to recall the prayer meetings for peace in Assisi (1986 and 2002) which Pope John Paul II held together with representatives of other religions, or more recently (2006) the joint quiet prayer of Pope Benedict XVI together with Imam Mustafa Cagrici in the Blue Mosque of Istanbul. It is also my own experience in common prayer meetings with Jews and Muslims: the common prayer does not only unite with God ('vertical' union) but also unites those who pray together ('horizontal' union). Common prayer creates a *unio mystica* in both directions. It opens my heart and my mind in such a way that the person praying at my side is not just any believer, but my Abrahamic brother, my Abrahamic sister. The intellectual and the ethical Golden Rule transforms itself, at this point of dialogue, into a spiritual path, which incorporates the heads, the hands and the hearts of the Christians and Muslims involved.

As a result of these experiences I felt committed to publish the first 'Book of Common Prayer' in Germany, for Jews, Christians and Muslims.[25] It was published in co-operation with a Rabbi and a female Muslim teacher of religion. A special edition with identical contents was printed simultaneously for pastoral care within the Federal Armed Forces. Christians and Muslims together form half of the world's population. If Christians and Muslims started speaking to one another, half of mankind would be in dialogue! Through dialogue both sister religions, Christianity and Islam, could finally overcome their family disputes – with the help of God.

25 Martin Bauschke, Walter Homolka and Rabeya Müller (eds), 2006, *Gemeinsam vor Gott. Gebete aus Judentum, Christentum und Islam*, Gütersloh: Gütersloher Verlagshaus (1st edn 2004).

12. Response to Bauschke

ATAULLAH SIDDIQUI

It is difficult to respond to a chapter in which one agrees with most of the argument. However, as a way of clarification I will highlight a few points here.

While I agree with the sentiments expressed in the very first sentence, that Christianity is a 'religion of love' and Islam is a 'religion of peace', this should not be seen as a mark of distinctiveness. Both faiths have both aspects in their heart and will remain so. As I have highlighted in my own presentation, earlier conflicts can largely be seen as a wider family dispute; however, as far as the central personalities of the two faiths are concerned – Jesus and Prophet Muḥammad – I believe they have not been treated equally. While Muslims would not accept Jesus as a part of redemptive history, they do accept his uniqueness. He alone is portrayed as the 'Word of God' and 'a spirit from Him' (4.171) and his miraculous acts such as curing the blind, healing the lepers (5.110) are exclusive to him. Muslims have bestowed, throughout the centuries, this special status, but they hardly ever received even a decent courteous response over the years concerning the Prophet. The Second Vatican Council's declarations *Nostra Aetate* and *Lumen Gentium*, I believe, are both watersheds in the Roman Catholic Church's understanding of Islam and its relations to Muslims. The documents urge us 'to forget the past' and call for 'sincere efforts be made to achieve mutual understanding for the benefit of all men' (NA 3); however, in order to mend the past, the central and crucial figure between the two faiths is the personality of the Prophet Muḥammad. While the issue of the Crusades and the various difficult paths that the two faith communities have travelled through the centuries has been well documented, what has largely been ignored is the Prophet Muḥammad and his place in our relationship. For Muslims he is the key, and central to all our beliefs and practices of faith. Muslims urged the

Second Vatican Council, while that was in session, to renounce any earlier 'statements' against the Prophet.

Bauschke hopes that if 'Christians and Muslims started speaking to one another, half of mankind would be in dialogue!' It is a very tall order. Our problem in dialogue with each other (inter-faith) is a lesser problem compared to our dialogue with members of our own faith (intra-faith). There are two issues: First, that dialogue between Christians and Muslims *together* has to go beyond the two faiths. People involved in dialogue between the two communities have to address our relations conscientiously, and as moral and religious obligations to defend the rights and welfare of all people. This is not taking place as much as it should be, probably because we meet largely through our commonly shared fears such as anti-religious discourse, and this is not helpful. Second, Muslims (as well as Christians) need to investigate our rich religious resources to connect with our own exclusive interpreters of Christianity. Sometimes it goes beyond prejudicial interpretations of the other to what is known as *ta'aṣṣub* (fanatically prejudiced). Al-Ghazālī describes beautifully how *ta'aṣṣub* 'usually comes together with man's disregard of his neighbour, and of his opinions, and the taking root in his heart of certain ideas which become so much a part of him that he fails to distinguish between right and wrong.'[1] This is a challenge for each of our faiths to address, and we seem to be unable to reach the heart of it. Unless we address this dark side of our own faith, reaching the other 'half of mankind' will remain a beautiful dream.

Bauschke argues for a 'confidence-building and peacemaking Christian theology of Islam' and correspondingly, an 'Islamic theology of Christianity'. I agree with the spirit of the statement. In order to open a serious theological exploration of Christianity, in my view, the prerequisite is trust. Unless one builds up deep respect for the other, through engagement and friendship, it will be difficult to overcome centuries of long-embedded understanding of Christianity. What is important now is a serious understanding of Christianity as Christians believe and practise it. This is, in my view, an urgent need, which Muslims have neglected. This is also important from another point of view. The understanding of religion and

1 Reza Shah-Kazemi, 2006, *The Other in the Light of the One: The Universality of the Quran and Interfaith Dialogue*, Cambridge: Islamic Text Society, p. 138.

its role in society, particularly in European society, has been provided by Christianity. It is one of the defining forces in European culture and civilization. Christianity in fact provided a soul for Europe. To understand this role of Christianity, Muslims need to enter into its understanding of itself.

As Bauschke has highlighted, the appropriate comparison would be between the Qur'ān and Jesus,[2] and not between Jesus and Muḥammad, for the Qur'ān and Jesus hold comparable positions within the respective faiths. Let me add to this two further aspects. The Qur'ān was an event in the life of Muḥammad. It was recited, memorized and became part of the community's spiritual life within the lifetime of the prophet. But how the prophet lived in the light of the Qur'ān was not recorded in his time; it was recorded later. The Gospels are about Jesus, but how he lived, what he did, etc., were recorded later. There is a time lag, and that has allowed a human interference in collection and compilation in both *ḥadīth* literature and the Gospels. Furthermore, Muḥammad's parallel would be Mary. Both were the bearer of God's Uncreated Word. If the Word is in the form of flesh, the purity is symbolized by the virginity of the mother who gives birth to the Word, and if it is in the form of a book, this purity is symbolized by the unlettered nature of the person who is chosen to announce this Word to the people.[3]

Bauschke has also raised the issue of prayer and 'common prayer' in particular. Here I want to highlight that Muslims use three different words to express their rituals and devotions. Worship (*'ibādah*) means purification of a person's soul. This includes working for a living, family life, pursuing education, etc. The daily life is part of *'ibādah*. It is said that good intentions change acts of habit (*'ādah*) into acts of worship (*'ibādah*). *Ṣalāh* is the renewal of faith – five daily ritual 'prayers' and other non-obligatory 'prayers' are performed in Arabic. This is a ritual exclusive to Muslims. *Du'a* in Islam is described as the essence of worship, which could be offered individually or collectively, in Arabic or in any language. I presume Martin Bauschke wants to connect here with Muslims in the sense of supplication or *du'a*.

---

2 Cf. Bauschke's chapter in this book, p. 148f.

3 Seyyed Hossein Nasr, 1944, *Ideals and Realities of Islam*, California: Aquarian, p. 44.

13. Response to Siddiqui

MARTIN BAUSCHKE

I can only agree when Ataullah Siddiqui says that '(t)oday's encounters between the two religions may generate tomorrow's theology of hate'.[1] In face of fundamentalist demagogues both sides have the responsibility to create an alternative to such a 'theology of hate', that is, a *theology of reconciliation and friendship between Christians and Muslims*. This theology needs to be developed jointly and, being a common Christian–Muslim theology, it is therefore different from either a 'Christian view of Islam' or a 'Muslim view of Christianity' as we have presented here. It would not only have the potential to contribute to peace between the two sides but would also be the basis of what Ataullah Siddiqui is rightly calling for: a Christian–Muslim 'co-action' and 'co-witness in a modern world'.

However, who are the Christians and Muslims that would be prepared to jointly develop a Christian–Muslim theology? And on which foundations could such a common theology be established?

In relation to the first question, both Siddiqui's and my own paper show that there is neither such a thing as *the* Christianity nor *the* Islam. Both world religions are marked by a huge diversity throughout space and time, being constituted by very different strands and schools. In both religions this broad spectrum can be differentiated into at least six types: there are conservatives, oriented towards tradition; liberals, ready for reform; those of a secular persuasion, for whom religion is reduced to religious folklore ('culture' or 'nominal' Christians or Muslims); mystics or esoterics, who often go their own spiritual ways; and, apart from this differentiated mainstream, there are the two further types of the extremists

1 Siddiqui's chapter in this book, p. 134.

and the radicals. The crucial question between these two is 'What do you think of violence?' To express my analysis differently, I feel that the idea of a gradual maturing of religions throughout history, as claimed for Islam by Muhammad Abduh,[2] is an abstraction. In fact, we find in both religions simultaneously children, adolescents, and wise elders.

To my mind, it is the liberal and mystically oriented Christians and Muslims who might be best prepared to develop a Christian–Muslim theology of reconciliation and friendship, and, as a matter of fact, they are already most committed to and involved in dialogue. But since they stand in competition with the theology of hate, as articulated on both sides primarily in extremist circles, the proponents of Christian–Muslim dialogue are at the same time confronted by the challenge of an *intra-religious dialogue* which Christians, and similarly Muslims, have to conduct among themselves.

The intra-religious dialogue is more difficult because, as my sketch of internal differentiation shows, the real fault-lines are not running between Christianity and Islam as such, but across the two religions along the borderlines of their various strands and types. Mohandas Gandhi, Anwar el-Sadat or Yitzhak Rabin – all peacemakers within their own religion – were assassinated by militant fundamentalists from their own camp who drew their justification from a theology of contempt of 'the Other' – referring not merely to the infidels of another religion but also and even more so to the members of another strand within their own religion. Courage is therefore needed, right from the start, if one wishes to initiate the joint development of a Christian–Muslim theology of reconciliation and friendship. This in itself would already be a form of Christian–Muslim 'co-action' and 'co-witness' – not in face of a secular world but in face of those extremists who believe 'like mad'.

As far as my second question about the possible foundations of such a common theology is concerned, Ataullah Siddiqui mentions two highly relevant aspects which I would like to pick up and elaborate a bit further.

A key starting point is thwarting *stereotypes and projections* as Siddiqui rightly demands in the first of his concluding remarks.

2 Cf. Siddiqui's chapter, p. 130.

'Recognizing the "otherness of the other"' entails seeing the others, as far as possible, 'as they see themselves'. A joint Christian–Muslim theology of reconciliation and friendship needs to be founded on respect for the self-understanding of the other. I must not distort the beliefs of my partner but allow them to challenge and irritate me, for only then his or her beliefs might also enrich and inspire my own ways of believing, thinking and acting. I am talking about the readiness to listen when the other tells me about him- or herself, in particular if this includes issues which make it difficult to listen, issues which are uncomfortable or painful because they may demand a confession of guilt, self-criticism and change.

A further aspect addressed by Ataullah Siddiqui is the need for a new way of relating to our sacred Scriptures. A common Christian–Muslim theology of reconciliation and friendship can only be developed through a joint study of the Bible and the Qur'ān. It will be seen as valid to the extent to which it is recognizably grounded in both sacred Scriptures. As a methodological principle *primae scripturae* would therefore mean that the *first reference texts* for dialogue should be the New Testament and the Qur'ān and less so the later doctrines and dogmas. Exegesis first, and then dogmatics! Yet how could Christians and Muslims jointly read their sacred Scriptures? In order to develop a Christian–Muslim theology of reconciliation and friendship we need a *common Christian–Muslim hermeneutics of their sacred Scriptures*. Let me briefly touch upon three relevant aspects:

1 The *exegetical primacy*: In jointly reading their sacred Scriptures it needs to be respected that Christians have a primacy in interpreting the New Testament and Muslims a primacy in interpreting the Qur'ān. No religion has the right to prescribe to another religion how it should understand its own sacred texts. To that extent, every sacred Scripture is primarily the 'property' of that religion which accepts it as 'sacred'.
2 The *acknowledgement of authenticity*: Jointly reading their sacred Scriptures raises the question of their mutual relation. If Christians and Muslims believe in the same God, they could appreciate both sacred Scriptures as authentic divine revelations, even if a Christian holds on primarily to the New Testament and the Muslim primarily to the Qur'ān. What is crucial is mutual

respect for the sacred Scripture of the other and their relationship and connectedness. That the latter is not free from contradictions does not count against their belonging together. For there are contradictions within both the Bible and the Qur'ān, but this does not revoke the inner unity of either of them. The acknowledgement of authenticity would entail, as Aḥmad Khān insisted against Ibn Taymiyya and Kairanawi,[3] abandoning, at last, the old accusation against the Christians that they manipulated the text of the Bible (*taḥrīf an-naṣṣ*) and conversely the Christian polemic that the Qur'ān is Muḥammad's fabrication.

3 The *right to co-interpret*: Should, under favourable circumstances, the dialogue indeed progress to a reciprocal acknowledgement of the authenticity of Bible and Qur'ān, this would result in the sister-religion's right to co-interpret the text and hence in a reciprocal *relecture*. Muslims are then entitled to reinterpret a New Testament text from their point of view and, conversely, Christians a Qur'ānic text. Then they may experience: God talks to me, as a Christian, no longer only through the New Testament, and to me, as a Muslim, no longer only through the Qur'ān. But God can and will talk to me as a Christian also through the Qur'ān. God can and will talk to me, as a Muslim, also through the New Testament.

3 Cf. Siddiqui's chapter, p. 129.

Part IV

Islam and Hinduism

14. A Muslim View of Hinduism

ASGHAR ALI ENGINEER

The Nature of Religious Differences

Generally it is thought that Hinduism and Islam, like any two religions, are not merely different, but contradictory to each other. Each religion is of course different but not necessarily contradictory too. However, the popular view is that they are not merely different but contradictory. Even if scholars prove otherwise, this popular view persists, thanks mainly to priesthood and politicians both trying to increase their flock.

Before we proceed with the subject of 'How Islam has viewed Hinduism', we must briefly discuss the nature of religion and also the nature of the differences between them. Only this can enable us to understand causes of clashes between different religions. Religions can be essentially divided into (1) ritual system, (2) thought system, (3) institutional system, and (4) value system.

Since each religion is the product of different cultures, societies, historical traditions and time periods, it is bound to differ from the other in ritual system, thought system and institutional system. But no two religions will differ from each other in value system. The main aim of every religion is basically to promote values in society and guide human conduct according to these values.

Also, it is important to note that the ritual system, thought system and institutional system are means to an end – and the end is to realize these values. These values are (1) truth, (2) love (of God and human beings), (3) equality (of all human beings), (4) justice, (5) peace, (6) respect for all forms of life, and (7) compassion for all those who suffer. There is hardly any religion which contradicts these values.

Each religion, depending on its cultural environment, social ethos and historical traditions, devises rituals, evolves a thought system (including certain beliefs and dogmas including those about life after death etc.) and fashions an institutional system to realize these values. In fact differences about rituals, thought system and institutional system should not create the illusion that religions clash with each other. They do not. On the contrary they complement each other through value systems. The differences are more apparent than real. Sometimes differences are only of language and expressions. All one can say is that each religion is unique and different from the other but not superior to the other. One often practises the religion that one is born in as it is coterminous with one's culture and family traditions. One likes one's religion because one is so familiar with it and has been so intimate with its beliefs and traditions.

Now we would like to throw some light on what promotes clashes or a sense of hostility between different religions. Mere uniqueness or differences cannot lead to a sense of hostility. We must trace the roots of hostility to something that is irreconcilable, namely, the interests of some sections of followers of a religion. The interests could be either political or controlling the religious establishment. The other important cause of hostility is prejudice born either out of sheer ignorance or created through propaganda. It is my considered view that religions per se do not clash.

Thus the view of religion of the other will depend on who views it, what is the level of understanding of the viewer and what interests are involved. Is the viewer a common person with prejudices born of ignorance or created through propaganda? Or does the viewer have political or 'religious' interests? Or is the viewer an objective scholar, having in-depth knowledge of the religious tradition he or she is studying?

Idol Worshippers and Polytheists?

The common Muslim in India looks down upon Hinduism as a religion of idol worshippers which Islam condemns, and in popular parlance Hindus are depicted as 'kafirs' (unbelievers) or *mushriks* (polytheists). This view of Hinduism taken by common Muslims in India has a long history and persists partly on account of ignorance of Hindu religion and partly because of hostile propaganda by vested interests. Similarly, common Hindus think of Muslims as 'fanatics', 'anti-Hindu' and now in modern times as 'anti-national'.

This view of Muslims is held by Hindus for the same reasons as those given for the Muslim view of Hindus.

Also, political hostility often turns into religious hostility and the political enemy becomes the religious enemy or the political other becomes the religious other. Thus one can hardly generalize from Muslim viewpoint of Hinduism as if it were the only viewpoint of Muslims of Hinduism, as there have been so many Muslim perspectives about Hinduism. That Hindus are kafirs and idol worshippers is held more extensively because common Hindus are seen worshipping idols in temples. The Qur'ān condemns idol worshippers and describes them as kafirs and *mushriks* (polytheists).

But many Muslim scholars and Sufi saints did not accept this point of view and refrained from describing Hindus as kafirs. 'Kafir' is an Arabic word which means one who hides (truth).[1] The Qur'ān described as kafirs those Qurayshites of Mecca (the Quraysh was the tribe to which the Prophet also belonged) who refused to accept the truth brought by Islam. However, every non-Muslim does not become kafir as non-Muslims have their own version of truth. Truth is often expressed differently depending on cultural and historical tradition, as pointed out above. It would be simplistic to consider Hindus as kafirs. We will elaborate on this further.

Many Muslim scholars have refrained from describing Hindus as kafirs because they have studied the Hindu religion through their own books (*śāstras*) and Hindu philosophy. Thus K. A. Nizami, a noted historian from India, observes, 'The accounts of India found in the works of Shahrastani, Masudi, Ibn Khurdazbih, Sulaiman Tajir and others are extremely valuable.'[2]

Al-Bīrūnī (973–1048) is another distinguished scholar who studied Hindu religion and its systems of philosophy through original sources and wrote his book *Kitāb al-Hind*, which has been translated by Edward Sachau as *Alberuni's India*.[3] Works like

1 See under 'kafir' in Imam Raghib Asfahani, *Mufradat al-Qur'an* (Lahore 1971), pp. 916–17.

2 See Foreword by K. A. Nizami to Muhammad Zaki, 1981, *Arab Accounts of India During the Fourteenth Century*, Delhi: Idarah Adbiyat-I-Delhi, p. vi.

3 Edward Sachau (ed.), 1983, *Alberuni's India*, Delhi: Munshiram Manoharlal.

these are good sources for understanding how Arabs and other Muslims viewed Hinduism when they came in contact with it.

In his book *Tuḥfat al-Albāb*, Abū Hāmid al-Gharnātī (1080–1169) observes about India

> the huge country, great justice, considerable wealth, good administration, constant convenience of life, and security on account of which there is no fear in the country of India and China. The Indians are the most learned people in the branches of philosophy, medicine, arithmetic and (skilled) in all wonderful crafts which it is impossible to imitate . . .[4]

Thus here one does not find any prejudice against Hindus or India, describing Hindus as kafirs but as most learned in philosophy, medicine, etc. Al-Gharnatī was writing as scholar and he described what he saw as a scholar, not as a religious preacher of Islam. Religious preachers are often ignorant of other religious teachings and are more interested in winning over converts and hence describe other religions either as false or as inferior to their own. A preacher, as opposed to a scholar, cannot maintain objectivity of observation.

Al-Bīrūnī, the learned scholar who read Hindu Scriptures in the original, understood why common people in India worship idols. His observation is quite interesting. He says,

> It is well known that popular mind leans towards the sensible world, and has an aversion to the world of abstract thought which is only understood by highly educated people, of whom in every time and every place there are only few. And as common people will only acquiesce in pictorial representation, many of the leaders of religious communities have so far deviated from right path as to give such imagery in their books and houses of worship . . . these words of mine would at once receive a sufficient illustration if, for example, a picture of the Prophet were made, or of Mekka and the Ka'ba, and were shown to an uneducated man or woman. Their joy in looking at the thing would bring them to kiss the picture, to rub their cheeks against it, and to roll themselves in the dust before it, as if they were seeing not the picture, but the original, and were in this way, as if they were present in

4 Quoted by Muhammad Zaki, *Arab Accounts of India,* p. 6.

> the holy places, performing the rites of pilgrimage, the great and small ones.

Then he goes on the explain that

> this is the cause which leads to the manufacture of idols, monuments in honour of certain much venerated persons, prophets, sages, angels, destined to keep alive their memory when they are absent or dead, to create for them a lasting place of grateful veneration in the hearts of men when they die . . .

Then Al-Bīrūnī continues to give examples from various religious traditions including those of Jews, Christians, Manicheans and so on and says finally about Hindus,

> Since however, here we have to explain the system and the theories of the Hindus on the subject, we shall now mention their ludicrous views; but we declare at once that they are held only by the common uneducated people. For those who march on the path to liberation, or those who study philosophy and theology, and who desire abstract truth which they call *sara* are entirely free from worshipping anything but God alone, and would never dream of worshipping an image manufactured to represent him.[5]

Thus we see that Al-Bīrūnī does not condemn Hindus for idol worshipping but explains it away as a popular practice from which the learned refrain. Also, another delicate question of eating cow's meat is dealt by him very objectively and in this case too he refrains from any unbecoming remark. First, he discusses the explanation given to him as to why Brahmans stopped eating beef. This explanation relates to digestion. But he is not satisfied by this explanation and says 'I, for my part, am uncertain, and hesitate in the question of origin of this custom between two different views.'

Then he gives his own explanation which is commonly advanced these days. He writes,

> As for economical reason, we must keep in mind that the cow is the animal which serves man in travelling by carrying his loads, in agriculture in the works of ploughing and sowing, in the household by the milk and product made thereof. Further, man makes

5 Sachau, *Alberuni's India,* pp. 112–13.

> use of its dung, and in winter-time even of its breath. Therefore it was forbidden to eat cows' meat; as also Alhajjaj forbade it, when people complained to him that Babylonia became more and more desert.[6]

Thus, by referring to Al-Hajjāj's ban on eating beef, he further justifies the ban on eating cow's meat by Hindus. Al-Hajjāj was governor of Iraq during the Umayyad period.

Sufi Views of Hinduism

Many Sufi saints looked at Hinduism very respectfully and tried to build bridges with Hindus. They maintained that Hindus possessed the truth as much as other peoples did. Miyān Mīr (1550–1635), a great Sufi saint belonging to the Qadriya school of Sufis, had very good relations with the Sikh Gurus. Guru Arjan Dev invited him to lay the foundation stone of Harmandir, which is also popularly known as the 'Golden Temple'. The Sikh Guru had the highest regard for Miyān Mīr of Lahore.

Dārā Shikūh (1615–59), the heir apparent of Moghul Emperor Shāh Jahān, acquired great scholarship in the Hindu Scriptures. Like Al-Bīrūnī before him, he acquired knowledge of the Sanskrit language and studied Hindu Scripture in Sanskrit. He was of the opinion that both religions have much in common and it is more a difference of language than substance. He translated the *Upaniṣads* into Persian and called it *Sirr-e Akbār* ('The Greatest Secrets'). I have seen a manuscript in his own handwriting in the library of Darul Musannifin, Azamgarh, Uttar Pradesh. What is most interesting is that he began by invoking Ganesha, the Hindu god, along with the Arabic and Islamic *Bismillah al-Raḥman al-Raḥīm.*

Dārā Shikūh describes the Upaniṣads as 'an ocean of *tawḥīd*' (that is, monotheism). He says that he examined the religious works of the Hindus, 'who do not negate monotheism', and found that the monotheistic verses contained in the four *Vedas* have been collected and elucidated in the *Upanikhat* (Upaniṣad), which is an ocean of monotheism. Dārā Shikūh even maintains that

> Any difficult problem or sublime idea that came to his mind and

6 Sachan, *Alberuni's India*, pp. 152–3.

was not solved in spite of his best efforts, becomes clear and solved with the help of this ancient work, which is undoubtedly the first heavenly Book and the fountainhead of the ocean of monotheism, and, in accordance with or rather an elucidation of the Qur'ān.[7]

Dārā Shikūh has so much respect for the *Upaniṣads* that he thought that the qur'ānic verses 56.77–79 refer to the Upaniṣads. He felt certain that the hidden book (or, *kitāb-i maknūn*) is a reference to this very ancient book'.[8] This is the highest tribute one can pay to the Scriptures of Hinduism. In fact Dārā Shikūh's *Majma' al- Baḥrayn* is a classical work on the unity of religion.

In this book Dārā Shikūh compares the religious terminology of Islam with that of Hinduism and conclusively shows that the difference is of language, not of the actual ideas behind it. He often refers to Hindus as *muwaḥḥidān-i Hind*, namely, the monotheists of India. He says the monotheists of India also believe in *qiyāmat-i kubra* (i.e. the Great Day of Judgement) and in Hindu Scriptures it is referred to as *mahāpralaya*. According to Dārā, Hindus also believe in heaven and hell and that after residing in heaven and hell *mahāpralaya* will occur. He also quotes verses from the Qur'ān like 72.9, 34.79, 68.39, 55.26–27 and 72.9 to prove his point.

He compares the concept of *mukti* with the Sufi concept of *fanā' fī Allah*, that is, merging with Allah as the ultimate liberation, and quotes the verse from the Qur'ān 72.9. He then throws detailed light on the concept of *mukti* (liberation) in the Hindu religion and considers *brahmāṇḍa* (the universe) as the body of God. According to him, *brahmāṇḍa* in Islam is referred to as *'Alam-i kubra*, which is the manifestation of Allah.[9]

Thus Dārā Shikūh's work is extremely important as far as Muslim attitudes towards Hinduism are concerned. Unfortunately this seminal contribution has been almost ignored by the scholars in evaluating Hindu–Muslim relations in contemporary India. This slim volume by Dārā Shikūh can serve as bridge between the two major communities in India. There is a great need to revive his work.

7 See M. Mahfuz-ul-Haq's Introduction to Dara Shikoh, *Majma'ul-Bahrain* (Mingling of the Two Oceans), reprinted by The Asiatic Society, Calcutta, 1982, p. 13.

8 Introduction, *Majma'ul-Bahrain.*

9 *Majma-'ul –Bahrain*, pp. 106–7.

Another Sufi saint, Mażhar Jān-i Jānān (1699–1781), also accepted Hindus as *ahl al-Kitāb*, that is, people of the book, a category created by the Qur'ān for Jews and Christians. He believed that Allah had promised in the Qur'ān to send guides to all nations (13.7) and Mażhar Jān-i Jānān argued from this that Allah could not possibly forget to send His guides to such a great country as India. Ram and Krishna, highly revered religious guides of India, might have been prophets of Allah.

He emphasised that Hindu Scriptures describe God as *nirakar* and *nirgun* (that is, without shape and attributes). Jān-i Jānān argued that this is the highest concept of *tawḥīd* (monotheism). Thus how can we describe Hindus as kafirs or *mushriks* when they believe in one God? He also explained, like Al-Bīrūnī before him, that the practice of idol worship was a popular practice not sanctioned by Hindu Scriptures. He went a step further and said that Hindus worship idols as intermediaries to God, not as God, just as Sufis need the help of a shaikh (master) to recognize Allah.[10] Thus he exonerated Hindus from being polytheists or kafirs.

He believed that Allah in His infinite mercy revealed the Vedas and sent an angel called Brahma for the guidance of the Indian people. The Vedas, according to Jān-i Jānān, are the books of *amr wa nahi'* (of Allah's commands and prohibitions). The Hindu *mujtahids* (interpreters of Vedas) have extracted six sects from them and they have based beliefs and dogmas upon them. It is like *'ilm-i kalām* (dialectics) in Islam.

On the question of ultimate liberation Jān-i Jānān takes a position which differs from Dārā Shikūh. According to Jān-i Jānān we should neither condemn Hindus as kafirs, nor should we say they will achieve *najāt* (liberation). He also argues that without proper proof one should not describe anyone as kafir. He even maintains that belief in *tanasukh* (transmigration of soul) does not lead to *kufr* (unbelief).[11]

Sufi literature is full of such references to Hinduism. One hardly finds hostile attitudes towards Hindus in Sufi literature. The only

10 See *Mirza Mazhar Jan-I-Janan ki Khutut* tr. from Persian into Urdu by Khaliq Anjum (Delhi, 1989), p. 131.

11 See Mażhar Jān-i Jānān's text of the letter in *Mirza Mazhar Jan-I-Janan ki Khutut*, pp. 131–4.

exception is perhaps *Mujaddid Alf-i thānī* (1564–1624) also known as Sirhindī. He launched a movement to purify Islam from Hindu influences and attached great importance to the purity of doctrines and advised his followers to practise a pure form of Islam. He also opposed bowing down to emperors, a practice widely prevalent among the courtiers. He opposed obeisance being performed before the Emperor Jahāngīr and he was imprisoned in Gwalior Fort by the emperor.

Mujaddid Alf-i Thānī also opposed the Sufi doctrine of *waḥdat al-wujūd* (Unity of Being) which held the revolutionary implication of accepting the truth of all religions, as according to this doctrine all manifestations are manifestations of Allah. Mujaddid, though a Sufi himself, opposed this doctrine and instead propounded another, namely, *waḥdat-i shuhūd* (unity of witnessing).[12] Thus Sirhindī was not hostile to Hinduism as such, but he launched a crusade against corruption in the basic doctrines of Islam and he blamed Sufis for this state of affairs as they accepted the validity of all religions.

With the exception of Mujaddid Alf-i Thānī, all other Sufis showed great respect for the beliefs of Hindus and based their opinion on Hindu Scripture and not on popular beliefs. The Sufis believed in the doctrine of *sulḥ-i kull*, that is, total peace and peace with all, and so Sufis should be considered as precursors of modern religious pluralism and multiculturalism. Akbar the Great was also inclined towards Sufism and was advised by his closest associates Abū al-Faḍl and Faizī, both of whom were Sufis. Both the brothers were persecuted by some narrow-minded 'Ulema and found refuge in Akbar's court and Akbar regarded them very highly and often consulted them in devising his policies towards other faiths.

Political Aspects

Now we would like to throw some light on Muslim rulers' attitude towards Hinduism and Hindus. Some communally minded Hindus select a few examples and maintain that all Muslim rulers humiliated Hindus. One cannot deny such instances in the history of more than 700 years of rule by various Muslim dynasties, but it cannot

---

12 Burhan Ahmad Faruqi, 1943, *The Mujaddids Conception of Tawhid*, Lahore.

be generalized in such a sweeping manner, as communalists seek to do.

The communalists on either side distort history. It is quite problematic to periodize Indian history on the basis of religion, namely, into the Hindu period and the Muslim period.[13] For example, it is misleading to call a period 'a Muslim period' because neither were the rulers all Muslims nor did all Muslims co-operate with each other, nor did they rule according to the principles of Islam. One Muslim dynasty fought against another Muslim dynasty, Khaljis fought against Tughlaqs and Tughlaqs against Lodhis and Lodhis against Moghuls and so on.

Some rulers were quite enlightened, liberal and tolerant, like Akbar (1542–1605), whereas others were orthodox in approach and tended to be intolerant, like Aurangzeb (1618–1707). Aurangzeb too has been much maligned as far as his treatment of Hindus is concerned. It is also alleged by communalists that Muslim kings demolished Hindu temples because idols were worshipped therein. This is a highly controversial issue – whether Muslim rulers really demolished temples because they hated idol worship and considered it against Islamic teachings or whether it was for political reasons.[14]

Maḥmūd of Ghazna (971–1030), who attacked and looted the Somnath temple in Gujarat, has been extensively quoted as an example of how Muslim rulers hated Hinduism and idol worship. However Romila Thapar, who specializes in the ancient and medieval history of India, has shown that he did not attack Somnath or revile Hinduism because he wanted to do away with idolatry but that he had motives of his own, which were primarily of an economic and political nature.[15]

Similarly, Aurangzeb's attitude to Hinduism and his demolition of a few Hindu temples has been highly controversial. He was undoubtedly no liberal like Akbar and was a strict follower of orthodox Islam. But at the same time he was a shrewd ruler and knew his

---

13 See Romila Thapar's essay in Romila Thapar, Harbans Mukhia and Bipan Chandra, 1969, *Communalism and the Writing of Indian History*, New Delhi: People's Publishing House.

14 See Asghar Ali Engineer, 1996, *Medieval History and Communalism*, Mumbai: CSSS.

15 Romila Thapar, 2004, *Somnatha: The Many Voices of History*, New Delhi: Penguin.

political interests well. He had more Rajput chiefs of higher status in his court than Akbar. He could defeat Dārā Shikūh only with the help of Mīrzā Rājā Jaisingh, who was ruler of Jaipur. Without his help he could not have defeated Dārā Shikūh, who was appointed the heir apparent by Shāh Jahān. He made Rājā Jaisingh one of the army chiefs and gave him high status in his court.

As for his demolition of temples, many scholars have pointed out that it was political rather than religious in spirit and he gave landed estates to many temples for their maintenance.[16] Thus the demolition of temples by some Muslim rulers should not be simplified. It was far more complex in nature. And Hindu rulers demolished Hindu as well as Jain and Buddhist temples. Raja Harsh, a Buddhist ruler of Kashmir in the late eleventh century, demolished several Hindu temples in the Valley.[17] Thus, various cases show that the demolition of temples should not always be taken as a religiously motivated hostile act towards Hindu religion.

Different Views dictated by Different Motives

As pointed out at the outset, it is important who views the other religion and with what motive. Is the clash between theologies or between political and other interests? One who transcends all interests would not demonize the 'other'. A human attitude towards the 'other' is never determined by any 'pure religious' consideration, though it may be posited as such. A human always looks at another religion with mixed motives.

In addition, the arrogance of power and political interests always play a very significant role. The religion of the ruling class seeks to play the dominant role simply because it is the religion of the ruling class. Religion per se may not promote such attitudes, but human beings following a religion always look at other religions from their own social status or power equation. Only those religious persons who do not have any such interests, like the Sufis among Muslims or mystics among Christians or *bhakti saints* among Hindus, can view other religions with equanimity and in true religious spirit.

---

16 Cf. Asghar Ali Engineer, 1996, *Medieval History and Communalism*.

17 See D. D. Kosambi, 1972, *The Culture and Civilization of Ancient India – in Historical Outline*, Delhi: Vikas Publishing House, pp. 186–7.

Even those theologians who are in any way part of religious or ruling establishments would view other religions from their own power perspective. Thus in India too, the *'ulamā'*, who were often part of the religious establishment or part of the ruler's court, viewed Hinduism as an inferior religion or as the religion of the *kuffars*. They had mixed motives, which were not purely religious.

The Sufis took a very different view of Hinduism because eminent Sufis always maintained their distance from power structures. They also refrained from developing their own establishment. Niẓām al-Dīn Awliya, who saw the reigns of five sultans, never paid court to any of them, and when Jalāl al-Dīn Khaljī wanted to visit his hospice and touch his feet, he did not agree to this and also rejected his offer of a village's revenue to cover his and his followers' upkeep.[18]

There was tension between Sufis and the *'ulamā'* as Sufis were open and tolerant and the *'ulamā'* were rigid and 'purist'. Since the *'ulamā'* were often part of the ruling establishment they also had the arrogance of the ruling class and considered Islam as the only true religion. The view taken by the chief qāḍī in the court of 'Alā al-Dīn Khaljī towards Hindus represents this attitude.[19]

Besides these factors, one's upbringing and family and social background also count in developing attitudes towards other religions. One either develops a sectarian, narrow mindset or a liberal and tolerant attitude, depending on one's family tradition. A narrow interpretation of religion also results from how one has developed since childhood. Preachers of religion often take a very rigid view of their religion as they wish to increase their flock, and this is not possible if they adopt liberal attitudes towards other religions. Also, the competition to control powerful religious establishments necessitates a rigid view of religion, as it helps tighten the grip over the establishment.

Today in democratic polity in multi-religious and multicultural society politicians are tempted to use the religious card to mobilize voters on the basis of religious identity and this is best done by vilifying other religions. The media, controlled by different kinds of vested interests also become part of the same game in demonizing a particular religion.

---

18 See Khaliq Ahmad Nizami, 1958, *Salatin-e-Delhi ke Mazhabi Rujhanat*, Delhi: Nadwatul Musannafin, p. 182.

19 Nizami, *Salatin-e-Delhi ke Mazhabi Rujhanat*, p. 232.

After the partition of India, Muslims were reduced to an insignificant minority in India and are now being targeted by the majority communal forces, and Islam is being maligned. Hindu religion or religious ethos has nothing to do with such vilification, but it is dictated by political need. After 9/11, Islam is being projected as a religion of terror by communal politicians and by media controlled by them.

Since Muslims are a marginalized minority in India today, their religious leaders' attitude has become quite defensive and the *'ulamā'* today are far more accommodating towards Hindus than ever before. For Muslims, security of life and property is far more important than religious doctrines and hence the *'ulamā'* are trying to cultivate harmonious relations with Hindus.

The media controlled by a section of the majority community tends to be quite prejudiced towards Muslims and hence the *'ulamā'* have to be quite careful in their statements, even about Islam and Islamic beliefs. Their statements are always under scrutiny. The BJP (Bharatiya Janata Party) representing the Hindu right has aggressively raised the issue of the demolition of temples by Muslim kings and during the 1980s the BJP tried to mobilize Hindu votes on this basis.

This BJP assault had a telling effect on how Muslims look at Hinduism in contemporary India. In Pakistan, which is a Muslim country where Hindus are an insignificant minority, Maḥmūd of Ghazna is a hero and his attack on Somnath temple is glorified as the act of a *mujāhid* (holy warrior) whereas in India Maḥmūd is a villain and the *'ulamā'* do not take such a glorifying attitude towards him and his attack on Somnath.

This example should suffice to show how political situations and security concerns can also dictate one's view of others' religion. Thus power equations play very important roles in viewing the religion of the other. In a multi-religious democratic society like that of India inter-religious harmony is most important and all religious leaders, whatever community they belong to, should do everything to promote tolerance, even respect, for others' religion.

Religion per se, as pointed out above, does not promote hatred or feelings of arrogance towards other religions; it is followers who develop theologies falsifying other religions in order to attract more people towards their own religion. The theologies developed in the

Middle Ages have to undergo constructive change to suit a democratic polity that enshrines equal rights for all citizens of a country.[20] All should be treated as equal partners in a democratic polity. Muslims in India today are no more rulers nor ruled but equal partners in a democratic set-up, constitutionally enjoying equal rights. Today polity and religion are far apart though some politicians of the right often misuse, as pointed out above, religion for political mobilization.

Muslim religious leaders should take the lead in promoting tolerance and respect for Hinduism as was advocated before by many eminent Sufis. Sufis, in a way, can be role models for Muslims today, and large numbers of Muslims have great respect and reverence for them. The Sufis played an eminent role, through their conduct and respect for all, in the spread of Islam in India. Their followers should take this task further by creating peace and harmony in society.

Hinduism is one of the great religions of the world, though its nature is very different from Semitic religions like Judaism, Christianity and Islam. It is not even a 'religion' in the technical sense of the word.[21] It is *dharma* meaning duties. Unlike Semitic religions it has no concept of one prophet, one book or well-defined doctrines, though it does have a concept of one God who is *nirakar* (without any shape) and *nirgun* (attributes). Its Scriptures, most importantly the Vedas, Upaniṣads and the Baghavadgītā, are inspired or revealed Scriptures, and the teachings embodied in these Scriptures exhibit, in terms of values and also in terms of concept of life after death, many similarities with other world religions. I, for my part, consider Hinduism to be a religion embodying truth. It is as valid a religion as any religion could be. The adherents of this religion follow universal principles as explicated in the Upaniṣads, and the Upaniṣads are among the highest achievements of human

20 See on this also: Asghar Ali Engineer, 2005 'Islam and Pluralism', in P. Knitter (ed.), *The Myth of Religious Superiority. Multifaith Explorations of Religious Pluralism*, Maryknoll: Orbis, pp. 211–19; Asghar Ali Engineer, 2007, *Islam in Contemporary World*, New Delhi: New Dawn Press.

21 It should be noted that the word 'Hinduism' does not occur in any of the traditional scriptures. It came into use during a much later period, probably since the eighteenth century, and became a formal name only during the British period in India.

thought and philosophy before the revealed Scriptures of Judaism, Christianity and Islam and must be admired and revered.

The theology of power should be transformed into a theology of respect towards all, and the fixation with the past should be considered as a great obstacle in the process of constructive change. Islam emphasized the rejection of the ancestral past and the construction of a new future based on faith (*īmān*) and good deeds (*'amal ṣāliḥ*). Morality is much more important in Islamic teachings than superiority, and excelling in good deeds (*istibāq al-khayrat*) is much more important than feeling a superiority of identity.

15. A Hindu View of Islam

CHAKRAVARTHI RAM-PRASAD

Beforehand: On 'Religion' and 'Identity'

The very idea of posing the question of what 'Hindu views' of 'Islam' are is one embedded in particular notions of religion and identity that are current in our times. We now take for granted that there are certain complex but coherent things called 'religions', which contain an identifiable set of beliefs, ritual practices, symbols, social values and ultimate goals that groups of people live by. This idea of a religion has been read into the welter of traditions that constitute Christianity, Judaism, Buddhism and – in our times, above all – Islam. With greater difficulty, Hinduism too has come to be seen as a single 'religion' in this way.

Over several centuries, but most importantly, during the period of Western European intellectual change known as the Enlightenment, the idea evolved that it was possible to define different religions, whose essence could be distilled through a set of doctrines.[1] On this view of the history of social reality across the world, there were clearly identifiable religions which, like any natural category, could be compared and contrasted through their beliefs and consequent practices; and the effort that began with Christianity[2] went on to other 'religions'.[3] The fact that beliefs were often shared across these

1 Cornelia Richter, 2006, 'The Productive Power of Reason: Voices on Rationality and Religion – A Sketch of the Development of the Enlightenment and its Aftermath', in Lieven Boeve, Joeri Schrijvers, Wessel Stoker and Hendrik Vroom (eds), *Faith in the Enlightenment? The Critique of the Enlightenment Revisited*, Amsterdam: Rodopi, pp. 23–38.

2 Nicholas Lash, 1996, *The Beginning and End of Christianity*, Cambridge: Cambridge University Press.

3 Jonathan Z. Smith, 1998, 'Religion, Religions, Religious', in Mark C.

different 'religions', that within each religion there were beliefs that could not possibly be held together at the same time, that practices often seemed not to be clearly tied to beliefs but had their own appeal, that various beliefs and practices seemed to merge with or separate out from one another across the boundaries of the separate religions – all these were deemed anomalous, to be explained away by appeal to historical developments, or the intrinsic incoherence of certain religions.

Tied to this scholarly taxonomy of religions was another, usually unrecognized presupposition: the people in whom these beliefs and practices were realized 'belonged' unambiguously to whichever religion was deemed to have those beliefs and practices. So, not only were there fixed bodies called the religions of Christianity, Islam and the rest, but there were determinate bodies of people called Christians, Muslims and so on. And just as religions could show anomalies, people could be confused, if they did not adhere to the beliefs and practices that were supposedly distinctive of the religion to which they were held to belong. It is surely a mark of the power of this idea that most of us would find this a natural thought: there are separate religions and, consequently, determinate religious identities. But why should it be natural to think thus?

If we look at the complex history (and present) of the sacred in the human imagination, we find that people have constantly moved between different conceptions of the good life and right actions. These movements have been impelled by a range of factors: the shifting psychology of the individual across a lifetime; interpersonal negotiations within marriage, family or local group; social stresses; climatic changes; political pressures; new and compelling narratives; charismatic figures . . . the list is long. And while some movements to new conceptions do bring about a critical rupture with the past, others do not. Conditions constantly change, and people move, as they deem appropriate, between conceptions of what to believe and do. Sometimes, novelty appeals without wiping out the settled comforts of older values. Traces of earlier thought-worlds remain in lives that are too crowded or urgent to allow for contemplative development of some one coherent narrative. Overarching considerations

---

Taylor (ed.), *Critical Terms for Religious Studies*. Chicago: University of Chicago Press, pp. 269–84.

– like desperate love or discriminatory taxes – compel people to slip back and forth between different traditions of doctrine and ritual.

It is this fluid reality that the imperial construction of determinate and separate religions and religious identity has both obscured and changed. It has obscured a history of multiple identities and blurred religious boundaries. But it has also changed that historical reality: arguably, the condition of modernity was brought about by the formation of rigid and exclusive identities derived from taking everyone to belong to some monolithic construct or the other. Of course, the construction of nations and national identity was probably the most potent such development (and can likewise be said to have been anything but natural), but religions and religious identity come a close second. All across the world, in the nineteenth and twentieth centuries especially, people accepted the idea that there were great cultural bodies formed by essential differences between religions. It became commonplace to think that there should be no difficulty in distinguishing Christians and Muslims and Hindus and Buddhists from each other. There should be no possibility of multiple identities, where a person or group could, in one locus, have many different ways of belonging. Nor could there be blurred boundaries, in which persons and groups could lead lives of hybridity, synthesis or other forms of epistemic freedom from determinate belonging to one set religion or another. For many people, identities are still fluid, in deliberate or unselfconscious resistance to the idea of monolithic and exclusive religious belonging. The tragedy is that fluid lives are being congealed by the force of this idea.

To be critical of the idea of monolithic religious identities is not to deny that, throughout history, people have taken beliefs and practices as the grounds for separating themselves into distinctive groups. Transpersonal identities of lesser or greater clarity are part of the evolutionary history of humanity. I am making a more specific point: an idea developed in modernity, that there were fixed and comparable/contrastive bodies of belief and practice called 'religions' and that individuals belonged determinately to only one of them, by virtue of which they came to possess a single religious identity. It is this idea that has taken hold all over the world, and influenced the way people think of themselves, others and the past. Once we become sensitive to how contestable and contingent this way of thinking is, we can approach the specific history and present of Hindu–Muslim relations with an understanding that it is all a matter of interpretation – and misinterpretation. In doing this, I am going to draw on the sophisticated recent scholarship on India, which abundantly demonstrates this point within a larger academic trend that recognizes both the fluidity of identities and the peculiar modern construction of religion and religious identity.

Fixing Hindu and Islamic Identities

While there is controversy over whether a sense of religious identity already played a role in motivating social violence between communities in pre-colonial India (violence based on clashes between religious communities is called 'communal' violence in India); arguably, the fixation of monolithic identities through the construction of pan-Indian religious communities was carried out through the administrative rationale of British rule in India and communal violence thereafter was clearly part of this colonial fixation of identities.[4] What had started as the intellectual project of the original orientalists – men of learning attempting to record and represent the history of Indian people who were coming under the power of the East India Company in the late eighteenth century – became, by the mid-nineteenth century, a way of controlling the native population by elaborate tabulations that separated communities and kept them from conceiving of themselves as part of any larger unity like a nation. While this involved hardening distinctions among Hindus through anthropologically simplistic definitions of caste, it also meant creating a deep divide between those classified as Hindus and Muslims that led directly into clashes between these two monolithically conceived 'communities'.[5]

Looking back at Indian history, one realizes that this British colonial project was by no means conjured out of thin air: after all, distinctions clearly existed between groups in Hindu society, and there were certainly pronounced distinctions between the commitments

4 Veena Das, 1990, 'Introduction: Communities, Riots, Survivors – The South Asian Experience', in Veena Das (ed.), *Mirrors of Violence: Communities, Riots and Survivors in South Asia*, New Delhi: Oxford University Press, pp. 1–36.

5 Bipan Chandra, 1984, *Communalism in Modern India*, New Delhi: Vani Educational Books.

of the established streams of Islam and those of the multifarious Hindu traditions. The fixation of a single Hindu identity, as one that held across a myriad of traditions, and was held to trump all other forms of self-reference, looks to be a colonial construct; and I am arguing that it is this that is relevant to the apparent naturalness of the Hindu-Muslim divide. This claim should be distinguished from another one, that there was no sense in which Hindus thought of themselves as Hindus, albeit in an infinite number of ways, in the pre-colonial period.[6] I am not disputing the historical claim to self-reference. Rather, I am saying that the colonial administration did create governmental processes in which the constant interflow between a plurality of traditions and communities was more or less dammed up, and the persistent shifting of collective identities across regions, languages and native kingdoms was stopped through a centralized bureaucracy that then fixed certain groups as belonging forever to one or another unified religion. The British administrative feat was, nevertheless, based on historical materials and contemporary narratives, although these were nothing like as conclusive as the resulting taxonomization of India suggested.

One of the crucial sources of the conclusion that there was a fundamental civilizational divide between Hindus and Muslims was the writing of a number of elite Muslims who had accompanied various armies that invaded the Hindu kingdoms of India or attended the courts of Muslim rulers. They were either of non-Indian origin (Arabs, Turks or Afghans in the main) or notable figures associated with the body of Muslim religious authorities (the '*ulamā*'). They tended towards a view of Islam which they self-consciously considered as doctrinally pure (even if they would have disagreed over the content of that purity). It was important for them to represent conquest and control as the triumph of a clearly defined Islam over the dark chaos of Hindu culture, as the bringing of India into true history, that of Islam.[7] But they were an interested party to the interpretation of events, and without looking at their background and imperatives, it is easy to conclude that their views of Islam

6 David Lorenzen, 2006, *Who Invented Hinduism?*, New Delhi: Yoda Press, pp. 1–36.

7 Harbans Mukhia, 1998, '"Medieval India": an Alien Conceptual Hegemony?', *The Medieval History Journal*, 1.1, pp. 91–105; 96–7.

represented the whole truth about how all Muslims saw Hindus. For example, naturally, these writers made exaggerated claims for the number of temples their masters destroyed in iconoclastic zeal – Maḥmūd of Ghazna is said to have destroyed 10,000 temples in the mid-sized city of Kanauj, and so on.[8] To take these accounts as representing a reliable whole historical account would be risible.

The British were not the only ones to read into these elite discourses the entire history of India as the violent clash of Islam with Hinduism, the utter rejection of every aspect of the latter's culture by the former, and the essential – even racial – difference between Muslims and Hindus. In the early twentieth century, as the political movement to gain independence from Britain grew, the Muslim League organization began to argue that if the principle of nationhood for Indians was to be granted, it would have to be applied equally to two disparate people, Hindus and Muslims. Called the 'Two Nations Theory', it was, for complex reasons, admitted by the British, and led to the partition of British India and the creation of Pakistan as a nation dedicated to the idea of an Islamic State. (That India was not created a Hindu State is a story to which we will eventually turn.)

Finally, there were also reasons why many Hindus themselves began to think in terms of a clear and distinct identity as Hindus, fundamentally different from – and historically opposed to – Muslims. In the nineteenth century, socially well-placed Hindu thinkers and leaders began to appreciate the need for resistance to British conceptions of their religious, social and even racial inferiority. Although this led to some sophisticated movements towards social reform, the most striking and fundamental shift occurred at a more ideological level, which saw the emergence of a discourse of identity derived from a reading of the distant past as a golden age of Hindu social and political achievement. Ironically, this discourse was dependent on colonial historiography, which itself represented India as the land of the Hindu 'race' before a Muslim invasion and conquest. The terms of this historiography already represented Hindus as a racially

8 Richard Eaton, 2002, 'Temple Desecration and Indo-Muslim States', in D. Gilmartin and B. B. Lawrence (eds), *Beyond Turk and Hindu. Rethinking Religious Identities in Islamicate South Asia*, New Delhi: India Research Press, pp. 246–81; p. 268.

defined group, and the original inhabitants of India. This retrieval of the past was meant by the British to demonstrate that their rule would be the inevitable culmination of Indian history: to the Hindus, the British offered freedom from Muslim political domination; to the Muslims, they offered a continuing place in India which they suggested would not be given them if the Hindus regained political power. We have already seen how this led some sections of the Muslim leadership to campaign in the twentieth century for a land within India just for Muslims. But equally, Hindus too began to see India as originally, and therefore truly, a Hindu land.

The emergence of a single unified Hindu identity as belonging to the religion of Hinduism (as opposed to the self-conception of many Hindus, which may go back well into the ancient period) – derived from the colonial construction of a single Hindu 'religion' out of organically interrelated but infinitely diverse traditions – ran closely with the idea of India as intrinsically a Hindu 'nation'. (The arrival of the problematic if also politically inspiring category of 'nation' to India also had major consequences, but we cannot deal with that notion in detail here. Suffice it to say that not only the birth and growth of the movement for independence from British rule, but also the conceptualization of what it was for which independence was being sought, were affected by the ideology of nationalism.) Many Hindus accepted this unified identity while nevertheless holding India to be a land of many religions. Nevertheless, seeing Hinduism as a single religion was intimately connected with the assumption that India was fundamentally a Hindu country. On this assumption, Islam – again, taken as a single, unified religion – was not essentially Indian, but an alien presence that erupted into the Hindu land through violent conquest. A fixed and unifying Hindu identity was defined in terms of a unique Indianness that pointedly contrasted with Islam.[9] The tragedy is that many Muslims accepted this clash-of-civilization reading of Indian history; only, they saw the entry of Islam as the inevitable triumph of divine will, religious truth and cultural superiority.

Islam, although clearly having a single founder, sacred text and

9 Neeladri Bhattacharya, 1991, 'Myth, History and the Politics of Ramajanmabhumi', in S. Gopal (ed.), *Anatomy of a Confrontation: The Babri Masjid-Ramajanmabhumi Issue*, New Delhi: Viking.

original body of authoritative codes, must be seen in the varied, local contexts in which it evolved, at once connected to the larger body of tradition and generative of indigenous variations. The key point about Indian Islam to this day is that, while Islam, it is also Indian.

Seen in this way, the contrast with Hinduism is not quite so sharp, since variations in local traditions appear to be common to both 'religions'. But the point about Hindu history's deep plurality is more directly made. Although a large number of similar regulative ideas, social formations and ritual performance are found across a range of Hindu traditions and communities, clearly Hinduism is not a religion with an essence – it has no single founder, text or core doctrine. Sometimes, it has been argued that pluralism itself is the central doctrine of Hinduism, but it is hard to see the staggeringly varied forms of life that are now called Hindu as, in any way, all commonly arguing for a doctrine of pluralism. (This is not to deny that there are specific texts which enunciate a view of difference that looks very like the modern concept of pluralism, as a doctrine that there can be a diversity of [sometimes incompatible] beliefs and practices within the same sphere of existence. But to read this view into every other Hindu tradition is an unfounded imposition.) At the same time, it should not be denied that modern history has seen the evolution of a common religious identity across the traditions called Hinduism. If anything, this commonality has been sharpened by recent moves by many marginalized groups of people to deny that they are in fact Hindus. To reject the possibility of a pan-Hindu identity today, simply by appeal to a more fragmented past, is to reject that history can happen to Hindus. (Why consider Europeans to be Christians, when after all, they were originally – historically – pagans?) There is, however, much virtue in appealing to this plural past in order to resist the use of Hindu identity for more hegemonic purposes – a point to which we will return towards the end of this essay.

A History

All that has gone before is meant to sensitize the reader to the extent to which the history of India is a construction out of questionable categories. Even the most careful of accounts, let alone a short one, is therefore bound to be embedded in interpretations that others will find questionable. That said, we need some sense of what happened over a thousand years in order to understand how Hindus and Muslims view each other. And this is so even if we are extremely cautious about expressing those views in terms of 'Hinduism' and 'Islam'.

It is likely that, because of the dense commercial connections across the Arabian Sea between Arabia and southern India, many Muslim communities were created in present-day Kerala and Tamil Nadu by Arab merchants and native people who took on Muslim identities over a few generations.[10] But there is no denying that by far the more forceful and consequential entry of Islam into India was through a series of invasions, which started from the Arab conquest of Sind by the end of the eighth century and gained momentum through a series of devastating raids against Hindu kingdoms made by Maḥmūd of Ghazna and then by Muhammad Ghor, from what is now Afghanistan. (It is a striking illustration of contested readings that whereas Ghazna and Ghor are the very epitome of destructive, plundering invaders in Indian history textbooks that instinctively collapse Hindu perceptions with Indian narratives, Pakistan's self-proclaimed Islamic State names its missiles – which strategically target India – after them, despite their origins from outside the area of the modern state.)

By the twelfth century, Muslim kingdoms had been established in the western reaches of South Asia, but it was under a series of dynasties from the twelfth to the sixteenth centuries, centred on Delhi (and thus called the Delhi Sultanate), that Muslim kings gained dominance over large parts of South Asia, reaching even deep into the peninsula. The nobility centred on the Delhi court was Turkish, but it entered into complex relationships with existing political formations, sometimes even forming flexible and open alliances.

Where there was strong Hindu political resistance, the Muslim elite tended to emphasize both the discourse of Islamic conquest and the adherence to a fundamental notion of Islam going back to its

---

10 Vasudha Narayanan, 2002, 'Religious Vocabulary and Regional Identity: A Study of the Tamil *Cirappuranam*', in D. Gilmartin and B. B. Lawrence (eds), *Beyond Turk and Hindu. Rethinking Religious Identities in Islamicate South Asia*, New Delhi: India Research Press, pp. 74–97; p. 75.

earliest cultural forms in Arabia. A notable manifestation of triumphalism as well as orthodoxy was the targeted demolition of temples associated with Hindu royal families (and therefore the sources of their sacred authority). But even then, over a period of time, the ideas and practices of Islam began to be translated into Indian languages and customs that had their origin in older, Hindu forms. In regions on the periphery of the traditional Hindu world, in present-day Bengal or Kashmir, Islam met with less political resistance and few pre-existing traditions of religious culture and authority. Here, there was much less emphasis on an original Islam, and a more obviously fluid accommodation with local, pre-Islamic practices.[11]

It is clear that Hindu sources – in contrast to elite Turkish-Muslim writers who stressed the idea of an Islamic triumph over native culture – usually took the invaders to be just another ethnic group, referring to them as *turuska*, Turks, rather than as Muslims. While Muslim beliefs were generally understood, their salience lay, for Hindu elites, in whether or not they cohered with the existing socio-political order, rather than in their theological commitments. If Muslim rulers, at any level, from local chieftain to the Sultan in Delhi, upheld practices like supporting Brahmin communities or pilgrimage centres, extracted only taxes that were considered the normal privilege of the ruler, and gave employment according to customary occupations, then they were assimilated into the existing social cosmology. The most striking example of this deeply pluralistic Hindu attitude lay in the Vijayanagar Empire. Often celebrated as the last Hindu political formation and interpreted as the final focus of resistance to Muslim invasion, Vijayanagar, especially at the height of its power in the early sixteenth century, was in fact a cosmopolitan land. Mosques were built with imperial support, European traders and soldiers employed in key areas, and – amidst the deliberate invocation of ancient Hindu rituals of kingship (since the Vijayanagar dynasties had no bloodlines running back to the traditional ruling elites of South India) – Islamic dress, courtly practices and even titles (the most notable being 'Sultan among Hindu kings') were adopted. Rather than seeing this as merely a ready Hindu adoption of Islamic cultural practices that had superior symbolic,

11 Richard Eaton, 1993, *The Rise of Islam and the Bengal Frontier, 1204–1760*, Berkeley: University of California Press.

practical and military value,[12] these features of Vijayanagar might be better seen as the natural consequence of a Hindu culture almost casually open to new ideas and practices.

The depth of the Turkish assimilation into the Indian landscape is seen in the way the volatile Sultanate was supported by Hindu rulers when the Mughals ('Mongols') invaded under Babur. But the triumph of the Mongol-Persian aristocracy over the Afghan nobility was completed within a generation, and the Mughals too, who had once pined for a return to their central Asian mountains from the hot plains of India, found themselves oriented completely to their new dominion. Once more, the same dynamics were played out – complex relationships of hostility, patronage and alliances with Hindu kingdoms, internecine battles between Muslim noble factions, the waxing and waning of imperial control. But there was one difference. By this time, Islam had been in India for half a millennium or more, and the rhetoric was no longer of its triumph over areas of chaos and darkness. Instead, more subtle conceptions of its place in India and relationship with Hindu traditions were articulated.

Europeans in the fifteenth century were seen as yet another group, and revealingly, Indian Muslim elites viewed the Portuguese and others as Hindus had viewed early Muslims, not as representatives of a particular, hostile religion but as a new group of interested actors on the Indian scene. The Europeans, on the other hand, saw them as 'Moors', as a people belonging to a religion that had to be vanquished . . . and in that bloody sense, history was to repeat itself, albeit in a different way.

Looking at the elite views of India during the establishment of Indian Islam, then, we find some asymmetries and variations. While Muslim elites were self-conscious about the victory of their particular faith over the native traditions, Hindu elites were more pluralistic and decentred in their reception of Islam, seeing Muslims as yet another ethnic group, their specific beliefs vectored into existing conceptions of power, authority and practice. But attitudes varied among Muslim elites too, especially under political pressure during

12 Phillip Wagoner, 2002, 'Harihara, Bukka and the Sultan: The Delhi Sultanate in the Political Imagination of Vijayanagara', in D. Gilmartin and B. B. Lawrence (eds), *Beyond Turk and Hindu*, pp. 300–26.

the formation of empire. Sometimes, the narrow purity of vision widened into an accommodation of Hindu cultural practices.

This accommodation crucially included the translation of many Muslim ideas into Indian languages. (The oft-noted point that, unlike the Bible, the Qur'ān is to be preserved in Arabic and therefore rigidly attaches Islam to Arabic culture, cannot be given too much weight in any account of the spread of Islam. Else we are left with no explanation for its weighty presence in South Asia, with its many non-Arabic cultures and languages – today's India, even after the partition of the British Raj into Muslim-majority Pakistan [and later, Bangladesh], has more Muslims than any other country apart from [again, non-Arabic] Indonesia, and roughly on a par with Pakistan and Bangladesh.) But this accommodation also included a brilliant range of Hindu figures who assimilated Muslim theological notions into popular Hindu belief and practice. Various mystics and poets from the lands under Muslim rule between the fourteenth and seventeenth centuries, known for their public commitment to an intense form of devotion (called *bhakti* in Sanskritic languages), used Islamic motifs and theological notions of God in an organic creation of popular Hindu worship and religious sentiment that is influential to this day; while reciprocally, so too were many aspects of Indian Islam influenced by Hindu culture, especially its music. Indeed, public devotionalism in many parts of India became a fusion of Hindu and Muslim motifs,[13] and brought into question clear distinctions between the traditions in many aspects of popular religion.

We have therefore been able to point to the nature of Hindu plurality and its consequences: first, the absence of any original perception of Islam as a distinct and alien presence in civilizational clash with some one tradition called Hinduism; and second, the gradual enculturation of Islam into India, both through its indigenization and through decentred and organic Hindu openness to its original theological ideas.

The fruitful interactions between Hindu and Muslim cultures did not at all imply some sort of edenic pre-modern India. For one thing, there is no denying that Islam took root across South Asia mostly in

---

13 R. S. McGregor (ed.), 1992, *Devotional Literature in South Asia*, Cambridge: Cambridge University Press.

lands that were first conquered by Muslim rulers. Military violence was a precondition of Islamization, apart from a few exceptional areas like the Kerala and Tamil coasts, which saw the formation of small Muslim communities in the eighth to tenth centuries. But equally, this does not mean that there was an edenic pre-Islamic India either. While their origins, self-professed faith, military organization and tactical skills might have distinguished early Muslim invaders from their Hindu opponents, their absorption into the Indian social cosmos was possible only because they were not seen as entirely alien. The land they entered had competing political formations, military-led expansion, social stratification, strategic alliances, and sustained contestation of power between martial nobility, religious authorities and mercantile or agrarian communities – features that the Afghans, Turks and Persians shared with native Indian society, albeit with different ideological bases.

Even though the invaders integrated into this new land, and many native groups gradually came to share their faith, Muslims did have large areas of existence in which they led lives parallel to their Hindu counterparts. Some religious figures, especially located in some Sufi communities, shared identity and following that were ambiguous between Islam and Hinduism,[14] but many aspects of religious performance, consanguinity, and the minutiae of daily life grew to be separate between Hindus and Muslims. Even before the establishment of the British Raj by the nineteenth century – which saw the elaborate imperial construction of differences between native groups for the purpose of administration and political hegemony – there were many differences between Hindus and Muslims, which has been likened to cultural apartheid. The sense of religious difference does appear to have played a part in violent confrontations between Hindus and Muslims by the eighteenth century,[15] although it is difficult to deny that these confrontations might have been driven by other considerations too, such as class.[16]

---

14 Tony Stewart, 1995, 'Satya Pir: Muslim Holy Man and Hindu God', Donald S. Lopez Jr. (ed.), *Religions of India in Practice*, Princeton: Princeton University Press, pp. 578–97.

15 Lakshmi Subramanian, 1996, *Indigenous Capital and Imperial Expansion: Bombay, Surat and the West Coast*, New Delhi: Oxford University Press.

16 Asiya Siddiqui, 1999, Review of Subramanian, *Indigenous Capital*

I would suggest that there is a *via media* between the two interpretations of Hindu–Muslim relations in pre-modern (that is, pre-colonial) India. It is not as if there was no sense of religious difference in violent clashes and parallel lives; the British did not invent the whole reality of India, after all. But the acceptance of this point should go hand in hand with an understanding of pluralism in Indian society. True, one could find in many Muslim practices and religious performance no trace of Hindu participation. But then, within any number of 'Hindu' communities themselves, one would not find any trace of participation by other 'Hindu' communities as well! The exclusion of low-status caste groups from most major temples is ample demonstration of further types of parallel lives in Indian society. So too – although less remarked upon – was the creation of a religious theatre of animal sacrifice and other rituals by low-status caste groups which, by virtue of being filled with practices considered at once polluting but also darkly powerful by higher castes, allowed spaces for these groups to invert their marginalization into spiritual assertion free of interference and organization by higher castes. And across sects, linguistic groups, and other divisions, many communities that were all Hindu, nevertheless led parallel lives too. So, one should not overstate the centrality of any divide between 'Hindus' and 'Muslims', any more than one can overstate the existence of free-flowing contacts and blurred boundaries between them. Differences in caste imposed divisions among Hindus, but there were also temple festivals and dominant deities that were common across many Hindu groups. In the same way, many Muslim and Hindu practices, figures and even texts were shared, while nevertheless deep differences in daily life also existed. To see nuances in Hindu–Muslim relationships is to see nuances in Indian society and history as a whole.

We have already seen how this interactive and blurred past was gradually elided by the development of monolithic conceptions of identity, through the nineteenth and twentieth centuries. By the time the movement for independence from British rule had become unstoppable in the 1930s, a sharp divergence over religion had taken place among the political elites of India. The Indian National Congress,

---

and Imperial Expansion, in *The Indian Economic and Social History Review*, 36.4, pp. 501–3.

dominant under Mahatma Gandhi and Jawaharlal Nehru, rejected the conception of India as a nation based on religion. Their nationalism was one that took the capacious view of India as a land of many religions: Gandhi because his deeply spiritual view of humanity committed him to seeing a fundamental commonality under all religious differences, Nehru because his optimistic modernism led him to believe that the true future of humanity lay beyond what he took to be the superstitions of religion itself.[17] Their political dominance held in control that wing of the Congress which felt that the very idea of India was embedded in the history of Hinduism – that is, an idea that pre-dated Islam. By contrast, Muhammed Ali Jinnah and his followers in the Muslim League argued that the India of the Congress would build in a permanent Hindu majority (of about 65 per cent of British India), and that true freedom for Muslims would only come from an Islamic state; the instinctive (and often natural rather than deliberately anti-Islamic) Hindu symbolism of the Congress in its mobilization of Hindu Indians[18] against British rule only added to this insecurity. This 'two-nations' theory prevailed for a variety of reasons, and India was partitioned, tearing up the richly mixed spaces of western and eastern India. Millions were forced to migrate, and a million were butchered, as Hindus and Sikhs left their ancestral lands in what had become Pakistan, and many Muslims went in the opposite direction from what had remained as India.

Independent India was created constitutionally as a 'secular' state, neutral to all religions. Vast numbers of Muslims remained in India under assurance of equality; they now formed above 10 per cent of the Indian population. (Practically all Sikhs – whose land lay on both sides of partitioned Punjab – chose India.) The colossal tragedy of Partition left permanent scars on Indian politics, over and above the vast human cost amply evidenced in unbearably moving narratives.[19] The newly born Indian and Pakistani states handled the

---

17 T. N. Madan, 2006, *Images of the World. Essays on Religion, Secularism and Culture*. New Delhi: Oxford University Press, Chapter 4, pp. 77–89.

18 William Gould, 2004, *Hindu Nationalism and the Language of Politics in Late Colonial India*, Cambridge: Cambridge University Press.

19 Mushirul Hasan (ed.), 1997, *India Partitioned. The Other Face of Freedom*, New Delhi: Roli Books, two volumes.

refugees badly, and left a legacy of distrust and maladministration. Muslims who had chosen India nevertheless felt the pressure from many Hindus to constantly demonstrate their loyalty, just because there now existed an explicitly Islamic state that claimed them for itself. To decry the tragedy of Partition for humane reasons became difficult, just because many Hindu nationalist groups had resisted it on the grounds that the whole, undivided India was a Hindu homeland and that Islam had no place in it. Finally, now that Pakistan had been created explicitly as an Islamic state, these Hindu groups became even more insistent that at least divided but independent India should now be considered a Hindu homeland.

Hinduism Today

We now have in India and in the diaspora a huge body of people who, whatever their history, consider themselves to belong to a 'religion' called 'Hinduism'. On the one hand, their collective sense of self is not very historically accurate; however, since history is not fixed for Hindus any more than it is for others, the accusation that historically there is no such thing as Hinduism is beside the point. But on the other hand, this assertion of a single Hinduism is often made for two disreputable purposes. One is to include forcibly within Hinduism many groups or communities – tribes and low-status castes as well as the Indic religions of Jainism, Buddhism and Sikhism – that do not see themselves as part of this religion and for whom there are few possible benefits in so seeing themselves. The other is to assert a civilizational difference with Muslims and charge that their religion is not intrinsically part of India. It is here that the history of Hinduism is politically relevant. It is here that the history of India itself, with its long history of many belongings, shifting categories of selfhood and a decentred openness to new forms of belief and practice is of vital importance to conceptualizing identity today.

In contemporary India, we see several dynamics being played out. The national politics of India was dominated for a while by the progress of parties that claimed adherence to Hindu nationalism – the claim that India was historically and fundamentally a nation of a unified Hindu people (even if that unity was just based on a doctrinal commitment to pluralism, it was supposed to be distinguishable from Islam and Christianity precisely for this reason).[20] The Bharatiya Janata Party (BJP), which represented this view at the national level, led coalition governments, but eventually lost its mandate – although it is still contested as to whether this was because it was not assertive enough or too assertive of its Hindu nationalist credentials. Nevertheless, whatever its performance in Parliament, the Hindu nationalist assertion of a natural Hindu majority has certainly taken root in urban India, even if voters are uncertain in their support of it at election time, when more fundamental questions of governance and even caste identity seem to supersede religion as factors.[21]

While political mobilization on the basis of pan-Hindu identity has waned in the middle of the first decade of the twenty-first century, there are many instances of continued violence at the local level, which model themselves on the major riots that have scarred urban areas from time to time over the decades. Typically, riots are started by the circulation of stories – occasionally accurate, usually exaggerated, often misrepresented, sometimes completely fabricated – about transgressions by the 'other' community. Under cover of growing anger and calls for retaliation, powerful agents mobilize ready-made groups of rioters, who skilfully recruit larger and willing numbers from their community and attack the 'enemy'. Considered on the whole, the majority of these attacks have been by Hindus on Muslims, without doubt, but Hindus have also died in cycles of violence. One fearful feature of Hindu attacks on Muslims has been that, in several cases, the state-level or local government appears to have either supported or at least deliberately allowed such attacks to go ahead: the most thoroughly documented being Gujarat in 2002.[22]

A new feature of violence since the 1990s has been the growth of a transnational movement of so-called *jihādī* Islam. India has, in fact,

---

20 Chakravarthi Ram-Prasad, 1993, 'Extracting the Fundamentals: Hindutva Ideology', *Contemporary South Asia*, 2, pp. 285–309.

21 Chakravarthi Ram-Prasad, 2003, 'Being Hindu and/or Governing India? Religion Social Change and the State', in G. ter Haar and J. J. Busuttil (eds), *The Freedom to do God's Will. Religious Fundamentalism and Social Change*, London: Routledge, pp. 159–96.

22 Siddharth Varadarajan (ed.) 2002, *Gujarat: The Making of a Tragedy*. New Delhi: Penguin.

seen rather more instances of symbolic and devastating attacks than Europe: on the Indian Parliament, on the Mumbai stock exchange and the city's rush-hour commuter trains, and on the occasion of various Hindu festivals. The obvious aim of these attacks – unlike riots, these are carried out by small, trained cadres – is to trigger retaliation against vulnerable Muslim communities, thereby increasing their sense of alienation, and recruiting them to the cause of a putative global Islam. Strikingly, unlike the conflagration that did follow a bomb blast in Mumbai in 1993, later attacks have not led to such violence. However, the rhetorical pressure on Muslim communities from the media and the Hindu middle-classes has remained. Very like in Britain and other Western countries, Muslims are expected to denounce such *jihādi* violence quickly, loudly and often. And given the diversity and sheer numbers of Indian Muslims, this is always going to be a problem, as some do not react with sufficient promptitude, some others simply do not have the wherewithal to express their feelings, and yet more do choose to assert their ideological commitment to the cause of an Islam that directly contradicts their national allegiance.

There are other things to be said about Hindu–Muslim relations in India today. Many Hindus have charged that India's constitution – under the influence particularly of the first prime minister, Jawaharlal Nehru – has given too many privileges to Muslims, by way of minority rights at the expense of 'ordinary Hindus'. While contestation over state provision has been a major feature of Indian politics, with competition between a bewildering variety of caste and other groups, provision for Muslims has been a particularly sharp point of debate. So, the somewhat strange exception made for Muslim private law – which allows, most potently, a Muslim man to have four wives, when the rest of the country is bound by the law against bigamy – has allowed Hindu nationalists to masquerade as supporters of Muslim women's rights, much to the embarrassment of traditional liberal critics of *sharī'a* laws. (That in fact, men from communities categorized as Hindu are more likely to commit bigamy than Muslim men are to marry a second wife is another matter.)

The evidence has mounted – most recently in the report of the 2006 Sachar Commission on the state of Muslims in India – that Muslims are not doing well on most socio-economic measures.

Some sections of the Muslim intelligentsia hardly help the case of ordinary Muslims by suggesting that the Indian State is so Hindu-centric that Muslims are unsurprisingly discriminated against; many Hindus counter that it is the very strength of religious identity among Muslims that explains why they do so badly despite special constitutional guarantees of their rights. The truth is somewhere in between: there is definite discrimination in low-level jobs, and – on the conventional and unfair basis of questioning their loyalty – in significant sections of the security services. But failure to get the meritocratic jobs in the central civil services or in the private sector comes from lack of education and social capital. But again, these shortcomings are because of mundane economic reasons: Muslims are concentrated in rural areas and urban slums.[23] But this is where those non-Muslims who too do not benefit from India's economic growth also live. Once again, the double-edged nature of thinking in terms of monolithic identities becomes evident: while undoubtedly helping to show large numbers of Muslims require help and support, it elides the fact that people from other ('Hindu') communities might, in similar socio-economic and demographic conditions, require similar support. So, when looking at hostile and critical Hindu responses to such reports, we must ask who these 'Hindus' are, and are likely to find that it is their own socio-economic background – from middle-class, dominant (if not necessarily upper) castes – that conditions the way they look at Muslims. But they might have the same disdain that all comfortable social groups show when blaming the victims for their own conditions; this is, after all, a nearly universal phenomenon. The other class of Hindus who are antagonistic towards Muslims or not sympathetic to their plight are those who share the same poor urban background and compete for the same resources, and are therefore resentful of any perceived inequality in the distribution of such resources. But again, unless they are deliberately mobilized against Muslims as such, these groups are equally worried about their fellow-Hindus from the same background, since India's complex politics of resource allocation might favour now one, now another group.

Everywhere, what looks like a problem of Hindu views of Muslims turns out, when we take a closer look, to be only tangentially related

---

23 *The Economist* 2006 'Don't blame it on the scriptures', 4 December.

to religion. One big difference, however, is the false impression of a monolithic Muslim community, which is created only partly by Hindu perceptions of the Other (to repeat, on closer examination, many 'Hindu' attitudes turn out to be those of particular groups of Hindus, who demonstrate the same attitude to their fellow-religionists whose economic conditions are the same as the majority of Muslims). Some Muslim leaders in India, and increasingly from within pan-Islamic globalism, deny the internal variety of Islam and Indian Islam in particular. They self-consciously seek to create a theologically narrow formulation of Muslim identity, decrying differences of local and syncretic practices, commitment to the nation, theological pluralism and, above all, the cultural accommodation of other traditions. Indian Muslim intellectuals agonize over the way in which the Indian roots of Indian Islam are decried by a brand of Islamist ideology that suggests that there is indeed a clash between their commitment to India and to Islam, between their acceptance of Hindu society around them and the purity of their faith.[24] This has put a great deal of pressure on Indian Muslims. In these conditions, Hindu nationalistic accusations of divided loyalties and hegemonistic intentions thrive, in a cycle of mutual antagonism fuelled by the artful creation of mutual grievances about the past.[25]

Under all these stresses, there is still much that is richly interactive and creative in Indian religious life, where identities still stubbornly resist collapse into the monoliths of modernity. Here, under the dynamics of political rationality and economic calculation, there are still signs of fluid self- and other-representation that go back to pre-modern society – not some ideal state of being of course, but ways of thinking of self and community in multiple ways that undermine the crashing simplification of 'Hindu vs Muslim' talk. This sort of daily life is there for all to see if their eyes are open, and careful anthropological work has done likewise.[26] It is this India of overlapping selfhoods that any committed person must strive to secure.

24 Rafiq Zakaria, 2004, *Indian Muslims. Where have they gone wrong?*, New Delhi: Popular Prakashan.

25 Sanjay Subrahmanyam, 2005, *Explorations in Connected History*, New Delhi: Oxford University Press; pp. 80–101.

26 Peter Gottschalk, 2000, *Beyond Hindu and Muslim: Multiple Identity in Narratives from Village India*, New York: Oxford University Press.

In Conclusion: Challenges

Given that Hindu–Muslim relationships are so closely tied to the idea and reality of the Indian nation-state, it is clear that India is at the heart of Hindu views of Islam.

The most radical view is one with which both radical Islamists and post-Marxist left-wing thinkers could agree upon: the nation-state is a construction anyway, and commitment to India should not matter at all in people's attempts to find themselves (howsoever they might disagree on the nature of that *telos*.) This becomes a difficult point to accept for most people who consider themselves Hindus, because of the historical association of their Hinduism with the spaces of the land now called India. (However, it should be pointed out that there is nothing intrinsically incompatible between considering oneself a Hindu and considering India as unimportant as a nation-state. If the purifying rivers flow and the much-loved temples stand, the sacred geography of India is eternally more important than the modern political formation . . .)

But it has now become difficult for life to be led without the ideal of a nation-state. Too much now depends for too many on the security and mental spaces that a state is supposed to offer. In any case, the overwhelming majority of Indians accept the centrality of the nation-state. It is in this context that any Islamic interpretation of the tenet that Allah's will is sovereign, as a denial of the legitimacy of national citizenship – namely, an interpretation that makes being an Indian incompatible with being a Muslim – is profoundly unhelpful for most Indian Muslims.

So, what is the idea of India against which Hindus can view Muslims? Another radical thought is that India should be a nation-state in which Muslims (and other minority groups) are allowed to think of India on their own terms, without questioning from others.[27] But this appealingly pacific criterion raises the pertinent objection that equality requires Hindus too to be allowed to think of India on their own terms – but this is just what would lead to ever-greater confrontations between imagined communities.

---

27 Partha Chatterjee, 1998, 'Secularism and Tolerance', in Rajeev Bhargava (ed.), *Secularism and its Critics*, New Delhi: Oxford University Press.

The challenge lies in finding a conception of India that allows for fluid, multiple and sometimes agonistic identities, within spaces of common consent. In such an India, the constructed nation-state is given its due but is also questioned when its apparatus fails in its task of providing for a decent life for all. Even if political processes do rationalize identities – as vote banks, as lobbying groups, as social movements and so on – these identities could shift and change. Indeed, this often happens in India, as alliances form and break across castes, religions and other groupings. (In central India in 2006, Dalits formed an electoral alliance with brahmins against intermediate castes and Muslims.) Furthermore, there is still a stubborn persistence of interaction across religions in daily lives, despite the pressures of identity politics. It is the retrieval of this life of multiplicity, a life drawn from the vibrant history of India but secured through the humane usage of the bureaucratic state, that offers the most optimistic possibility for Hindu–Muslim relationships.

For this to happen, political processes must emerge that do not function on the premise of fixed and monolithic identities. As both a precondition and a consequence of such an emergence, Hindus must strive to re-conceive their manifold pasts, their many and varied theologies and practices, while critically purging their inheritance of its many savage exclusions. There is now a pan-Hindu identity which cannot be wished away, but must be worked with, and it is upon its creative understanding of multiple truths and life-forms that its relationship with both itself and Islam (as well as with other groupings) will depend. Above all, following through the concept of multiple identities, not only the many ways of being a Hindu but also the ways of belonging to other forms of collective identity, whether social, geographic or some other, must be recognized. Seen this way, there would be no single monolithic identity (a 'majority').[28] It is for those who call themselves Muslims in India to articulate and live out their relationship with 'Hinduism', but only among many other relationships based on other identities and relationships too.[29]

---

28 Gyanendra Pandey, 2006, *Routine Violence*, New Delhi: Permanent Black, p. 191.

29 Ranbir Samaddar, 2006, 'Identity Assertions as Contentious Acts', in S. Saberwal and H. Mushirul (eds), *Assertive Religious Identities. India and Europe*, New Delhi: Manohar, pp. 271–93; pp. 291–2.

16. Response to Ram-Prasad

ASGHAR ALI ENGINEER

I must say Ram-Prasad's views of Islam are quite objective and rational. He is free of prejudices, which are prevalent among non-Muslims. His paper is scholarly and well documented. What he says about Islam is to my mind quite agreeable. However, his treatment of the subject is more historical and political rather than theological. He also concentrates on Indian Islam rather than universal Islam.

Before we deal with this aspect of the problem, I must mention a very valid point Ram-Prasad makes. He observes that the pan-Indian religious identities were created by British colonialists:

> While there is controversy over whether a sense of religious identity already played a role in motivating social violence between communities in pre-colonial India . . . arguably, the fixation of monolithic identities through the construction of pan-Indian religious communities was carried out through the administrative rationale of British rule in India and communal violence thereafter was clearly part of this colonial fixation of identities.[1]

This is not only a valid observation but also is the key to understanding and solving communal problems. Construction of pan-Indian religious communities and identities was a colonial political project, which is being perpetrated by our political leaders in post-colonial, post-independence India. One has, therefore, to emphasize multiple identities in Indian lives, but one also has to realize that the idea of pan-Indian religious communities is going to pose political problems.

But then Ram-Prasad also maintains, with some justification of course, that

1 Ram-Prasad's chapter in this book, p. 189.

> ... one realizes that this British colonial project was by no means conjured out of thin air: after all, distinctions clearly existed between groups in Hindu society, and there were certainly pronounced distinctions between the commitments of the established streams of Islam and those of the multifarious Hindu traditions.[2]

He points out that 'the fixation of a single Hindu identity, as one that held across a myriad of traditions, and was held to trump all other forms of self-reference, looks to be a colonial construct; and I am arguing that it is this that is relevant to the apparent naturalness of the Hindu–Muslim divide.'[3]

However, the problem does not start only with the construction of a single Hindu identity as a colonial project, it also lies in the sense of 'civilizational divide', as Ram-Prasad puts it, created by the writings of a number of Muslim elite who had accompanied various armies that invaded the Hindu kingdoms of India or attended courts of Muslim rulers. But again use of words like 'Hindu kingdoms' and 'Muslim rulers' are somewhat problematic. This is again to fall prey to colonial construction of identities. No such identity as 'Hindu' or 'Muslim' existed. There were different Buddhist, Rajput, Brahman dynasties which were invaded, and those who invaded should not be bracketed within universal Muslim identity; they too belonged to Ghaznavid, Slave, Tughlaq or Khalji dynasties who were fighting against each other. Using words like 'Hindu' or 'Muslim' rule or 'Hindu and Muslim' period leads to supporting the colonial project.

Muslims themselves were divided not only among various invading dynasties but also among those who came from outside and those who were converted, again for myriad reasons to Islam. Those converted were despised by the ruling classes who came from outside. The latter looked down upon the indigenous Muslims. Also, the indigenous Muslims like Hasan Mewati, refused to side with invaders like Babur and instead fought with Rana Sanga and thousands of Mewati Muslims (indigenously converted) fought along with the Rana and courted death.

Thus Indian social reality is extremely complex and defies any

2 Ram-Prasad's chapter, p. 183f.

3 Ram-Prasad's chapter, p. 184.

neat categorization, however carefully made. The Pathans, whom the Moghuls had defeated, never saw eye to eye with them and always sided with those who fought against Moghuls. Then also Rajput clans were fighting against each other, and some Rajput rulers, like Raja Mansingh, sided with Moghuls whereas others, like Rana Pratap, fought against them. And a Pathan like Ḥakim Khān Sūr fought against the Moghul army along with soldiers of Rana Pratap. Thus a Rajput fought a Rajput and a Muslim (Akbar) fought a Muslim (Ḥakim Khān Sūr).

Likewise, among elite Muslim writings, one finds no homogeneity. As I have shown in my paper ('A Muslim View of Hinduism') some '*ulamā*' took what could be described as an anti-Hindu view as if there was 'civilizational divide', others like Dārā Shikūh, Mażhar Jān-i Jānān and several others took a diametrically opposite view and came to the conclusion that Islam did not clash with the Vedas and Upaniṣads, the indigenous Scriptures. Dārā Shikūh, particularly, believed in a complete harmony between the Scriptures of the two religions.

The crucial divide was political, rather than theological. Those '*ulamā*' who were part of ruling political establishments tended to be more hostile towards followers of indigenous religious traditions (as party of power politics and courting favour with rules) than those who grappled with religious differences outside the charmed circle of political power. Dārā Shikūh studied 'Hindu' religion seriously as a non-political theological project and hence he found great similarities between the two.

Ram-Prasad also points out that 'The British were not the only ones to read into these elite discourses the entire history of India as the violent clash of Islam with Hinduism, the utter rejection of every aspect of the latter's culture by the former and the essential – even racial – difference between Muslims and Hindus.'[4] He then continues, 'In the early twentieth century, as the political movement to gain independence from Britain grew, the Muslim League organization began to argue that if the principle of nationhood for Indians was to be granted, it would have to be applied equally to two disparate people, Hindus and Muslims.'[5] It is true that the Muslim League

4 Ram-Prasad's chapter, p. 185.

5 Ram-Prasad's chapter, p. 185.

almost agreed with the British reading of Indian history based on the assumption of 'clash of civilization'. The Muslim League's clash with the Hindus as a whole (ignoring that a large number of Hindus led by Gandhi and Nehru stood for secular India) was a political project. Jinnah neither knew nor was interested in knowing the fundamentals of Hindu religion (he hardly knew of Islam either). Jinnah was fighting in the political arena.

It would be wrong to assume that the Muslim League was the only sinner, for the Hindu communal forces were no less to blame. Thus, as pointed out by Ram-Prasad, the emergence of a single unified Hindu identity derived from the colonial construction of a single Hindu 'religion' out of organically interrelated but infinitely diverse traditions, came close to the idea of India as a 'Hindu nation'. And for Leaguers too 'Hindu India' was more acceptable than secular India. Together they carried the cross of partition.

Coming to contemporary India, Ram-Prasad deals with the communal situation. He feels that whatever the performance of Hindutva forces in Parliament might be, the Hindu nationalist assertion of a natural Hindu majority has certainly taken root in urban India, even if voters are uncertain in their support of it at election time, when more fundamental questions of governance and even caste identity seem to supersede religion as factors.

Ram-Prasad also refers to bomb blasts and attacks by *jihādī* groups and even feels that these transnational *jihādī* attacks are more in number and devastation than in Europe. This further compounds the situation though these attacks have not made a real dent on Hindu–Muslim relations.

He also deals with the socio-economic situation of Muslims in India and refers to the recently published Sachar Committee report. However, Ram-Prasad feels that though there is discrimination against Muslims at lower levels of government jobs, it is the lack of education and merit which results in the poorer representation of Muslims in the higher echelons. But at the same time he admits that the lack of education is also partly the result of the economic situation and not necessarily a lack of interest in modern education.

Thus on the whole it seems that Ram-Prasad deals with the subject fairly objectively though one may differ from him in certain assertions here and there. However, he does not deal, for whatever reason, with the theological aspects of the Hindu view of Islam.

The Hindutva forces are attacking today certain theological aspects of Islam, like the concept of *kufr* (disbelief) and rejection of non-Muslims and also *sharī'a* laws. I think that the theological aspects cannot and should not be excluded. In fact, Ram-Prasad's paper presents more a 'Hindu View of Muslims' rather than 'A Hindu View of *Islam*'.

Despite the lack of this aspect, his paper is helpful and he deals with his subject quite sensitively. Certainly his idea of the colonial construction of a single Hindu identity is quite useful and, if understood properly, can dispel many myths being woven around the concept of a single Hindu identity by the Hindutva forces in contemporary India and its harmful effects on the secular foundation of Indian politics. The Muslim leaders also should not insist on such singular Muslim identity.

17. Response to Engineer

CHAKRAVARTHI RAM-PRASAD

In his heartfelt plea for a sustained understanding between Muslims and Hindus, Asghar Ali Engineer draws on both history and his own theoretical understanding of religion. The reader will see that his narrative of the long and complex history of Islam in India resembles mine in most respects; possibly, I stress more than he does the fluidity of identity between the traditions, but we are agreed that it is folly to represent Indian history as the endless onslaught of 'Islam' on 'Hinduism'.

I am somewhat less sure of following him into his theological position. In the face of the destructive exclusivisms of today, Engineer's stance is a brave one. He argues that religions are complementary to each other – each provides a way of approaching a common truth that is not inconsistent with other ways. The ethical impulse behind this is laudable. I have three worries about this position.

The first worry is epistemological. How is it possible for anyone to assert the commonality of truth among the traditions? At the level of specific articulations about the nature of the truth, in the conceptual vocabulary deployed, in the interpretative traditions in which they are embedded, in their explicit claims about the means of access to that truth – in all these, different traditions (howsoever they are defined) are incompatible. If we are to say that, despite all this, they are really – truly – talking of the same thing begs the question of how one could claim this. Where is the perspective from which one can look at all the traditions and assert their commonality? I think there could be three responses.

First, there is a distant possibility that, like the nineteenth-century figure Ramakrishna Paramahamsa, one could experiment in different traditions for periods of time and conclude that the experiences in all were at their core the same; but that only puts the burden on the person concerned, for how do we rule out the idea that highly specific conceptual, cultural and psychological facts were in play? Ramakrishna himself could be said, quite fairly, to express a form of Hindu mystical tradition.

Alternatively, the argument could be a transcendental one, in the technical sense: only the (unseen, ultimate) commonality of truth among all apparently different religious traditions can explain the nature of religious experience. But religious experience is fantastically diverse, so it is difficult to see how it can be explained by appeal to a common truth.

Finally, there is the line of argument put forward by Engineer himself, that there is a set of values that any tradition claiming to be religious holds (or ought to hold – it is not clear which). Even if we grant that different traditions do espouse commitment to justice, love and the like, this only explains that all religions fulfil the same functions and are defined as religions by virtue of these commitments. This is not the same as saying that therefore all religions ultimately lead to the same truth. In fact, one could say it is quite the opposite: it is precisely because they lay claim to the same values but through different narratives that religions compete or clash with each other.

The second worry is theological. While Engineer cites such examples as the wonderful Dārā Shikūh to make the point that Hindu and Muslim theology can be reconciled, he does not adequately acknowledge that Dārā and others were extraordinarily creative in forming their own view of religious tradition. It is not only obscurantism that prompts objections to such new theologies. There is the very real exegetical question of taking traditions seriously. What the Upaniṣads mean by the concept of *brahman* has been debated over many centuries; Dārā's claim that the Upaniṣads were really talking of the Allah of the Qu'rān, while daring, does some considerable interpretative violence to the dense conceptual context of the Upaniṣads. Conversely, what it does to the understanding of Allah in the Qu'rān is even more striking.

Furthermore, while there is a strain in Hindu thought that devalues the role of imagery, it is not a major one. Dismissing the inescapable role of images in the overwhelming majority of Hindu lives as ludicrous simplicity is not a good way of going about establishing common ground. At the other end of theological reflexivity from popular Hindu practice, such key thinkers as Rāmānuja and Madhva

– founders of dominant schools of Vedānta – take the divine form to be of utmost importance. In general, Hindu thought, whether popular, mystical, devotional or philosophical, understands the divine to be accessible through qualities (*guṇa*s); and here, crucially, they take qualities not only to include love, knowledge, power, grace and the like, but also form. The Islamic disjunction between the abstract qualities (which are attributed to Allah) and the concrete ones (which are denied) is generally not made in Hinduism. Equally, the concept of *brahman* as the supreme principle of being that transcends all qualities renders moot the question of comparing it with any conception of God, for *brahman* – so conceived as beyond qualities – is as much beyond love and grace as form. By all means one can conceive of a theology that draws on Hindu and Islamic sources, but one should recognize that these involve taking great liberties with traditions taken as a whole.

The third worry is sociological and psychological. The religious dimension is highly explanatory in people's narratives of their lives; even when people pick and choose, change their commitments, transgress boundaries, shed beliefs or get unwittingly drawn into collective religious performances, they attach very specific value to the sacred that they sense in this dimension. As such, when they are told that the specific beliefs and actions to which they are committed are actually partial, illusory or otherwise not completely compelling, people do not as a rule take kindly to it. This is a pragmatic point. Of course, often people are at some stage of their lives when challenges transform them; but mostly, resistance to such challenges is the norm. So, if a key way to build bridges between Hindus and Muslims is to say that actually any differences they perceive are not ultimately real (and therefore not completely truthful), then we have an uphill task on our hands. Only those whose religious lives are already centred on the idea of commonality will accept this – but preaching to the converted is a mug's game . . .

I have taken some effort to delineate my worries, not because I do not wholeheartedly endorse Engineer's moral vision of a peaceful and pluralistic India (or the world) but because I am not sure that his narrative of ultimate commonality is the best way forward. Instead, I would suggest a more piecemeal and painful process of negotiating a pluralistic coexistence. In this, the issue is not whether religions are ultimately the same or not, but whether we can draw on our own traditions to find a way of living with others on their terms. Key to this will be to understand that we may not have the same truth commitments ultimately, but we can make many different commitments to the truth as we see it, at all times. We can try and see how our own commitments also allow us to give space to the commitments of others. This is what I have suggested towards the end of my own essay.

Part V

Islam and Buddhism

18. A Muslim View of Buddhism

MAJID TEHRANIAN

The 2001 Taliban destruction of the Buddha statutes in Bamiyan, Afghanistan, may have left no doubt in the public mind that Muslims do not approve of the Buddhist habit of venerating statutes. This essay attempts to set the record straight. Historically, Buddhism and Islam have been neighbours for centuries in Asia. They have heavily borrowed from each other. As a result, new religious traditions (for example, Sufism) have emerged that contain elements from both. Although many of the ideas in this paper are the result of my own spiritual search, and the influence of Sufism upon me, they may be relevant to a globalizing world that is bringing various religious traditions into greater contact, clash or dialogue.

This essay, first, provides an example of a Buddhist–Islamic dialogue in my own personal experience. Second, it reviews the need for that dialogue. Finally, it puts the Buddhist–Islamic dialogue in a historical perspective by examining Sufism as a bridge between the two religious traditions.

My Dialogue with Daisaku Ikeda

In 1996, I was approached by representatives from Soka Gakkai International (SGI), a Buddhist sect originating in Japan, to be the first director of a new peace research institute honouring their second president.

'Why me?' I responded.

'Because you are neither Japanese, nor a Buddhist, nor a member of SGI,' came the reply. 'We are trying to reach out to the rest of the world.'

That was music to my ears. In a world torn by profound religious differences, here was a religious group that wished to reach out to others. I accepted the offer, and we embarked on the organization of a research institute that came to be known as The Toda Institute for Global Peace and Policy Research.

Prior to this event, in 1992, I had the pleasure of meeting Daisaku Ikeda in Tokyo. Following Tsunesaburo Makiguchi and Josei Toda, Ikeda is the third president of SGI. In 1992, I was embarking on a long trip along the ancient Silk Road. I was taking a route directly opposite to the one that Marco Polo had taken in the thirteenth century. I was travelling from Honolulu to Tokyo, Kyoto, Beijing, Xian, Urumchi, Almaty, Dushanbe, Samarkand, Bukhara, Ashkhabad, Baku and Tehran.

At our first meeting, Ikeda and I entered into a dialogue about the Silk Road and its significance in Asian intercultural relations. He was highly informed about Asia and its cultural traditions. I suggested that we should enter into a more serious discussion on the theme of dialogue of civilizations. He readily agreed, and for the next eight years, we corresponded. The outcome was a book, *Global Civilization: A Buddhist-Islamic Dialogue*.[1] The book has now been translated into seven languages, Japanese, French, Italian, Thai, Persian, Malay and Chinese. It seems to have struck a respondent chord in Asia. It represents an awakened need for understanding among Asian civilizations.

Revolving around the land mass of Eurasia, the Old World is reasserting its place in history. China and India, the two most populous countries in the world, are fast industrializing. Following a period of experimentation with communism to build their necessary infrastructures, Russia and China have returned to commercial regimes in order to catch up with the digital West. Other smaller countries are similarly in the grip of social, economic, political and religious transformation. Such ancient religions as Hinduism, Buddhism, Christianity and Islam are responding to the spiritual needs of an atomized modern world. Under such circumstances, a dialogue among major religions and civilizations seems necessary if not inevitable.

Buddhism antedates Islam by some 1,000 years. Islam grew out of the Abrahamic traditions. Buddhism was born out of the Hindu

1 Daisaku Ikeda, Majid Tehranian, 2000, *Global Civilization: a Buddhist-Islamic Dialogue,* London: British Academic Press.

world. On the surface, the two religions seem to have little in common. Like Judaism and Christianity before it, Islam is primarily preoccupied with the monotheistic plans for the universe. By contrast, Buddhism does not very much concern itself with that issue. Buddhism is rather preoccupied with human suffering and how to alleviate it. The starting points of the two traditions are different, yet complementary. They are both concerned with human conditions of frailty, fragility and finitude.

We live in a secular world, but the hunger for religious faith seems to be on the ascendant. What are the origins of this hunger? It seems to me that the roots are to be found in the human condition. As our illnesses show, we are all fragile. Moreover, most of us fail to live up to our own ideals. And we all face the mathematical certainty of death. These conditions would be better accepted if we could believe in an invisible world. Most religions offer us that world-view. Isn't it ironic that a world-view designed to give solace to the human condition is today employed to sow discord?

The Need for Buddhist–Muslim Dialogue

My dialogue with a Buddhist leader focused on the emergence of a new phenomenon, namely a new civilization whose shape and contents are still in the process of formation. Because it encompasses the contributions of all previous civilizations, we chose to call this new civilization, Global Civilization. We tried to make the book that emerged from our dialogue accessible to all. After introducing Buddhism and Islam, the book takes up such global issues as religious resurgence, clash and dialogue of civilizations, global ethics, and the problems of war, peace and dialogue.

It was a great pleasure to collaborate with Ikeda in this enterprise. He has the gift of human communication at a level that is at once simple and complex. At the time, Professor Samuel Huntington had published his article (1993) and book (1996) on clash of civilizations. In the post-Cold War era, his thesis had found a ready audience in Washington, DC. The enemy was no longer communism, which was defeated after all. According to Huntington, the new struggle is between 'the West and the rest'. The terrorist act of 11 September 2001 seemed to confirm Huntington's thesis. Islam, in particular, seemed to be the historical enemy of the West. In the

Crusades, the Christian and Islamic worlds had crossed swords. In the modern world, the West had dominated and in many cases colonized the Islamic world. With the discovery of oil in the Middle East, the stakes were raised. From Mohammad Mossadeq in Iran to Gamal Abd El-Nasser in Egypt and Saddam Hussein in Iraq, the challenges against Western domination were continuing. They had to be stopped. The question was, how?

The first impulse was to respond to terrorism with counter-terrorism. But that response produced greater terrorism. Subsequently, a more spiritual and less violent response had to be found. The new Global Civilization demands a new faith. That faith has to transcend all existing faiths. An inter-faith dialogue is desirable. But in an age of imperial domination, can you have a genuine inter-faith dialogue? Yes, people of good will are sponsoring such a dialogue. And this is not the first time in history that constructive encounter between different faiths has taken place.

Sufism as a Bridge between Buddhism and Islam

The histories of Buddhism and Islam could not be any more different. Buddhism emerged in present-day Nepal out of a princely domain. The historical Buddha, Śākyamuni, is said to have been a prince who left his father's palace after he encountered the three human sufferings, illness, old age and death. After his Enlightenment he proclaimed a path along which human beings should find ultimate liberation. In its birthplace, India, Buddhism flourished for about 1,500 years but subsequently declined. However, it also spread north and east, to South East Asia, Central Asia, China, Korea, Japan, and now to the West. In Central Asia, its main political vehicle was the Kushan Dynasty, which ruled from North India to Central Asia from the second century BCE to the third century CE.

Buddhism more or less followed one of the most travelled routes of the Silk Road. It left behind such monuments as the statues of Buddha in the Bamiyan plain near Kabul. The tallest of these statues was 53 metres high, built into the mountainside in front of residential monasteries. In 1972, I was witness to this majestic sight. The statues were destroyed by the Taliban regime of Afghanistan in 2001. The Bamiyan plain used to be a Buddhist Mecca attracting Buddhist pilgrims from all over the Buddhist world in Asia. Afghanistan and Iran may have been partly Buddhist lands before the advent of Islam. The Barmakid family from Greater Khorasan were Buddhist before they converted to Islam. They acted as the first ministers for the 'Abbāsid court in the eighth century, but they were soon massacred. Some of the Ilkhanid[2] emperors, descendants of the Mongols, who controlled much of the region in the thirteenth century, were Buddhists before they became Muslims. As they looked to the West, they discovered a primarily Muslim constituency. Before the advent of Islam, Buddhism was thus a going concern in the Central Asian region.

Islam emerged out of totally different circumstances. Islam followed in the traditions of Judaism and Christianity. It came out of the Arabian Peninsula. Within the first 100 years of its birth, it had conquered a vast empire stretching from India to North Africa. Islam's appearance in a commercial oasis such as Mecca in a sea of nomadic civilization cast its character. Firmly in the tradition of the Hebrew prophets the Prophet Muḥammad based his new faith on the continuity of God's intervention in human history. From an Islamic view, there were some 42,000 prophets from Adam to Muḥammad sent by God to guide humanity. Islam has always accepted Moses and Jesus as two of the greatest of such prophets. I have argued elsewhere that Islam owed its success perhaps to the emergence of a commercial civilization in the Indian Ocean basin.[3] Others have argued that Islam tried but failed to conquer Europe because of contrary 'winds'.[4] 'Islamic culture proved almost as hard to spread against the wind as the Islamic conquest.'[5]

As it evolved, the new Islamic faith developed a body of law known as the *sharī'a*, based on the *Qur'ān*, the *Sunna* (the tradition of the Prophet and his four Rightly Guided successors), *qiyās* or analogy, *ra'y*, the individual judgement, and the consensus of the learned men of Islam known as the *'ulamā'*. The *sharī'a* was useful in the management of a vast empire. But it must have soon proved problematical.

---

2 'Ilkhanids', in Cyril Glasse (ed.), 1989, *The New Encyclopaedia of Islam*, 1989, New York: Roman & Littlefield Publishers, p. 211.

3 See Majid Tehranian, 2007, *Rethinking Civilization: Resolving Conflict in the Human Family*, London: Routledge.

4 Felipe Fernandez-Armesto, 2002, *Civilizations: Culture, Ambition, and the Transformation of Nature*, New York: Free Press, pp. 331–2.

5 Fernandez-Armesto, *Civilizations*, p. 332.

Some believers known as *Sufi* (wool wearers) emerged to question it. They juxtaposed the *ṭarīqah* (the Way) to the *sharī'a* as their creed. The tension between the *sharī'a* and the *ṭarīqah* has stayed with us. In some Islamic countries, it has led to the persecution of Sufis. In one well-known instance, it led to the execution of Husayn ibn Manṣūr Ḥallāj (244–309 AH in the Islamic calendar/857–922 CE in the Christian calendar). The 'Abbāsid police had allegedly found 'a great number of documents, written on Chinese paper, some of them in gold ink. Some were mounted on satin or silk, and bound in leather'.[6]

Whatever the truth of the matter, Ḥallāj has become a saint for many Sufi orders. He travelled far and wide, performed miracles, was allegedly heading a resistance movement, had followers in high places, and arguably declared himself God (*'anā al-ḥaqq*).[7] That expression may be translated as 'I am the truth,' or 'I am God.' Whichever, that made him a dangerous man. The Qarmatian revolt was under way. The Fatimid Dynasty was rising in Egypt. As a Persian, Ḥallāj also may have been suspected of sectarian (*shū'ubiyya*) sympathies. No wonder that the 'Abbāsids had to get rid of him on the pretext of defending Islamic orthodoxy.

The theological controversy between those who view God as transcendent and those who view Him as immanent was ripe in Islam as it has been in most religions. Ḥallāj was taking the side of immanence. He was following the qur'ānic verse that said God is as near to you as your jugular vein (50.16). He was also following in a tradition set by Mani (216–76/7 CE). He was probably expressing the more urbanized views of divinity vis-à-vis the more abstract, desert views. Our views of divinity seem to be profoundly affected by the natural environment we occupy. The views of God differ fundamentally among the people of the sea, deserts, jungles, prairies and congested urban environments.[8]

A word should be said about Mani and Manichaeism. Manichaeism has suffered a bad press in the West. It has been represented as a

---

6 'Sufism', in Cyril Glasse (ed.), 2002, *The New Encyclopedia of Islam*, Walnut Creek: Altamira, p. 164.

7 There is controversy as to what Ḥallāj meant. Strictly speaking, '*anā al-ḥaqq*' means 'I am the truth'. But some may view that statement to mean, 'I am the Truth', namely God.

8 See Fernandez-Armesto, *Civilizations*.

doctrine of extreme dualism between matter and spirit. But in religious history, Manichaeism seems to have bridged Zoroastrianism, Judaism, Christianity and Buddhism. According to the *Berkshire Encyclopedia of World History*:

> Manichaeism was a religion founded in Mesopotamia during the first half of the third century CE that incorporated aspects of Zoroastrianism, Judaism, Christianity, and Buddhism. It was the only sect emerging from the Near Eastern Gnostic traditions to survive beyond the first three centuries CE and to attain global status. At various points in medieval times, its influence extended from France to China and its popularity rivalled that of Catholic Christianity and Buddhism. While almost universally attacked by the mainstream religious traditions of the West, the teachings of Manichaeism came to shape debates with Judaism, Christianity, Islam concerning the nature of good, evil, humans, and the world.[9]

For some ten years, Manichaeism was the religion of St Augustine before he converted to orthodox Christianity. According to *The Encyclopaedia Britannica* ('St. Augustine'), Manichaeism was known as a Christian sect. It penetrated the Roman Empire all the way to North Africa where St Augustine was born. The conversion of St Augustine had practical consequences. It allied him with the Eastern Roman emperors and religious orthodoxy.

Enough has been said to illustrate that mutual influence and constructive encounters among religions and civilizations have been going on for centuries. All religions seem to be an outcome of such interaction.

Sufism's Principal Doctrines

As the intellectual fruit of the human condition, religions respond to that condition. Sufism is no exception. In Islam, Sufism represents a reaction against the excessive emphasis on the *sharīʿa*, the letter of the law, as opposed to the spirit of the law, the *ṭarīqah*. However,

9 William H. McNeill, et al. (eds), 2005, *Berkshire Encyclopedia of World History*, Great Barrington, MA: Berkshire Publishing Group, p. 1179.

Sufism is also heir to the Zoroastrian, Platonic, Semitic, Hindu and Buddhist Gnostic traditions. The genius of the Sufi poets and philosophers is to have synthesized these traditions into a practical way of life. Briefly, the central features of Sufism can be summarized as follows:

Tawḥīd Borrowed from its Semitic sources, the emphasis on *waḥdat al-wujūd* is central to an understanding of Sufism. The Sufi believes that God's manifestations in nature are infinite and unique. In one of his celebrated poems, Rūmī seems to come close to the Hindu–Buddhist doctrine of reincarnation. He argues that because he has a chance to elevate himself in the hierarchy of being, death does not diminish him. But beyond diversity in nature, the Sufi also believes in the unity of God. This belief puts Sufism at peace with all monotheistic religions.

Love The Sufi's ultimate desire is *fanā bi'llah* (death in God) in order to achieve *baqā bi'llah* (immortality in God). God's manifestations in the visible universe are infinite. He is manifested in the inner life of the self. The kingdom of God is within you. But the Sufi must emancipate himself from his own ego standing between him or her and God. Achieving the death of selfhood (*fanā bi'llah*), the Sufi can attain *baqā bi'llah* (immortality in God). For Rūmī, death was devoutly to be wished, because it united him with God. He called his own death the Bridal Night (*shab-i 'arūs*) and had it celebrated by music and dancing.

The Sufis believe that 'love' provides the bridge between the individual and what Paul Tillich has called 'the ultimate ground of being'. Love is the cornerstone of all human relations with their environments. Love transforms the entire universe. Rūmī sings, 'It is love that stirs the wine; it is love that blows music in the reed.' In the Sufi view, wine and music are thus manifestations of the divine.

The Way (Ṭarīqah) The Sufi believes in the natural spirituality of all humanity. But each individual has to travel his or her own road. Some have divided the road into seven stages. The Bahā'ī prophet, Bahā'u'llāh, has written a book modelled after Aṭṭār's *manṭiq al-ṭayr* ('The Logic of the Birds').[10] It conceives of the seven valleys,

10 In modern Persian, *manṭiq* translates into 'logic'. However, as Sheila and Amin Banani say, Aṭṭār's work is usually referred to as the 'Conference

including the valleys of search, love, knowledge, unity, contentment, wonderment and nothingness.[11] Each of these valleys has its own demands and rigours. Others have conceived of only three paths, including *makhāfah* (fear), *maḥabbah* (love) and *ma'rifah* (knowledge). This corresponds to the Vedāntine ternary *karma* (action), *bhakti* (devotion) and *jñāna* (knowledge).[12]

The Pīr Each individual's spiritual journey is best guided by a *pīr*, a teacher or a guru, who has gone through them.

The Khānqāh Without denying the sanctity of the mosque, the Sufi religious life is focused on the *khānqāh*. That opens the door to the diversity of Sufi orders or brotherhoods. Such orders have played an important role in the bonds of community and power politics. For example, the Sanūsiī Dynasty in Libya and the Ṣafavid Dynasty in Iran emerged out of Sufi orders.

Poverty The concept of poverty here has a layered meaning. On the surface, it means that the Sufi is inattentive to the material aspects of life. Sufism began as an ascetic way of life. The typical dervish carries a begging bowl. That may have been borrowed from the begging bowls carried by Buddhist monks. More generally, however, poverty implies an abandonment of the trappings of the ego.

Fanā' bi'llah The ultimate purpose of the Sufi is the dissolution of his or her own ego into the vast ocean of being. That may or may not be compared to the Buddhist doctrine of *nirvāṇa*. As with *fanā'* the literal meaning of *nirvāṇa* is 'fading out'. The term *nirvāṇa* often

---

of the Birds'. Dick Davis has done an outstanding translation (in verse) into English published as a Penguin Classics volume. Bahā'u'llāh's work is entitled in English 'The Seven Valleys'. It doesn't coincide with Aṭṭar's sequence of 'valleys'. His work was written to answer specific questions. Bahā'u'llāh writes that since God is an 'unknowable essence', human beings cannot 'know' God or the Divine directly. Cf. Farid al-Din Attar, 1984, *The Conference of the Birds*, translated with an introduction by Afkham Darbandi and Dick Davis, New York: Penguin Books.

11 In Persian, the seven valleys are called *ṭalab, eshq, ma'rifat, istighnā', taḥīd, ḥayrat, faqr* and *fanā'*. See Said Naficy, 1377/1998, *Sarchishma-yi taṣawwuf dar irān: taṣawwuf-i irān az nażar-i falsafī* ('The Origins of Sufism in Iran: Sufism from a Philosophical Perspective'), Tehran: Intishārāt-i furūqī, p. 118.

12 *The New Encyclopedia of Islam*, 2002, p. 438.

refers to Enlightenment or total understanding. But it may be also considered as godhood or an unconditioned reality. What is 'fading out' are the three Buddhist vices: greed, hatred and delusion.[13] In Buddhism, enlightenment happens when and if the individual has renounced all attachment to the material world. 'The aim of Buddhist practice is to be rid of the delusion of ego and thus free oneself from the fetters of this mundane world. One who is successful in doing so is said to have overcome the round of rebirths and to have achieved enlightenment.'[14] In contrast to Islam, which seems to be focused on historical success, Buddhism seems to consider freedom from *saṃsāra* (the cycles of birth and rebirth) as the beginning of *nirvāṇa*. The Sufis' goal of overcoming one's ego and their spiritual understanding of 'poverty' in the sense of non-attachment to the material aspects of life show an affinity to Buddhist spirituality. And on the other hand, Buddhism has developed its own ways of responsible action in and for the world. Particularly in Mahāyāna Buddhism it is affirmed that Nirvāṇa is ultimately not different from *saṃsāra*.

Music and dance The Western world knows Sufism via the Whirling Dervishes. This group goes back to the Mowlavi Order, which allowed music and dancing as channels for spiritual growth. In Orthodox Islam, music and dance are arguably prohibited. Sufism, and the Whirling Order in particular, brought back music and dance as spiritual pursuits. The Whirling Dervishes move in a circular motion parallel to the circular motion of the Cosmos. They emulate the heavenly bodies and collapse finally in utter ecstasy. Dance is thus practised as a special form of meditation or contemplation.

Poetry The greatest contribution of the Sufis is perhaps in their poetry. Most poetry in Persian, and some in Arabic, Turkish and Urdu, is imbued with Sufi enthusiasm. It is hazardous to name any specific poets. I mention only those that I have read and appreciated personally: 'Aṭṭār, Rūmī, Sa'adī, Ḥāfiż, and Suhrāb Sipihrī. Among these poets, Rūmī is the best known in the West. Embodying Sufi

---

13 P. Schmidt-Leukel, 2006, *Understanding Buddhism* (Edinburgh: Dunedin Academic Press), pp. 48ff.

14 Cf. 'Buddhism', in *Encyclopaedia Britannica*, 2006, http://www.britannica.com/eb/article-68656.

doctrines, Rūmī is perhaps the greatest. Living in the 13th century and travelling from Balkh in present-day Afghanistan to Konya in Turkey, he was initially a respected judge in the Saljuq Empire's capital. But according to legend, after meeting a dervish by the name of Sham ad-Dīn Tabrīzī, he experienced a spiritual transformation. His poetry took on a much more lyrical tone, but it also revealed his command of the sciences of his time. He combines Islamic beliefs with Greek, Persian, Hindu and Buddhist knowledge.

Conclusion

Our age has been called the Age of Globalization. This is a mixed blessing. For the first time in human history, different peoples and civilizations are coming into direct contact. The encounters are not always pleasant or harmonious. We need the wisdom of the great spiritual traditions to guide us through these perilous times. I have tried to show that two such great traditions, Buddhism and Islam, have been historically in communication for many centuries. Out of their interaction, Sufism, the mystical form of Islam, received strong inspiration and shows various affinities to Buddhism. But mysticism is present in all great religious traditions. The esoteric and exoteric have lived side by side. In Judaism, there is the Kabbalah. In Christianity, Meister Eckhart is the greatest known Christian mystic. In Islam, Rūmī is best known to most of the world. Taoism in China seems to convey its best mystical traditions. Buddhism also has had its own mystical path.

> Buddhist mysticism (including the philosophical school of Chan), like other forms of mysticism, insists on the ineffability of the mystical experience, because it is not intelligible to anyone who has not had a similar experience. Mystical knowledge is not intellectual but is 'felt knowledge' that views things in a different perspective and gives them new significance. The experience is both ineffable and timeless, which means that the mystic seems to be outside time and space, oblivious to his surroundings and the passage of time.[15]

---

15 'Buddhism', in *Encyclopedia Britannica*, 2006, http://www.britannica.com/eb/article-68656.

Together with the ethical and spiritual values that Buddhism and Islam have in common, mysticism seems to be the place where Buddhism and Islam come fairly close and where, at the same time, they transcend the boundaries of their different religious identities. In this sense the following verses, ascribed to Rūmī, have a message for our times:[16]

What shall I say, O Muslims?
I know not myself.
I am neither a Christian, nor a Jew,
Nor a Zoroastrian, nor a Muslim.
Neither of the East, nor of the West,
Nor of the desert, nor of the sea
Neither from the land, nor of the sky.
Neither of the earth, nor of water,
Nor of wind, nor of fire.
Neither of the high, nor of low,
Nor of space, nor of time,
Neither an Indian, nor Chinese
Nor Bulghar, nor Saksin
Neither of Iraq, nor of Khorasan
Neither of this world, nor of the next
Nor of paradise, nor of hell.
Neither of Adam, nor of Eve
My Place is the placeless
My sign is the signless
There is neither a body nor a soul.
For I am of the Beloved.

16 Dīwān-ī Shams-i Tabrīz no. 31. Rūmī's authorship is debated.

19. A Buddhist View of Islam

ALEXANDER BERZIN

With concern about the problems of globalization and global warming becoming increasingly widespread, the importance of what His Holiness the Fourteenth Dalai Lama calls 'universal responsibility'[1] is becoming increasingly evident. Sustainable development, and even survival, depends on nations, cultures, religions and individual persons taking shared responsibility to try to solve these universal problems. One of the most essential bases for such co-operation is mutual understanding. Through education about other cultures, we may hopefully avoid the disastrous effects of any possible future 'clash of civilizations'.[2]

Two such civilizations are the Buddhist and Islamic worlds. Over history, the two civilizations have interacted in both constructive and problematic ways. When they have clashed, religious doctrine may have been used to rally the troops. But deeper analysis shows that the motives behind the conflicts have centred primarily on economical, political and strategic military issues.

At present, there are very few areas in the world where traditional Buddhist and Islamic groups are living together. In some of those regions where they do intermix – such as Tibet, Ladakh and southern Thailand – the interaction is so strongly affected by the actions of other cultural and national groups that one cannot meaningfully isolate specific Buddhist–Muslim issues outside of their wider context. In others, such as Malaysia and Indonesia, the Buddhist population consists of overseas Chinese, and the interaction between

1 Bhikshu Tenzin Gyatso, the Fourteenth Dalai Lama, 1980, *Universal Responsibility and the Good Heart*, Dharamsala, India: Library of Tibetan Works and Archives.

2 Samuel Huntington, 1996, *The Clash of Civilizations and the Remaking of World Order*, New York: Simon & Schuster.

them and the native Muslims is primarily dictated by economic factors. In short, religious doctrinal differences seem to play little role in present-day Buddhist–Islamic relations.

What, then, is the purpose of fostering Buddhist–Muslim dialogue? Doctrinal differences between the two religions will always be there and, of course, these need to be known and acknowledged so as not to cause inadvertent offence. However, by discovering and affirming shared basic human values – such as the facts that everyone wishes to be happy and not to suffer, and that all of us are interconnected – members of all communities, not only the Buddhist and Muslim ones, can pool their resources and focus their efforts on trying to solve pressing issues of global concern.

Here, we shall briefly survey the history of Buddhist–Muslim interaction during the first millennium after the Prophet,[3] focusing on the level of knowledge that the Indo-Tibetan Buddhist tradition has had of Islam, and the points that it has identified as being either harmonious or problematic.[4] The problematic points indicate some of the issues that require mutual tolerance so as to avoid any rejection of cooperation. The common points, on the other hand, suggest some of the positive foundations that can be strengthened for building mutual respect and coordination of efforts.

Historical Survey of the Interaction between the Buddhist and Islamic Worlds

Śākyamuni Buddha lived in north central India from 566 to 485 BCE, while Muḥammad lived in Arabia from 570 to 632 CE. Thus, for most of its formative years in India, Buddhist literature contains no

---

3 For a fuller discussion, cf. Alexander Berzin, *The Historical Interaction between the Buddhist and Islamic Cultures before the Mongol Empire*, http://www.berzinarchives.com/cms/en/archives/e-books/unpublished_manuscripts/historical_interaction/pt1/history_cultures_01.html

4 It is beyond the scope of this paper to include an account of the interaction between the two religions during the Il-Khānate period in Iran when, between 1256 and 1295 CE, the Mongol rulers there patronized and spread Tibetan Buddhism before their conversion to Islam. Also omitted is an analysis of the Uyghur Buddhist response to the progress of Islam in their domain in East Turkistan (present-day Xinjiang, China) between the eleventh and fourteenth centuries CE.

references to Islam or to its teachings. However, even after the time of the Prophet, Buddhist sources make only scant reference to the tenets of the Islamic faith. Any interaction that occurred between the two peoples was based on very little knowledge of each other's beliefs.

Buddhists under Umayyad and ʻAbbāsid rule

During the early centuries following the time of the Buddha, Buddhist teachings had spread from the Indian subcontinent to present-day Afghanistan, eastern Iran, Uzbekistan, Turkmenistan and Tajikistan. Both lay and monastic Buddhist communities flourished there. When, starting three decades after the time of the Prophet, these regions came under Arab Islamic rule with the Umayyad and then the ʻAbbāsid Caliphates, the Buddhists there received *dhimmī* status. This meant that, as non-Muslims, they were allowed to follow their own religion, but the laypeople among them were required to pay an extra poll-tax. The few persecutions that did occur were short-lived, and the Buddhists were allowed to rebuild any of their monasteries that had been destroyed. The Buddhist community living with *dhimmī* status, however, does not appear to have taken any interest in or to have written about Islam.

Many Buddhists in these areas also converted to Islam during this period. The reasons for their conversion varied from region to region and person to person. It appears, however, that the main factors were economic and political incentives, rather than because of religious conviction or conversion by the sword. There do not seem to be any written accounts by these converts explaining the reasons – doctrinal or other – for their conversion.

Buddhist scholars in Baghdad

The earliest serious contact between Buddhist and Muslim scholars began in the mid eighth century CE, during the ʻAbbāsid period. At that time, Caliph al-Manṣūr constructed in Baghdad a House of Knowledge[5] for the study and translation of literature from the Greek and Indian cultural worlds, particularly concerning scientific

5 Ar. *Bayt al-Ḥikmat*.

topics. As part of this programme, his son, Caliph al-Mahdī, invited Buddhist scholars from India and from the huge Nava Vihāra monastery in Balkh, Afghanistan.

It is difficult to say that the Buddhist monks in Baghdad were actually formally associated with the House of Knowledge. However, it seems that they did have discussions at that time with Islamic scholars. Evidence for this comes from *The Book of Religions and Creeds*,[6] a treatise on Islamic heresies, in which the twelfth-century Ismā'īlī theologian, al-Shahrastānī, gives a brief account of the image the Islamic scholars of that time had of Buddhism. As their main interest lay in Greek thought, however, their study of Buddhism was not in depth.[7]

Correspondingly, the Buddhist scholars in Baghdad seemed to have shown little interest in Islamic doctrines. Although the monks at the Buddhist monastic universities at that time in present-day Afghanistan and the Indian subcontinent vigorously debated the assertions of the various non-Buddhist Indian tenet systems, there is no evidence that any debates occurred with Muslim scholars. No mention of Islamic beliefs appears in any of the Sanskrit Buddhist philosophical treatises, either then or afterwards.

The destruction of Buddhist monasteries on the Indian subcontinent

Many Buddhist monasteries were destroyed during the various invasions of the Indian subcontinent, first by Umayyad forces in the first half of the eighth century CE and then by the armies of assorted Islamic Turkic vassal states under the 'Abbāsids from the early eleventh to the mid thirteenth century CE. The monasteries did not recover from this destruction and, although many Buddhists on the subcontinent subsequently converted to Islam, the majority became absorbed into the general Hindu population.

The Turkic invasions appear to have been motivated primarily by considerations of military, political and economic gain, rather

6 Ar. *Kitāb al-Milal wa al-Nihal*.

7 Dr Hamid Tahir (Dean of Dar al-'Ulūm Faculty of Islamic Sciences, Cairo University), private discussion with author (Cairo, Egypt, 3 October 1996).

than by religious zeal. Nevertheless, one cannot dismiss the descriptions, found in Muslim, Buddhist and Western historical accounts, of the atrocities and religious fanaticism that occurred during these campaigns. Regardless of what the motives for the destruction might have been, the Buddhist literature of the time does not reveal any further information about the Buddhist view of the Islamic teachings.

Muslims in Tibet under the Fifth Dalai Lama

Because of widespread famine in their homeland in the mid seventeenth century CE, a group of Kashmiri Muslim immigrants settled in Lhasa, Tibet, during the political reign of the Fifth Dalai Lama. As part of his policy of religious tolerance, the Fifth Dalai Lama granted the Muslims special privileges. He granted them land for a mosque and a cemetery, permitted them to elect a five-member committee to supervise their internal affairs, allowed them to settle their own disputes independently according to the *sharī'a* laws, and exempted them from tax. Although these privileges indicate Buddhist respect for the autonomy of the Muslim community in Tibet, they give no indication that any inter-faith dialogue took place at those times.[8]

Conclusion

The conclusion that can be drawn from this survey is that, although the Indo-Tibetan Buddhist world had both peaceful and problematic contact with the Islamic world on many occasions over the first millennium following the Prophet, there was hardly any Buddhist interest in learning about the teachings of Islam.

---

8 Cf. Alexander Berzin, *Historical Sketch of the Muslims of Tibet*, http://www.berzinarchives.com/cms/en/archives/study/islam/historical_interaction/overviews/history_muslims_tibet.html

The Kālacakra Literature as the Source for the Classical Buddhist View of Islam

The only place where Buddhist reference to the Islamic doctrines appears during this period is in the Sanskrit Kālacakra literature.[9] Kālacakra, meaning cycles of time, is a Mahāyāna Buddhist system of tantric practice for gaining enlightenment to be able to benefit all beings as much as is possible. It describes three parallel cycles of time: external, internal and alternative. The external cycles refer to planetary motion, astrological patterns and historical cycles, including periodic invasions by foreign forces. When speaking of these invasions, the basic texts address themselves to a Hindu audience. Internal cycles refer to biological and psychological rhythms. Alternative cycles are repetitive meditation practices aimed at overcoming being under the control of the external and internal cycles.

The Islamic references in the Kālacakra literature most likely emerged partially in the Buddhist monasteries of present-day eastern Afghanistan and partially in the homeland of tantra, Oḍḍiyāna (north-western Pakistan), during the tenth century CE. Both regions were under Hindu Shāhi rule at that time.[10] By the end of that century, this literature reached the Indian subcontinent, where, in Kashmir, it was probably conflated with the experiences of the Ghaznavid invasions (1001–1025 CE). Shortly thereafter, this literature was transmitted to Tibet; however, it has always remained a relatively minor feature of the Indo-Tibetan Buddhist tradition. Thus, one must keep a proper perspective concerning the prevalence of Buddhist knowledge of Islamic thought. For the most part, Buddhists have remained uninformed about the Islamic teachings.

---

9 For a general introduction to Kālacakra and its literature, see Geshe Lhundup Sopa, Roger Jackson and John Newman, 1985, *The Wheel of Time: The Kālacakra in Context*, Madison, Wisconsin: Deer Park Books.

10 Cf. Alexander Berzin, *Historical Sketch of Buddhism and Islam in Afghanistan*, http://www.berzinarchives.com/cms/en/archives/study/islam/historical_interaction/detailed_histories/history_afghanistan_buddhism.html

The Ismā'īlīs of Multān as the primary form of Islam referred to in the Kālacakra literature

To avoid misunderstanding the past Buddhist view of Islam, it is important to identify the form of Islam that the Kālacakra literature describes. The texts are not referring to Islam as a whole and certainly not to Islam as it is understood and practised in its wide range of forms today. The texts speak, more specifically, of a foreign people who, in the future, will threaten an invasion of the kingdom of Shambhala – the mountainous land in which the Kālacakra teachings flourish. From the description of the beliefs of these future invaders, they appear to be followers of the early eastern Ismā'īlī Shī'ite tradition.

The main evidence supporting this hypothesis comes from *The Regal Abridged Kālacakra Tantra*[11] I.153. This verse presents a list of the eight prophets of the future invaders:

> Adam, Noah, Abraham, and five others – Moses, Jesus, the White-Clad One, Muhammad, and Mahdi . . . The eighth will be the blinded one. The seventh will manifestly come to the city of Baghdad in the land of Mecca, (the place) in this world where a portion of the *asura* (caste) will have the form of the powerful, merciless *mlecchas*.[12]

This list is the standard Ismā'īlī list of seven prophets, with the addition of the White-Clad One. It can be argued that the White-Clad One is Mani, the third-century CE founder of Manichaeism. However, although early Ismā'īlī thinkers might have had some

11 Skt. *Laghu-kālacakra-tantra-rāja* (Tib. *bsDus-pa'i rgyud-kyi rgyal-po dus-kyi 'khor-lo*) or, as given in the *sDe-dge bsTan-'gyur*, vol. 11, 1A, Skt. *Śrīmad-ādibuddhoddhṛta-śrīkālacakra-nāma-tantra-rāja* (Tib. *mChog-gi dang-po'i sangs-rgyas-las phung-ba rgyud-kyi rgyal-po dpal dus-kyi 'khor-lo*). Biswanath Banerjee (ed.), 1985, *A Critical Edition of Śrī Kālacakratantra-rāja (Collated with the Tibetan Version)*, Biblioteca Indica, Series 311, Calcutta: The Asiatic Society, p. 39.

12 For a fuller analysis, see Alexander Berzin, *The Kalachakra Presentation of the Prophets of the Non-Indic Invaders, Full Analysis*, http://www.berzinarchives.com/cms/en/archives/study/islam/kalachakra_islam/kalachakra_presentation_prophets_in/kc_pres_prophets_islam_full.html

Manichaean influence from so-called 'Manichaean Islam',[13] Ismā'īlī theologians have concurred with the general Islamic condemnation of Manichaeism as a heresy.

One possible reason for the Kālacakra list of prophets numbering eight is to make a parallel with the eight incarnations of Viṣṇu enumerated in the immediately preceding verse (I.152). In Buddhist cosmology, the asuras, a type of jealous demigods, are rivals of the Hindu gods and always wage war against them. If there are eight incarnations of the Hindu god Viṣṇu, then there would need to be eight *asura* prophets to vie against them. Another explanation, according to an early Indian commentary to the verse, *A Commentary on Difficult Points Called 'Padmani'*,[14] is that the White-Clad One is another name for Muḥammad. In any case, the Sanskrit terms that the Kālacakra literature uses to refer to the followers of these prophets help us to postulate the location of this Ismā'īlī group. It would appear that they are the Ismā'īlīs of Multān, situated in northern Sindh, present-day Pakistan, during the second half of the tenth century CE. This is suggested by the reference to the followers of the prophets as members of the *asura* caste.

The Kālacakra literature regularly refers to the invaders as *mleccha*, the traditional Sanskrit name given to foreign invaders of the Indian subcontinent, starting with Alexander the Great and including the Kushans and the Hepthalite Huns. The term connotes people speaking unintelligible non-Indic languages. Mleccha are characterized by their merciless invading armies. The other main term used for the invaders is '*Tāyi*', a Sanskrit phonetic transcription of the Arabic *taiy* (plural: *tayayah*, *tayyāyē*) or the Persian form of it, *tāzī*. The Tayayah were the strongest of the pre-Muslim Arab tribes, the Tayy'id, and '*Tāzī*' became the Persian word for Arabs. '*Tāzī*' was the term used in reference to the Arab invaders of Iran, for example, by the last Sāssānid ruler, Yazdgerd III.[15]

The Kingdom of Multān was a vassal state of the Ismā'īlī Fātimid

13 Marshall G. S. Hodgson, 1974, *The Venture of Islam: Conscience and History in a World Civilization*, vol. 1, *The Classical Age of Islam*, Chicago: University of Chicago Press.

14 Skt. *Padmani-nāma-pañjika* (Tib. *Padma-can zhes-bya-ba'i dka'-'grel*), *sDe-dge bsTan-'gyur*, vol. 13, 135B.

15 Cf. 'Letter from Yazdgird III', http://www.bozorgbazgasht.com/yazdgird.html

Empire, centred in Egypt. Surrounding the crumbling 'Abbāsid Empire on both sides, the Fātimids and their Multānese vassals posed a serious threat of invasion in their quest for supremacy over the Islamic world. Thus, it is reasonable that the foreign invaders mentioned in the Kālacakra texts refer to these Multānese Ismā'īlīs. That conclusion correlates with the postulation that the Kālacakra literature originated in the Afghan and Oḍḍiyāna regions under Hindu Shāhi rule, sandwiched between Multān and the 'Abbāsid regions at that time.

The Kālacakra Description of the Tāyi beliefs

The Kālacakra texts mention some of the customs and beliefs of the Tāyi *mlecchas*. Most of these beliefs are fundamental to Islam as a whole. Some seem to be specific to the Ismā'īlī thought of the time, while others contradict that thought. This discrepancy perhaps indicates that the compilers of the Kālacakra literature had incomplete information about Ismā'īlī beliefs held in Multān, and therefore filled in their account with information gleaned from other forms of Islam they had met. Alternatively, it could indicate that the theological views expressed by the main Ismā'īlī thinker of the time – Abū Ya'qūb al-Sijistānī,[16] a strong supporter of the Fatimid state – were not yet widely disseminated in Multān. This could have been the case, although al-Sijistānī's works were the official Fatimid doctrine prevalent at that time in the eastern Ismā'īlī regions.[17]

In any case, we must be careful not to mistake the Kālacakra description of the Tāyi beliefs as representing the view of all of Islam by the entire Buddhist population of Asia throughout history. The description is limited to a specific place, at a specific time, within a specific politico-historical context. Nevertheless, the Kālacakra accounts are relevant because, to this author's knowledge, they are the only classical Buddhist texts that address any Islamic beliefs. Thus, they are unique as primary sources that actually reveal a classical Buddhist view of Islam.

16 Lived mid to late tenth-century CE.

17 Cf. Farhad Daftary, 1990, *The Isma'ilis: Their History and Doctrines*, Cambridge: Cambridge University Press, pp. 240 ff.

Creation and obedience to Allah

The *Regal Abridged Kālacakra Tantra* (II.164cd) states:

> Created by the Creator is everything that arises, moving and unmoving. From pleasing him, as the cause for liberation for the Tāyis, there is heaven. This is indeed the teaching of Rahman for men.

Puṇḍarīka elaborates in *Stainless Light: A Commentary Explaining 'The Regal Abbreviated Kālacakra Tantra'*,[18]

> Now, as for the assertions of the Tāyi *mlecchas*, the creator Rahman[19] gives rise to every functional phenomenon, both moving and unmoving. The cause for liberation for the Tāyis, namely the white-clad *mlecchas*,[20] is pleasing Rahman, and this definitely brings a higher rebirth (in Paradise) for men. From not pleasing him, comes (a rebirth in) Hell. These are the teachings of Rahman, the assertions of the Tāyis.

According to al-Sijistānī, Allah, through His command or word, created the universal 'intellect'. The universal 'intellect' is an eternal, motionless, unchanging and perfect primal being. It is an undifferentiated universal encompassing everything and is somewhat like a universal 'mind,' but in the form of a being. The universal 'intellect' emanated a universal 'soul,' which is likewise eternal, but is always in motion and is imperfect. Within the universal 'soul', the physical world of nature emerges. The universal 'soul' has two contrary dispositions: movement and rest. Within physical reality, movement creates form and rest creates matter. Matter remains inert and static, while its forms are continually in motion and changing.[21]

---

18 Skt. *Vimalaprabhā-nāma-laghu-kālacakra-tantra-rāja-ṭīkā* (Tib. *bsDus-pa'i rgyud-kyi rgyal-po dus-kyi 'khor-lo'i 'grel-bshad dri-ma med-pa'i 'od*), *sDe-dge bsTan-'gyur*, vol. 12, 20A-B.

19 Arabic for 'compassionate one', and epithet of Allah.

20 The reference to the Tāyis as being clad in white may perhaps refer to Muslim pilgrims wearing simple white robes during the Hajj to Mecca.

21 Cf. Paul E. Walker, 1993, *Early Philosophical Shi'ism: The Ismaili Neoplatonism of Abu Ya'qub al-Sijistani*, Cambridge: Cambridge University Press, pp. 81 ff. Cf. also, Daftary, *The Isma'ilis*, pp. 241 ff.

Thus, it is perhaps in reference to al-Sijistānī's explanation of creation that *The Regal Abridged Kālacakra Tantra* notes: 'Created by the Creator is everything that arises, moving and unmoving.' Although the concepts of a universal 'intellect' and a universal 'soul' have remained prominent in Ismā'īlī thought, they do not occur in other forms of Islam.

Al-Sijistānī, however, does not assert pleasing Allah – in the general Islamic sense of obeying the *sharī'a* laws or, in the general Shi'ite and later Ismā'īlī sense, of acknowledging the infallibility of the line of imāms – as the cause for 'a higher rebirth in Paradise'. His explanation of the cause for going to Paradise is quite different.

For al-Sijistānī, the universal 'soul' gives rise to individual, particular souls that descend into the physical world of matter and form. Within each particular individual human being, the individual soul appropriates an individual portion of the universal 'intellect', which is thus partial and limited. The cause for going to Paradise is an individual soul's discrimination whereby it turns away from the delights of the physical world and turns, instead, toward the pure realm of the universal 'intellect.' In doing so, an individual soul learns the distinction between truth and falsity, and between good and bad.[22]

Circumcision, the Ramadan fast and halāl

Puṇḍarīka, in *The Glorious Deepest Service*,[23] explains:

> According to others, the cause for a higher rebirth (in Paradise) is having the skin from the tip of one's own penis cut off and eating at the end of the day and the beginning of the night. This is certainly what the Tāyis do. They do not enjoy the flesh of cattle that have died (a natural death) by their own karma. Rather, they eat those that have been slaughtered. Otherwise, there is no going to a higher rebirth (in Paradise) for men.

Puṇḍarīka amplifies the second part of this line in *Stainless Light*:[24]

> With a cleaver, they slit the throats of cattle with the *mleccha*

22 Walker, *Early Philosophical Shi'ism*, pp. 95 ff.

23 Skt. *Śrīparamārtha-sevā* (Tib. *dPal don-dam-pa'i bsnyen-pa*), *sDe-dge bsTan-'gyur*, vol. 13, 17B.

24 *sDe-dge bsTan-'gyur*, vol. 11, 129A.

> God's mantra *Bishimilla*,[25] and then eat the flesh of those cattle that have been slaughtered with their God's mantra. They do not eat the flesh of those that have died (a natural death) by their own karma.

These passages indicate the general Islamic customs of circumcision, eating only after sunset during the Ramadan fast, and obeying the injunctions concerning the restrictions of the ḥalāl dietary laws.

Ethics, prayer and injunction against statues of God

In *The Essence of the Further Tantra of the Glorious Kālacakra Tantra*,[26] it is stated:

> In keeping with the teachings of those whose women wear veils . . . the hordes of Tāyi horsemen destroy in battle any statues of gods there may be, without exception. They have one caste, do not steal, and speak the truth. They keep clean, avoid others' wives, follow definite ascetic practices, and remain faithful to their own wives. (First) having washed themselves, then, at an individually desired time during the pitch-black night and at noon, twilight, mid-afternoon, and when the sun rises over the mountains, the Tāyi non-Buddhists[27] pay homage five times (each day), prostrating on the ground facing their holy land and taking singular refuge in the 'Lord of Those with *Tamas*'[28] in the heavenly realm above the earth.

Here, the Kālacakra text also explains beliefs common to all Muslims: not making 'idolatrous' statues, honouring the equality of all men in Islam, keeping strict ethics and praying five times a day.

---

25 Ar. *Bismillah*, 'in the name of Allah'.

26 Skt. *Śrī-kālacakra- tantrottaratantra-hṛdaya* (Tib. *dPal dus-kyi 'khor-lo'i rgyud phyi-ma rgyud-kyi snying-po*), *sDe-dge bKa'-'gyur*, vol. 77, 141B.

27 Skt. *tīrthika*.

28 According to *The Regal Abbreviated Kālacakra Tantra*, I.153, the prophets Moses, Jesus, Mani, Muḥammad and Mahdī are 'Those with the *Tamas*.' *Tamas* is one the three constituent features (Skt. *triguṇa*) into which the Indian Sāṃkhya philosophical system divides the universe.

Problematic points mentioned in the Kālacakra texts

The Kālacakra literature points out two problematic features of the Tāyi teachings that might prevent religious harmony. It is significant, however, that the literature does not indicate that these problematic features will be the causes for a future invasion by the Tāyi forces. Invasions are a periodic occurrence in the Kālacakra vision of cycles of time, and are to be understood as mirroring and representing periodic invasions of each person's mind by disturbing emotions and attitudes.[29] Moreover, neither of the problematic points is unique to Multanese Ismā'īlī thought, let alone to Islam in general. They are points shared by other religions as well.

Sacrificial slaughter of animals

The first feature that the Kālacakra texts find problematic was also found among the Hindus of the time. The problem concerns the slaughter of cattle in the name of the Tāyi god, Bismillah. Thus, Puṇḍarīka, in *Stainless Light*,[30] mistakenly takes the ḥalāl method of slaughter to signify a sacrifice to God, similar to the Vedic ritual. Addressing himself to a Hindu audience, Puṇḍarīka states, 'You will consider that (Tāyi) teaching to be valid, because of the words in your (Vedic) scriptures, "Employ cattle for the sake of sacrifice."'

The Buddhist teachings strongly prohibit animal sacrifice. According to the Buddha, sentient beings take repeated rebirth as any life form that has a mind, including both human and animal. Consequently, any animal that one might sacrifice could have been one's mother in a previous life. Although the Kālacakra texts misunderstand the ḥalāl method of slaughter as a sacrifice and make no reference to the ritual sacrifice of sheep by pilgrims on the *hajj*, sacrificial slaughter was and still remains a problematic area between Buddhism and Islam.

Buddhist doctrinal difficulty concerning sacrificial slaughter, however, is not limited to the presence of this practice in Islam. It also pertains to certain forms of Hinduism. The problem extends even to certain forms of Buddhism that are mixed with indigenous customs. For instance, during the Kālacakra initiation conferred by

29 Cf. *The Regal Abridged Kālacakra Tantra*, II 48–50.
30 *sDe-dge bsTan-'gyur*, vol. 11, 129A.

the Dalai Lama in Bodh Gaya, India, in January 1975, the Dalai Lama strongly advised Buddhists attending from remote Himalayan regions that they must stop all animal sacrifice.[31]

In modern times, Buddhists no longer seem to associate the ḥalāl method of slaughter with sacrifice. During the pre-communist period in Tibet, for example, not only were the local Muslims permitted to slaughter animals in the ḥalāl manner, but also many Tibetan nomads brought their livestock to Muslim butchers to be slaughtered and sold as meat. Most Tibetans, in fact, felt that the best meat dishes were served in the Muslim restaurants and had no qualms or hesitation in patronizing them.

The afterlife

The second problematic area between the two belief systems mentioned in the Kālacakra texts concerns the nature of the afterlife. *The Regal Abbreviated Kālacakra Tantra* (II.174) states:

> Through an (eternal) afterlife, a person experiences (the results of his) earlier committed karmic actions of this world. If that were so, then depletion of humans' karma from one birth to another would not occur. There would be no exiting from *saṃsāra* and no entering into liberation even in terms of immeasurable existence. That thought, indeed, appears among the Tāyis, although dismissed by other groups.

Puṇḍarīka elaborates on this passage in *Stainless Light*:[32]

> The assertion of the *mleccha* Tāyis is that humans who die experience happiness or suffering in a higher rebirth (in Paradise) or in Hell with their human bodies, through Rahman's decision.

This passage refers to the general Islamic belief in the Day of Judgement, when all men will rise from the dead in their human bodies and will be judged by Allah. Based on their past deeds, they will pass to either eternal happiness in Paradise or eternal suffering in Hell, still retaining their human bodies. The Ismā'īlī tenet, however, as formulated by al-Sijistānī, denies the resurrection of the

31 Personal recollection of the event by the author.
32 *sDe-dge bsTan-'gyur*, vol. 12, 26B–27A.

human body. According to al-Sijistānī, the happiness of Paradise and the suffering of Hell are experienced purely mentally by the individual soul, without any physical aspect.[33]

Buddhism, on the other hand, with its teachings of karma, asserts recurring rebirth (Skt. *saṃsāra*) by the force of one's karmic actions motivated by disturbing emotions and attitudes. Destructive actions, motivated by anger, greed, attachment or naivety about behavioural cause and effect, result in rebirth in a hell, or as a ghost, or an animal. Naivety may be due to either lack of knowledge or an incorrect understanding. Constructive actions which are still associated with naivety about reality, result in rebirth as a human, an *asura* ('anti-god') or in a heaven. Each of these types of rebirth that anyone may experience – including rebirth in a heaven or a hell – has its own type of body specific to that realm. One cannot be reborn in a heaven or a hell with a human body.

Moreover, Buddhism teaches that the karmic aftermath of any karmic deed ripens into happiness or suffering for only a limited period of time. Once that karmic aftermath has finished ripening, it is depleted. One then dies from a heavenly or hellish rebirth and is reborn in yet another saṃsāric realm. From a Buddhist point of view, rebirth in a heaven or a hell cannot be eternal. However, one's recurring saṃsāric rebirths will continue eternally, one after the next, unless one completely rids oneself of their true causes. Moreover, even the happiness of a heavenly rebirth is a form of suffering, since it never satisfies and eventually comes to an end.

Thus, Buddhism teaches that if one rids oneself of all disturbing emotions and attitudes, one stops committing karmic actions that would lead to continuing saṃsāric rebirth, whether in a heaven, a hell, on this earth, or elsewhere. Likewise, one gets rid of the karmic aftermath already accumulated. Then, on the basis of constructive deeds done without any naivety about reality, one gains an eternal, peaceful, joyous state of *nirvāṇa*, liberation from recurring saṃsāric rebirth. There is no Day of Judgement and no judge. Continuing saṃsāric rebirth is not a punishment, and the attainment of *nirvāṇa* is not a reward. The connection between behavioural cause and effect operates purely in a mechanical way, without divine involvement.

---

33 See Walker, *Early Philosophical Shi'ism*, p. 134.

As was the case concerning animal sacrifice, the problematic area of the nature of the afterlife and of an eternal Heaven or Hell is not limited to a difference of assertion between Buddhism and Islam. It is an issue between both Buddhists and Hindus on the one side, and Muslims and Christians on the other.

Battle with the mleccha Tāyi according to the Kālacakra literature

The Regal Abridged Kālacakra Tantra (I.158–66) describes an invasion of Shambhala by the mleccha Tāyis, 1800 years after the founding of their religion, and their defeat in battle by the Shambhala armies. In the next chapter (II.48–50ab), however, the text explains the inner equivalents for the battle in terms of meditation methods. These verses conclude (II.50cd):

> The battle with the lord of the mleccha is definitely inside the body of embodied beings. On the other hand, the external (level of the battle) is, in fact, an illusory form. (Thus,) the battle with the mleccha in the case of Mecca is not (actually) a battle.

The fifteenth-century Tibetan commentator, Kaydrubjey, in his *Illuminating the Very Nature of Reality. An Extensive Explanation of 'Stainless Light,' the Great Commentary to 'The Glorious Kālacakra Tantra'*,[34] elaborates:

> This explanation in the second chapter is the definitive meaning of the description, in the first chapter, of the battle that exemplifies it. It must be applied to the yoga arising from piercing the vital points of one's own body. . . . When it says in the text that this (external level) is an illusory form, this means that the battle in the first chapter has, as its intention, what is described here in the second chapter. And, except for showing a manner of battle that is an emanation, like an illusory form, its (intention) is not (for people) to act in the manner of causing great harm through fighting against the mleccha and killing them.

---

34 mKhas-grub rje dGe-legs dpal-bzang. *dPal dus-kyi 'khor-lo'i 'grel-chen dri-ma med-pa'i 'od-kyi rgya-cher bshad-pa de-kho-na-nyid snang-bar byed-pa*, II.45B.

Thus, although, on the surface it might appear as though the Kālacakra literature is predicting a great war between the Buddhists and the Muslims, the texts and commentaries make it clear that the battle must be understood merely as a representation of an inner battle against the forces of one's own disturbing and destructive states of mind.

Common points, but having different interpretations in each system

Buddhism asserts that Buddha, being skilful in methods and wishing to benefit everyone, taught in many varying ways to suit different mentalities. Thus, Buddha gave teachings that paralleled certain assertions made by other belief systems. Although Buddhism and these other systems had different understandings of the points made in these teachings; nevertheless, the commonality could form a basis for religious harmony, understanding, and peaceful co-operation. The Kālacakra literature demonstrates this principle.

The nineteenth-century CE Tibetan commentator Mipham, in his *Illumination of the Vajra Sun, Clarifying the Meaning of the Words of 'The Glorious Kālacakra Tantra', Commentary to Chapter (Five), Deep Awareness*,[35] explains:

> The *mlecchas* have two (philosophical points) that they hold. They hold external phenomena to have the nature of a collection of atoms, and they hold the existence of a self of a person that temporarily takes birth or that has an aspect that takes birth in *saṃsāra*. The goal is to achieve the happiness of the gods as the fruit. Aside from this, they do no assert any other type of *nirvāṇa*.

The nature of atoms

Mipham does not provide a specific text in which Buddha spoke of matter being composed of atoms. However, by following his discussion of the invaders' views with a progressive presentation of the four schools of Indian Buddhist philosophy, Mipham implies

---

35 Mi-pham 'Jam-dbyangs rnam-rgyal rgya-mtsho. *dPal dus-kyi 'khor-lo'i rgyud-kyi tshig don rab-tu gsal-byed rdo-rje nyi-ma'i snang-ba, Ye-shes le'u'i 'grel-chen*, 117B.

that the Tāyi assertions fit in with the Buddhist presentations. He explains that the Vaibhāṣika and Sautrāntika schools of Hīnayāna Buddhism assert indivisible, partless atoms; while the Cittamātra and Madhyāmaka schools of Mahāyāna Buddhism assert atoms that are endlessly divisible.

Similarly, among the philosophical views that had developed within Islam before the mid tenth century CE, certain writers asserted indivisible atoms. They included al-Ḥakam and al-Nazzam, within the Shī'ite Mu'tazili school of disputation, and the Sunni theologian al-Ash'arī. Most other Islamic theologians of that time, as well as afterwards, asserted atoms as being infinitely divisible. Al-Sijistānī, however, seems to be unclear about the divisibility of atoms.[36]

The Buddhists and the Muslims used significantly different arguments, however, for refuting the indivisibility of atoms. The Buddhists argue that it is illogical for atoms not to have at least directional parts or sides; otherwise, it would be impossible for two atoms to join together. For two atoms to join, they would have to join on only one side, in which case they can be divided, at least mentally, into directional parts.[37] The main Islamic argument is that if atoms were indivisible, that would imply a limitation in Allah's powers. As Allah is omnipotent, he must be able to divide an atom infinitely.

The nature of persons or souls

Mipham continues,

> Knowing their dispositions and thoughts, Buddha taught *sūtras* of what they (the Tāyis) could accept. For instance, in *The Sūtra of Carrying Responsibility*,[38] Buddha said that persons carrying

36 Ibrahim K. Taufik, 2002, 'Ancient Heritage in Kalam Philosophy', in *Values in Islamic Culture and the Experience of History*, ed. Nur Kirabaev and Yuriy Pochta, Cultural Heritage and Contemporary Change, Series IVA, Eastern and Central Europe, vol. 13, Series IIA, *Islam*, vol. 9, Washington DC: Council for Research in Values and Philosophy.

37 Cf. Śāntideva, *Bodhisattvacāryāvatāra* (Engaging in Bodhisattva Behavior, Tib. *Byang-chub sems-dpa'i spyod-pa-la 'jug-pa*), trans. Alexander Berzin, IX.93–95, http://www.berzinarchives.com/cms/en/archives/e-books/unpublished_manuscripts/bca_shantideva/translation/engaging_bodhisattva_09.html

38 Tib. *Khur 'khu-ba'i mdo*.

> responsibility (for their actions) do exist, but without speaking of the soul of a person as being either permanent or impermanent. These points are true on the face of their (Tāyi) assertions. Buddha's intended meaning is that persons do exist as continuities of a self that bears responsibility for karma, but which is merely imputed onto a continuum and, by nature, is neither permanent nor impermanent.

Buddhism teaches that there is a finite, but uncountable number of individual persons and of mental continuums. An individual person is something imputed on an individual mental continuum, much like a habit can be imputed on a continuum of repeated forms of similar behaviour.

The continuity of each individual person, like the continuity of each individual mental continuum, is eternal, but non-static. These continuities are eternal, in the sense of having no beginning and no end. However, they are non-static in the sense of changing from moment to moment. In each moment, each person does something different, such as cognizing a different object.

While under the influence of naivety, each person commits karmic actions and bears responsibility for those actions. The karmic legacies of these actions ripen into the person's experience of saṃsāric happiness or suffering through a continuity of rebirths. When a person is able to maintain continuous correct awareness of reality, the person becomes liberated from ever experiencing the ripening of these legacies. In this way, the continuity of the saṃsāric existence of that person ceases forever and the person attains liberation, *nirvāṇa*. Nevertheless, the everchanging continuity of that individual person and of the mental continuum on which that individual person is imputed, go on eternally, even after the attainment of *nirvāṇa*.

In short, according to Mahāyāna Buddhism, the Buddhist branch to which Kālacakra belongs, an individual person is not permanent in the sense of being static; nor is an individual person impermanent in the sense of being temporary. Moreover, the saṃsāric existence of an individual person is not permanent in the sense of being eternal; nor is the nirvāṇic existence of an individual person impermanent in the sense of being temporary.

From an Ismā'īlī perspective, al-Sijistānī also asserts that persons – in this case, souls – bear responsibility for their actions and are neither permanent nor impermanent. However, the metaphysical basis for his assertions is quite different from the Buddhist one. The universal 'soul' is not permanent in the sense of being static, but rather it is in constant motion and flux. However, it is also not impermanent in the sense of being temporary, but rather it is eternal.

According to al-Sijistānī, all individual souls of men are parts or portions of the same universal 'soul'. When an individual soul leaves a human body, its temporary bodily existence comes to an end. It reverts to the undifferentiated universal 'soul' and does not take further bodily rebirth before the Day of Judgement. Nevertheless, an individual disembodied soul somehow retains its individuality. At the time of resurrection and judgement, the individual soul attains the mental pleasures of eternal Paradise if it has gained sufficient rational knowledge of the truth, through its association with an individual intellect while embodied. If the individual soul remained enmeshed in corporeal sensuality while embodied and did not acquire rational knowledge of the truth, it attains eternal mental tortures in Hell.

Thus, the individual soul is not permanent, in the sense that it is not eternally in its embodied state. However, it is also not impermanent, in the sense that after resurrection and judgement, it continues forever, bearing responsibility for its actions while embodied.[39]

The nature of the creator

Buddhism does not assert an omnipotent creator of the universe that directs what happens in it. Nor does it assert an absolute beginning or end of the universe or of individual beings. However, the Kālacakra literature does speak repeatedly about an eternal, individual clear-light mind within each being. By the force of the karmic aftermath that each being has built up from previous behaviour, this deepest level of mind creates all the appearances of both saṃsāric and nirvāṇic existence that this being individually and subjectively experiences. Because this clear-light level of mind has all the potentials that allow for each being to become an enlightened Buddha, the Kālacakra literature refers to it as ādibuddha, a first or primordial Buddha. It is 'first' in the sense of being the first or deepest source of Buddhahood.[40]

39 Cf. Walker, *Early Philosophical Shi'ism*, pp. 134 ff.
40 Cf. Mi-pham, *dPal dus-kyi* . . . (see fn. 35).

In order to conform to the first of the five *pancasila* principles that structure the philosophical basis of the Indonesian state – namely, belief in the one and only God – Indonesian Buddhists have asserted that ādibuddha is the Buddhist equivalent of God.[41] Although ādibuddha is not an omnipotent creator or judge in the sense in which Allah is; nevertheless, each individual's clear-light level of mind shares certain features of Allah as asserted by al-Sijistani. To know either Allah or ādibuddha, one needs to negate all qualities from it and then negate that negation as well. Both are beyond words and concepts. In the case of al-Sijistānī, this process establishes the absolute transcendence of Allah;[42] whereas, in Kālacakra, this establishes that the clear-light mind is devoid of all levels of mind that conceptualize about existence or non-existence. Moreover, unlike the general Islamic view that Allah can never have a graphic representation, ādibuddha can be conventionally represented by the four-faced, twenty-four-armed Kālacakra Buddha-figure.

Summary

In short, if one does not look in depth at the metaphysical explanations of the Buddhist Kālacakra literature and of the Ismā'īlī theologian al-Sijistānī, the two systems agree that a person or soul is neither permanent nor impermanent, and yet bears ethical responsibility for its actions. Both systems also emphasize the indispensable role that ethical behaviour and knowledge of the truth play in gaining everlasting happiness – whether that happiness be in *nirvāṇa* or in an eternal Heaven. These points of agreement indicate the type of approach that can be used today for furthering Buddhist–Islamic co-operation and harmony.

Current Buddhist–Islamic Interaction

At present, there are five major regions in which Buddhist and Muslim populations are living either together, or in close proximity,

41 Cf. Alexander Berzin, 'Islamic-Buddhist Dialogue', http://www.berzinarchives.com/cms/en/archives/study/islam/general/islamic_buddhist_dialog.html

42 Wilfred Madelung, 1987, 'Isma'iliyah' in *Encyclopedia of Religion*, editor-in-chief Mircea Eliade, vol. 13, New York: Macmillan, pp. 248–60.

and interacting with each other. These are in Tibet, Ladakh, southern Thailand, Malaysia and Indonesia. In each of the five, however, the interaction between the two groups is influenced primarily by economic and political factors, rather than by their religious beliefs.

Tibet

Relations between the native Tibetan Buddhist population and the centuries-old Kashmiri Muslim settler community have continued to be harmonious, based on the policies of the Fifth Dalai Lama. In current days, the members of this Muslim community are fully accepted as Tibetans by the other Tibetan groups, both inside and outside Tibet, and they continue to play an integral role in Tibetan society in exile in India.[43]

On the other hand, there have been significant problems in the relations between the Tibetan Buddhists and the Chinese Hui Muslims. These two groups have lived side by side for many centuries in the traditional north-eastern Tibetan region of Amdo, currently divided between Qinghai and Gansu provinces of the People's Republic of China.[44] Although, at times, Hui warlords have exercised strong control over parts of this region, the Buddhists and Muslims living there had worked out a *modus vivendi*. In the last decades, however, the PRC Government has promoted Tibet as the land of economic opportunities. Consequently, Hui merchants have moved in significant numbers into traditional Tibetan regions, not only in Amdo, but also in Central Tibet (the Tibetan Autonomous Region). The local Tibetans view these new arrivals as foreign competitors and thus there is a great deal of resentment.[45]

Both the Buddhist and Muslim groups living in the traditional Tibetan regions within the PRC face serious restrictions on the prac-

---

43 Cf. Masood Butt, 'Muslims of Tibet,' *Tibetan Bulletin* (January–February 1994): 8–9, 16.

44 Cf. Alexander Berzin, 'Historical Sketch of the Hui Muslims of China', http://www.berzinarchives.com/cms/en/archives/study/islam/historical_interaction/overviews/history_hui_muslims_china.html

45 Cf. Alexander Berzin, 1996, 'The Relation of the Hui Muslims with the Tibetans and the Uighurs', http://www.berzinarchives.com/cms/en/archives/study/islam/modern_interaction/relation_hui_muslims_tibet_uighurs.html

tice of their religions.[46] Especially in Central Tibet, the lay communities have almost no access to religious instruction. Thus, the confrontations that arise between the two groups are not based on religious differences. The problem is not that the new settlers are Muslims, but that they are Chinese and are threatening the economic welfare of the native population. Religious dialogue and co-operation are extremely difficult in the current situation, when the PRC authorities encourage and exploit cultural differences in order to maintain control.

Ladakh

Ladakh, with its Tibetan Buddhist population, is currently part of the Indian state of Kashmir and Jammu. The attention of the Ladakhis' Muslim neighbours in the Kashmiri part of the state is focused primarily on the Hindu–Muslim political conflict concerning whether to join Pakistan, remain within India, or become an independent state. Moreover, the traditional trade route between Kashmir and Tibet, through Ladakh, is closed due to Chinese Communist control of Tibet. Thus, the Kashmiri Muslim traders no longer have contact with the Buddhist community in Tibet, or even with the growing Muslim community there.

Conflict between the Buddhists and Muslims in Ladakh is fuelled mostly by competition for developmental aid. With the living Buddhist tradition no longer viable in Tibet, Western tourists flock to Ladakh to witness Tibetan Buddhism practised in a traditional setting. Developmental projects, sponsored by Indian and international agencies, have followed in the wake of growing tourist traffic. With the situation so volatile in the Kashmiri part of the state, far less attention has been paid to developmental projects there. Naturally, many Kashmiri Muslims are resentful of the aid projects that go to Ladakh. People do not seem to feel that Buddhist–Muslim interfaith dialogue can play any significant role in finding a solution to this problem.

---

46 Cf. Alexander Berzin, 1996, 'The Situations of Buddhism and Islam in China', http://www.berzinarchives.com/cms/en/archives/study/islam/modern_interaction/situation_buddhism_islam_china.html

Southern Thailand

Southern Thailand has a primarily Muslim population, which has more in common with the Muslims of Malaysia than it does with the Buddhist population of the rest of Thailand. The conflicts there concern the Muslims' wish for greater political autonomy. Religious issues seem to be irrelevant.

Malaysia and Indonesia

Malaysia and Indonesia both have majority Muslim native populations, interspersed with minority Buddhist communities, consisting mostly of overseas Chinese and some South East Asians. The Muslim and Buddhist groups keep strictly to their own religious traditions. In fact, in Malaysia, ethnic Malays are forbidden, by severe laws, to convert from Islam to Buddhism, or even to attend a Buddhist teaching or ceremony. The main conflicts between the groups in each country, however, seem to derive from economic competition.

Conclusion

Fostering and intensifying good relations and dialogue between Buddhists and Muslims in Tibet, Ladakh, southern Thailand, Malaysia, and Indonesia is important and certainly very beneficial. It can resolve or alleviate the tensions between the two religious groups, even if its capacity to solve the economic and political causes for conflict is limited.[47] The main focus for the development of Buddhist–Muslim mutual understanding and co-operation, then, has fallen on the efforts of religious leaders of the two faiths outside of the context of the situations in which Buddhist and Muslim populations are actually living side by side today.[48]

---

47 For an account of an important Buddhist–Muslim dialogue that took place in Bangkok, Thailand, June 2006, see 'Buddhists and Muslims in Southeast Asia: Working towards Justice and Peace', *Seeds of Peace* 22, no. 3 (2006), pp. 15–28. This dialogue led to a joint declaration (Dusit Declaration) and the decision to set up a permanent Buddhist–Muslim Citizens' Commission for Southeast Asia.

48 See also Bhikkhuni Liao Yi, Maria R. Habito (eds), 2005, *Listening. Buddhist-Muslim Dialogues 2002–2004*, Taipei: Museum of World Religions Development Foundation.

The Position of His Holiness the Dalai Lama regarding Islam and Inter-faith Harmony

Over many years, His Holiness the Fourteenth Dalai Lama has repeatedly met with Muslim religious leaders in inter-faith events held in numerous parts of the world. The Dalai Lama's message is clear. Following a press conference that the Dalai Lama held at the Foreign Correspondents' Press Club, New Delhi, India, on 8 October 2006, Agence France-Presse reported,

> The Dalai Lama has warned against portraying Islam as a religion of violence, saying Muslims have been wrongly demonized in the West since the September 11 attacks. Promoting religious tolerance, the world's most influential Buddhist leader said Sunday that talk of 'a clash of civilizations between the West and the Muslim world is wrong and dangerous.' Muslim terrorist attacks have distorted people's views of Islam, making them believe it is an extremist faith rather than one based on compassion . . . All religions have extremists and 'it is wrong to generalize (about Muslims). They (terrorists) cannot represent the whole system.' . . . The Dalai Lama said he had cast himself in the role of defender of Islam because he wanted to reshape people's views of the religion.[49]

The Dalai Lama repeated this theme at the conference on 'The Risks of Globalization: Do Religions Offer a Solution or Are they Part of the Problem?' sponsored by Forum 2000, Prague, Czech Republic, on 10 October 2006. There, he said, 'In the past, like today, there have been divisions in the name of religion and to overcome them we should have a continuous dialogue between different religions . . . If you truly believe your religion comes from God, then you have to believe other religions are also created by God.'[50]

Here, the Dalai Lama was echoing the words of Dr Sayyid M. Syeed, secretary general for the Islamic Society of North America. At an interfaith meeting, entitled 'A Gathering of Hearts Illuminating

---

49 'Dalai Lama Warns against Talks of 'Clash of Civilizations." Agence France-Presse, 9 October 2006.

50 Radio Free Europe, 12 October 2006.

Compassion', held in San Francisco, California, on 15 April 2006, attended by the Dalai Lama, Dr Syeed said, 'The Quran instructs Muslims that humanity would consist of people of only one faith if it had been so deemed by Allah.'[51]

The contemporary role of the Kālacakra initiation as a venue for Buddhist–Muslim harmony

A noteworthy corollary of the growing development of a Buddhist–Muslim dialogue is the role that the Kālacakra initiation has played as a venue for this dialogue. For example, Prince Sadruddin Aga Khan attended, as a guest of honour, the Kālacakra initiation conferred by the Dalai Lama in Rikon, Switzerland, in July 1985. The late prince was the uncle of His Holiness Prince Karim Aga Khan IV, the present spiritual head of the Nizārī branch of Ismā'īlī Shī'ism. Seven years later, Dr Tirmiziou Diallo, the hereditary Sufi leader of Guinea, West Africa, attended the Kālacakra initiation conferred by the Dalai Lama in Graz, Austria, in October 2002.

Moreover, during the Kālacakra initiation that the Dalai Lama conferred in January 2003 in Bodh Gaya, India, the holiest site in the Buddhist world, the Dalai Lama visited the local mosque located next to the main stūpa. According to the official report of the visit by the Department of Information and International Affairs of the Central Tibetan Administration, Dharamsala, India,

> His Holiness was received there by Maulana Mohammad Shaheeruddin, the Imam of the mosque and the Rector of a religious school attached to the mosque. Addressing the teachers and students, His Holiness said that though we follow different religions, but basically we all are the same human beings. All religious traditions teach us to be a good human being. So, it is for us to work towards this end.[52]

51 *San Francisco Chronicle*, 16 April 2006.

52 http://www.tibet.net/en/flash/2003/0103/180103.html

Universal responsibility as a basis for Buddhist–Muslim co-operation

The Dalai Lama has often stressed that inter-faith co-operation, whether between Buddhists and Muslims or among all world religions, needs to be based on universal truths acceptable within the religious framework of each group. Two such truths are that everyone wishes to be happy and no one wishes to suffer, and that the entire world is interrelated and interdependent. As with the example from the Kālacakra literature concerning the shared Buddhist–Islamic teaching that persons bear ethical responsibility for their actions, these two maxims have different philosophical explanations in the two religions. Buddhism explains the two points in terms of logic, while Islam explains them in terms of the equality of all God's creations. Nevertheless, we find voice to similar sentiments in both religions that support the policy of universal responsibility.

The eighth-century CE Indian Buddhist master, Śāntideva, wrote in *Engaging in Bodhisattva Behaviour* (VIII 91): 'Just as despite its many parts, with divisions into hands and so on, the body's to be cared for as a whole; similarly, despite the differences among wandering beings, yet in regard to happiness and pain, they're all equal to myself in wishing to be happy, and thus form a whole.'[53]

A *ḥadīth* preserved by Nu'man ibn Bashir al-Ansari similarly records the Prophet as saying,[54] 'The similitude of believers in regard to mutual love, affection, and fellow-feeling is that of one body; when any limb of it aches, the whole body aches because of sleeplessness and fever.'

Through such teachings as these and the continuing efforts of not only Buddhist and Muslim spiritual leaders, but also the participation of members of the two religious communities, the prospect for religious harmony between the Buddhists and Muslims and, in general, among all world religions, looks hopeful.

53 Śāntideva, *Budhisattvacāryāvatāra*, http://www.berzinarchives.com/cms/en/archives/e-books/unpublished_manuscripts/bca_shantideva/translation/engaging_bodhisattva_08.html

54 Quoted in http://www.mountainofflight.co.uk/spiritual_hadith.html

20. Response to Berzin

MAJID TEHRANIAN

Alexander Berzin has provided a thoughtful and learned account of the dialogue between Buddhism and Islam through the ages. Given that the contacts between the two faiths have been tangential to their histories, this is a great contribution. Thanks to the forces of globalization in recent decades, however, the two faiths have increasingly come into more direct contact. In Afghanistan, Thailand, Indonesia, Malaysia, Tibet and Ladakh, these contacts have caught the attention of the world.

To face the global challenges, Berzin calls for global responsibility. I fully agree with him. All great religions share in the global responsibility for human survival, sustainable development and equitable growth. Facing the threats of nuclear annihilation, global pollution and the widening chasms in wealth and power, humankind needs the wisdom of traditional religions. But traditional religions cannot effectively contribute to this global dialogue unless they learn to talk to each other while engaging secular science and its emerging global civilization.

What can be the ground rules for such a dialogue? First, in order to understand rather than debate, we are well-advised to limit the dialogue on doctrines and rituals. Second, we need to focus on ethics in order to understand the underlying reasons for ethical conversions and diversions. Third, we need to develop a common ground by focusing on rules for international and inter-faith tolerance, coexistence, and co-operation.

Let us take up each of these ground rules for Buddhism and Islam. The two great religions emerged out of totally different ecological conditions and reflect some of their origins with respect to their doctrines and rituals. Buddhism came out of the Hindu world and reveres the images of Lord Buddha. The statues of Buddha at

Bamiyan, for example, told the worshippers that there is Buddha nature in all of us, showing that the right path is to overcome greed and worldly possessions. Islam emerged out of the Arabian Peninsula, propagates strict monotheism and calls for the destruction of images. No wonder that the encounter of the two religions has recently led to bitter conflicts. There seems to be no room for compromise here. Although miniature painting found a place in the Islamic world, the dominant art form is called *Arabesque*. This consists of abstract designs before cubism was born. Calligraphy was another art form. The Arabic script lent itself to a diversity of abstract designs. It combined the beauty of calligraphy with the symbolic power of abstraction. You can yourself witness the outcome in some mosques.

In my own paper I showed that a kind of dialogue and exchange between the Muslim and Buddhist civilizations has been at work for a long time indeed. However, the problems today are appreciably larger. We can count the most pressing as follows: human survival in the face of weapons of mass destruction; sustainable development in the face of a polluting global environment; equitable growth in the face of the widening chasms in wealth and power. To address such problems, great religions have to avoid falling into the trap of debating doctrines and rituals. Religions differ in their theology and rituals. This may be a blessing in disguise. The diversity in humankind calls for diversity in doctrine and rituals. However, such diversity need not be the cause for division and conflict. We may bring great religions into a more meaningful dialogue if we can focus them on the ethical problems they commonly face.

Both Buddhism and Islam have strong claims on ethics. Buddhism recommends the Noble Eightfold Path: right view, right thought, right speech, right conduct, right livelihood, right effort, right mindfulness and right meditation. This is not far away from the Zoroastrian dictum: noble thoughts, noble speech and noble deeds. With some imagination, it can be interpreted to mean Christian love, Islamic charity (*iḥsān*) or Greek *agape*. Great religions have always taught us how best to live together. The above ethical principles provide the keys to such a puzzle.

Violence is abhorred in all great religions. Although Islam has been demonized since the 9/11 tragedy, it can be argued that *jihād* has two critical dimensions, including the inner and the outer. Inner *jihād* in Islam is the struggle of the human soul to overcome its ethical shortcomings. Humans are heir to what the Muslims call *nafs al-ammara*, the unbridled self. To overcome all the temptations of greed, jealousy and anger, the Muslim must turn to God. Outer *jihād* consists of the exertion to overcome the resistance in accepting God's peace, that is, *Islam*, etymologically derived from *salama* (peace). Islam does not legitimize violence except in self-defence. Obviously, the interpretation of this doctrine may vary greatly among Muslims. But the point can be made that all great religions consider faith something personal. In Buddhism, this principle comes out very clearly:

> Believe in nothing just because a so-called wise person said it. Believe in nothing just because a belief is generally held. Believe nothing because it is said in ancient books. Believe nothing just because it is said to be of divine origin. Believe nothing just because someone else believes it. Believe only what you yourself test and judge to be true. (cf. Aṅguttara Nikāya 3:66)

The Muslims also believe in the same principle. As the Prophet Muḥammad once said, 'there is no compulsion in faith' (Qur'ān 2.256). Both views are in conformity with our contemporary scientific world-view. There are, of course, many events in history that violate the principle of religious toleration. But that is the price we have had to pay for the chasm between ideals and realities in all societies. In Islamic societies, it is well known that the People of the Book (Jews, Christians, and increasingly Zoroastrians, Hindus and Buddhists) were given autonomy to be managed by their own religious authorities. They were tolerated so long as they paid their taxes as *dhimmīs* (protected ones).

That brings us to the most controversial issue: the relations between religion and politics. Ever since the American Constitution of 1776, the principle of the separation of religion and politics has come to be accepted as the hallmark of a liberal society. That principle is now being challenged all over the world – in Iran, Israel, India and the United States, among others. It must be recalled that the principle of the separation of religion and politics is a fairly new one. It cannot be dated long before the French Revolution (1789), a secular revolution that denied the validity of all religion in favour of modern science. Since then, the world has been increasingly divided between nomadic, agrarian, commercial, industrial and digital societies.[1] As a result of modernization and globalization, the traditional nexus of tribes and families has also weakened. In other words, societies have been increasingly atomized. Mass movements and traditional religions have provided refuge for the individual. Witness the Nazis, the Fascists, and the religious fundamentalists. It is not surprising therefore that secular and religious fundamentalism is on the rise. After two centuries of retreat, traditional religion is coming back with a vengeance.

This may not be a passing phenomenon. Conditions of frailty, fragility and finitude have not changed in the human condition. The human condition seems to call for an invisible world in which we can take refuge. Human suffering can be moderated by modern science, but it cannot be alleviated. We are left with no choice except epistemological pluralism. We must accept the findings of science and the insights of religion side by side. From a logical standpoint, that may prove uncomfortable. But the position can be reconciled if we accept the teachings of religion as symbolic rather than literal, while we experiment with the teachings of science in a progressive fashion. We must ultimately accept that we are all global citizens with global responsibilities. That is the lesson of globalization. So long as they do not trample upon the rights of others, differences must be tolerated and celebrated.

---

1 Cf. Majid Tehranian, 2007, *Rethinking Civilization: Resolving Conflict in the Human Family*. London: Routledge.

21. Response to Tehranian

ALEXANDER BERZIN

In his article, Tehranian underlines the importance and need for a 'global civilization' that encompasses the values of the world's various religious traditions. In my paper, I similarly cited the call of His Holiness the Dalai Lama for 'universal responsibility'. Global civilization and universal responsibility both depend on meaningful dialogue among world religions, such as Buddhism and Islam. Such dialogue can occur on the level of religious leaders, as well as on the level of the general public. Moreover, it can occur on the level of generalizations, as well as the level of well-documented specific detail.

As mentioned in my paper, both leaders and followers of Buddhism and Islam have been largely unaware, in the past, of each others' beliefs. This situation is slowly changing at present, but requires greater effort. Thus, in this context, the internet is becoming an increasingly valuable medium for spreading information and dialoguing, particularly among the public, and even more particularly among young people. Users of the internet, however, are faced with the formidable task of sifting through the mass of often conflicting information available, in order to locate reliable, unbiased sources. In meeting this challenge, Tehranian's outline of similarities between Sufism and Buddhism goes in the right direction concerning generalities, but needs to be supplemented with detailed analyses of specific cases, in order to avoid misunderstanding.

For example, Tehranian writes, 'Historically, Buddhism and Islam have been neighbours for centuries in Asia. They have heavily borrowed from each other. As a result, new religious traditions (for example, Sufism) have emerged that contain elements from both.'[1]

---

1 Tehranian's chapter in this book, p. 213.

There is a big difference, however, between two religions having contact with each other and the two 'heavily borrowing from each other'.

Tehranian is indeed correct when he asserts, 'They are both concerned with human conditions of frailty, fragility, and finitude.'[2] Nevertheless, the fact that both deal with similar issues does not lead to the conclusion that either of the two necessarily influenced the other in formulating its resolution of those issues. This does not discount, however, the possibility that certain ideas may have been borrowed from one religion to another. But assertions of such borrowing need to be delineated with precision and specificity in order to be credible. After all, both Sufism and Buddhism have long histories, wide geographic ranges, and great diversities of schools and masters, each with its own individual assertions.

For example, Abū Yazīd Bisṭāmī (804–74 CE) introduced into Sufism the concepts of *fanā* (cessation of existence – the total destruction of the individual ego in becoming one with Allah) and *khud'a* (deceit or trick, as the description of the material world) from the influence of his teacher, Abū 'Alī al-Sindī. Zaehner has argued convincingly that al-Sindī, known to have been a convert from another religion, most probably derived the former concept from the *Chāndogya Upaniṣad* and the latter from the *Svetāśvetara Upaniṣad*, as interpreted by the Advaita Vedānta founder, Śaṅkara (788–820 CE).[3] Although all forms of Buddhism deal with the similar topic of *nirvāṇa* (release from recurring rebirth) and many Mahāyāna schools assert that the world of appearances is similar, although not equivalent, to *māyā* (illusion), it is hardly likely that any of their formulations played a role in the development of Sufi thought.

On the other hand, we can find examples of literary borrowings from Buddhism into Sufism. For instance, the Buddhist image of a group of blind men each describing an elephant differently, based on each touching a separate part of the animal, found its way into Sufism in the writings of the Persian scholar Abū Ḥāmid al-Ghazālī (1058–1111 CE).[4] Advocating philosophical scepticism, al-Ghazālī

2 Tehranian's chapter, p. 215.

3 R. C. Zaehner, 1960, *Hindu and Muslim Mysticism*, London: University of London Athlone Press.

4 Zaehner, *Hindu and Muslim Mysticism*.

used the image to illustrate how Islamic theologians possess only partial truth, while Buddha used it in *The Sutta of the Non-Buddhist Sects*[5] to demonstrate the futility of the non-Buddhist philosophers debating their views with each other.

Other Buddhist influences on Sufism occurred in the sphere of ritual practice. Tehranian alludes to this in his brief reference to the Mongol Il-Khānate rule of Iran (1256–1336 CE). In more detail, five of the first six Il-Khān rulers were followers of Tibetan Buddhism, the exception being Ahmad Tegüder (r. 1282–4 CE).[6] The sixth Il Khān, Ghazan (r. 1295–1304 CE), converted to Islam with the Shī'ite Sufi master Ṣadr ad-din Ibrāhīm Ḥammuya.[7] The increasing emphasis, from this time onwards, on the veneration of the tombs of Sufi saints was perhaps influenced by the Buddhist veneration of stūpa relic monuments.

Buddhist borrowings into Islam, however, were not limited to Sufism. Tehranian's mention of the role that Manichaeism played as a bridge suggests, as a possible example, the account of previous lives of the Buddha as a bodhisattva, known in medieval Christian sources as *Barlaam and Josaphat*.[8] It is well known that Manichaean Sogdian versions of these accounts[9] were written prior to their first appearance in an Arabic version as *The Book of Bilawhar and Yudasaf*,[10] compiled by Aban al-Lahiki (750–815 CE) in Baghdad. This Islamic rendition incorporated parts of the Arabic account of Buddha's previous lives, *The Book of the Buddha*,[11] also prepared at that time, based on translations into Arabic of two Sanskrit texts,

5 Pāli: *Titthiya Sutta*, found in *Udāna*6:4–6 (*Utterances*), the third book of the *Khuddaka Nikāya* (*Shorter-Length Discourses*).

6 Bertold Spuler, 1968, *Die Mongolen in Iran: Politik, Verwaltung und Kultur der Ilchanzeit 1220–1350*, Berlin: Akademie Verlag.

7 John Spencer Trimingham, 1971, *The Sufi Orders in Islam*, Oxford: Clarendon Press.

8 Zaehner, *Hindu and Muslim Mysticism*.

9 David Marshall Lang, 1957, 'The Life of the Blessed Iosaphat: A New Oriental Christian Version of the Barlaam and Iosaph Romance', *Bulletin of the School of Oriental and African Studies* 20:1/3, pp. 389–407. Cf. also David Marshall Lang, trans., 1966, *The Balavariani (Barlaam and Josaphat): A Tale from the Christian East*, Berkeley and Los Angeles: University of California Press.

10 Ar. *Kitab Bilawhar wa-Yudasaf*.

11 Ar. *Kitab al-Budd*.

A Rosary of Previous Life Accounts[12] and Aśvaghoṣa's *Deeds of the Buddha.*[13] Since al-Lahiki's text is no longer extant, it is unclear how much material he also incorporated in it from Manichaean sources. If some were, it would most likely have been through the influence of dialogue between Buddhist and Manichaean Muslim scholars present, at that time, in the 'Abbāsid court.[14]

Moreover, Buddhist borrowings into Islamic civilization were not limited to the religious or literary spheres. They also occurred in the field of medicine. Tehranian's mention of the influence of the Barmakid family in the 'Abbāsid court refers to the rule of the fourth 'Abbāsid caliph, Hārūn al-Rashīd (r. 786–809 CE), and his chief minister Yaḥyā ibn Barmak, a Muslim grandson of one of the Buddhist administrative heads of Nava Vihāra Monastery in Balkh, Afghanistan. Although, Buddhist scholars were already present at the House of Knowledge in Baghdad at that time, Yaḥyā invited yet more Buddhist scholars, especially from Kashmir. No Buddhist philosophical texts, however, were translated into Arabic under Yaḥyā's patronage. Rather, the focus was on translating, from Sanskrit into Arabic, Buddhist medical texts, specifically Ravigupta's *Ocean of Attainments.*[15]

A far more delicate issue than religious, literary and scientific borrowing, however, is the issue of a shared ethic as the basis for both global civilization and universal responsibility. For example, Sudan, Pakistan, Iran and Saudi Arabia have criticized the Universal Declaration of Human Rights, signed at the United Nations in 1948, as not taking into account the values of non-Western religions and cultures. Their objections led to the Cairo Declaration on Human

---

12 Skt. *Jātakamālā*.

13 Skt. *Buddhacārita*. Cf. Alexander Berzin, *The Historical Interaction between the Buddhist and Islamic Cultures before the Mongol Empire*, http://www.berzinarchives.com/cms/en/archives/e-books/unpublished_manuscripts/historical_interaction/pt2/history_cultures_10.html

14 Cf. Alexander Berzin, *The Kalachakra Presentation of the Prophets of the Non-Indic Invaders (Full Analysis)*, http://www.berzinarchives.com/cms/en/archives/study/islam/kalachakra_islam/kalachakra_presentation_prophets_in/kc_pres_prophets_islam_full.html

15 Skt. *Siddhasāra*. Kevin van Bladel, 'The Bactrian Background of the Barmakids', Paper delivered at the conference 'Islam and Tibet: Cultural Interactions,' Warburg Institute. London, 18 November 2006.

Rights in Islam, adopted by the ministers of 48 Islamic countries in 1990 at the Organization of the Islamic Conference. This document recognizes only those human rights that accord with Islamic law, *sharī'a*.[16]

In reference to Islam and Buddhism, Tehranian suggests 'Sufism as a bridge between the two religious traditions'. One of the reasons, he states, is: 'In Islam, Sufism represents a reaction against the excessive emphasis on the *sharī'a*, the letter of the law, as opposed to the spirit of the law, the *ṭarīqah*.' Great caution, however, is required here. Various Sufi schools may be present in many of the Islamic countries today, but the fact that all the Islamic countries signed the Cairo Declaration indicates that any ethical basis for either global civilization or universal responsibility needs to take *sharī'a* into account. Therefore, as a basis for further dialogue in formulating such an ethic, it is essential to undertake further detailed analysis and identification of points of ethics shared in common by the world's various religious, as well as secular systems.

As for Tehranian's thesis that Sufism can facilitate Buddhist and Muslim interest in learning more about each other, I believe that this may be the case, but only to a limited extent. In finding common points between the two religions, I do not think it is helpful, however, to emphasize mysticism. 'Mysticism' is a technical term used primarily in theistic systems for methods of achieving some type of ecstatic union with God. Such terms are not relevant to Buddhism. More relevant would be the importance of the spiritual master and of meditation methods, such as those for the development of love, breathing exercises, repetition of *mantras* or *dhikrs*, and visualization. Such topics, however, will probably be of interest and relevance to only a limited audience of Buddhists and Muslims, and not to the general public among traditional followers of the two religions. Therefore, in addition to well-documented online and printed information and comparative studies concerning Buddhism and Islam, wide media coverage of inter-faith services held by leaders of not only the two religions, but of as many religions as possible, might have an even greater positive impact for establishing religious harmony, global civilization and universal responsibility.

---

16 http://en.wikipedia.org/wiki/Cairo_Declaration_on_Human_Rights_in_Islam

Subject and Name Index

Also published by SCM in the Gerald Weisfeld Lecture series

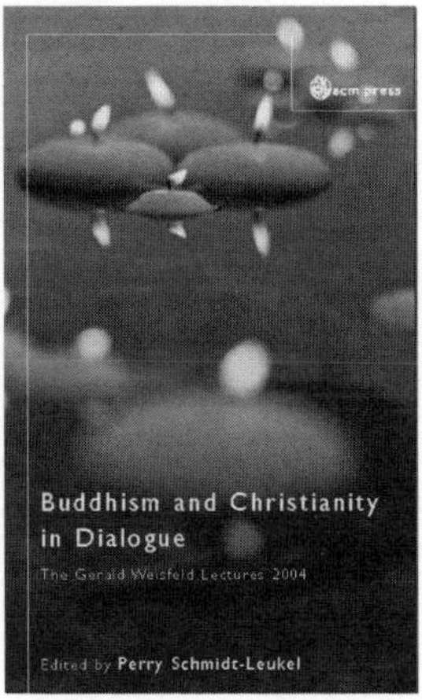

Buddhism and Christianity in Dialogue
Edited by Perry Schmidt-Leukel

A unique and groundbreaking book, which introduces basic topics of the relation between Buddhism and Christianity. Four Buddhist and four Christian contributors write comparatively about both traditions, explore new ways of mutual understanding and engage in a lively dialogue.
2005, ISBN 978 033404008 8

War and Peace in World Religions
Edited by Perry Schmidt-Leukel

A collection of essays by eminent British and German authors, providing an excellent grounding in a wide range of world religions and their attitudes to war and peace.
2004, ISBN 978 033402938 0